SETON HALL UNIVERSITY   MAIN
BF441 .W32
Psychology of reasoning;

3 3073 00063679 3

D0934683

Psychology of Reasoning

Structure and Content

Psychology of Reasoning

Structure and Content

P. C. Wason

P. N. Johnson-Laird

SETON HALL UNIVERSITY
McLAUGHLIN LIBRARY
SO. ORANGE, N. J.

Harvard University Press, Cambridge, Massachusetts

1972

BF
441
W32

© P. C. Wason and P. N. Johnson-Laird
All rights reserved

First published 1972
Library of Congress Catalog Card Number 78–189160
SBN 674–72126–8

Printed in Great Britain

Contents

Acknowledgments

The research described in this book owes a particular debt to our colleagues, especially Dr A. R. Jonckheere and Dr Sheila Jones of University College London, and Dr Paolo Legrenzi and Dr Maria Sonino Legrenzi of the University of Trento, for many fruitful discussions and ideas.

The first author is particularly indebted to the Medical Research Council for continuous and generous support since 1953. In addition, we are both indebted to the Medical Research Council for a grant for scientific assistance from 1968 to 1971. We should like to thank our assistant, Mrs Diana Shapiro, during this period, for conducting our experiments with enthusiasm and devotion.

It will be quite evident that this book owes a great deal to the following students and assistants who have collaborated closely with us over the years: Beryl Boydell, Dr Susan Carey, Dr Elizabeth Cornish, Dr Jonathan Evans, Angela Fine, Tirril Gatty, Graham Gibbs, Roger Goodwin, Dr Judith Greene, Penelope Hayes, Dr Athol Hughes, Dr Martin Katzman, Robert Marsden, Dr Jonathan Penrose, Jean Phillips, Joanna Tagart, Peter Thompson, Jeremy Tridgell and Jean Waddington.

We should also like to thank Susan Churchill for deciphering our illegible hand-writing, and typing the manuscript with exemplary efficiency, and Rosemary Stevenson for preparing the indexes.

Finally, we are most grateful to Professor G. C. Drew, Professor D. B. Fry and Professor Frieda Goldman Eisler who provided us with a most congenial atmosphere and every facility with which to pursue our research.

P. C. WASON
P. N. JOHNSON-LAIRD

'Is there any other point to which you would wish to draw my attention?'
'To the curious incident of the dog in the night-time.'
'The dog did nothing in the night-time.'
'That was the curious incident', remarked Sherlock Holmes.

A. CONAN DOYLE *Silver Blaze*

This book is primarily about our own research into the psychology of reasoning. There is, of course, no clear boundary surrounding this topic. It is obvious, for example, that when an individual draws a conclusion from premises according to the traditional Aristotelian laws of logic, he is engaged in reasoning. It is also feasible to assert that an individual solving a crossword puzzle, planning to buy a new house, or determining the best route from one town to another, is also engaged in reasoning. But what about an animal, who has learnt separately the parts of a maze, and then proceeds to put the parts together? Some psychologists would call this activity reasoning. In our view, it is fruitless to argue about definitions of terms, and we shall be concerned with how humans draw explicit conclusions from evidence.

Like most psychologists we set out not quite knowing where we were going, but certain issues excited our interest. Perhaps the most fundamental problem was the extent to which most individuals can be considered naturally rational thinkers. It is important to understand what is meant by 'rational' in this context—such words tend to evoke a whole set of connotations which can be misleading. Some people, specialists perhaps concerned with creativity, seem to think that man is too rational, in the sense that he is prone to proceed in a strictly linear fashion, and is inept at thinking of original ideas. Others, psychoanalysts perhaps, or specialists in intelligence testing, seem inclined to think that man is too irrational to be a disciplined thinker. Our concern is simply this: given a set of assertions, to what extent can the individual appreciate all that follows from them by virtue of logic alone, and remain unseduced by plausible, but fallacious conclusions? We are not concerned with whether these assertions are true or false, nor with whether the individual holds them among his beliefs, nor with whether they are sane or silly. The rational individual, in our sense of the word, is merely one who has the ability to make inferences; he may not be rational in any other sense of the word.

At a more tangible level, however, we were interested above all else in a number of apparently simple deductive problems which so many intelligent people almost invariably got wrong. The important point was not simply that they got them wrong, and departed from the canons of formal logic, but that they usually came to realize their mistakes. Moreover, these mistakes were nearly always of a particular kind rather than being random. Hence we were interested in their determinants, the factors which governed 'performance', and made it fail to reflect logical 'competence', to borrow a distinction drawn by Noam Chomsky.

The reader may expect from us a discussion of the use of reason in arguments, or controversies, in daily life. In fact most arguments of this kind do not involve points of logic. They involve emotional decisions to accept or reject premises, the relevance of questions of fact, equivocation, and differences in interpretation. The following extract from an interview of Enoch Powell by David Frost (Smithies and Fiddick, 1969) is a good example.

FROST ... Didn't you have a fantastic duty to check that story, to find out if it was true?

POWELL I haven't the slightest doubt it was, but may I—

FROST But have you—did you check it at all?

POWELL I haven't the slightest doubt—

FROST Did you check it at all?

POWELL I haven't the slightest doubt, and I verified the source from which I had that information. Now—

FROST Did you verify the story?

POWELL I verified the source and I haven't the slightest doubt that it is—

FROST But what do you mean you verified the source?

POWELL —that it is as true as it is typical.

FROST But it's not typical, I mean, I'm not saying it hasn't happened.

POWELL Ah—well now—

FROST I'm not saying—you say it's typical.

POWELL Yes, I do.

FROST You see, you keep using words like typical (Yes) as though there's millions of piles of excrement dropping through letter boxes (Yes) (Laughter) up and down our green and pleasant land (Yes) to use your own—and that's not happening, and if you're quoting a specific case—

POWELL Well, you say it's not happening—

FROST And you verify—it's not millions?

POWELL Well, clearly not millions.

FROST Typical? Typical?

POWELL Typical of what happens in areas where the immigrant population is increasing in numbers and is taking over—

FROST Naughty, naughty, naughty. Not typical. Not typical.

POWELL Well, we can argue about this as a matter of fact—

FROST The word typical—

POWELL —but that it is a—

FROST I'm not saying it's never happened. (No) I'm saying its incredibly untypical.

POWELL No, I don't agree with you—

In contrast, arguments today which hinge primarily on points of logic are mainly confined to philosophical problems. The following extract from a radio debate between Bertrand Russell and F. C. Copleston (Russell, 1957), on the existence of God, clearly shows the distance between discourse of this kind and ordinary talk.

COPLESTON ... The fact that we gain our knowledge of causality empirically, from particular causes, does not rule out the possibility of asking what the cause of the series is. If the word 'cause' were meaningless or if it could be shown that Kant's view of the matter were correct, the question would be illegitimate I agree; but you don't seem to hold that the word 'cause' is meaningless, and I do not suppose you are a Kantian.

RUSSELL I can illustrate what seems to me your fallacy. Every man who exists has a mother, and it seems to me your argument is that therefore the human race must have a mother, but obviously the human race hasn't a mother—that's a different logical sphere.

COPLESTON Well, I can't really see any parity. If I were saying, 'every object has a phenomenal cause, therefore, the whole series has a phenomenal cause', there would be parity; but I'm not saying that; I'm saying, every object has a phenomenal cause if you insist on the infinity of the series—but the series of phenomenal causes is an insufficient explanation of the series. Therefore, the series has not a phenomenal cause but a transcendent cause.

RUSSELL That's always assuming that not only every particular thing in the world, but the world as a whole must have a cause. For that assumption I see no ground whatever. If you'll give me a ground I'll listen to it.

COPLESTON Well, the series of events is either caused or it's not caused. If it is caused, there must obviously be a cause outside the series. If it's not caused then it's sufficient to itself, and if it's sufficient to itself it is what I call necessary. But it can't be necessary since each member is contingent, and we've agreed that the total is no reality apart from its members, therefore, it can't be necessary. Therefore, it can't be uncaused—therefore it must have a cause . . .

RUSSELL . . . The physicists assure us that individual quantum transition in atoms have no cause.

COPLESTON Well, I wonder now whether that isn't simply a temporary inference.

RUSSELL It may be, but it does show that physicists' minds can conceive it.

There is, of course, a need for the study of all kinds of argumentation, but it is, to revert to a classical distinction, primarily concerned with rhetoric rather than with reason. However, this is not to suggest that reasoning does not occur in everyday life—of course it does, but it is all too often contaminated by all the rhetorical devices which we have mentioned. What we have tried to do is to isolate the components of inference, the basic steps of any kind of deductive activity, in order to determine the psychological processes involved in them.

Such steps are, by definition, simple and it is often easy to imagine how they might be performed by an intelligent individual. In fact, there may be several different ways in which they could, in principle, be carried out. For example, in the psychological literature, there are at present at least three different theories about the way in which the following problem is solved. 'A is not as bad as B; C is not as good as B. Who is the worst?' For this reason, we have relied upon the techniques and methods of experimental psychology rather than on our own subjective impressions and judgments. There is another advantage to the experimental approach: totally unanticipated phenomena are often discovered by it. We almost feel inclined to say that we consider an experiment a failure when it fails to surprise us. (And perhaps psychology, as a science, could also be said to have come of age when its theories are surprising.)

In general, the experimental approach involves presenting tasks to individuals (subjects) under standardized, controlled conditions, and then observing their overt responses. However, we have sometimes put rather more emphasis than usual upon the pattern of individual responses rather than merely collapsing them into group averages, just because of the number of different ways in which problems can be solved. To do full justice to this, we have also asked the subjects how they went about the tasks. Such introspective reports are potentially dangerous because in the past they led to an ultimately futile controversy about whether thought could be devoid of imagery (see Humphrey, 1951). As a method of probing the contents of consciousness, introspection is of limited scientific value, but as a method for revealing the processes of reasoning it is a very useful auxiliary technique (see Newell, Shaw and Simon, 1958).

On the whole, we have not presented our problems in the form of straightforward learning tasks, correcting the subject when he is wrong, rewarding him when he is right. In our experience, if a reasoning problem is sufficiently difficult to demand such a procedure, the experimenter (and the subject) learns little from its adoption. What we have done in such cases is to engage the subject in a sort of therapeutic dialogue, in which the experimenter, by progressively confronting the subjects with inconsistencies in their deductions, attempts to allow them to gain some insight. Of course, not all our problems are sufficiently difficult to need this technique.

In at least one respect, research on reasoning is like research on perception: it is often most revealing when 'error' occurs. A fallacious inference, in fact, is in some ways like both an optical illusion and a pathological delusion. Both illusions and delusions however, tend to persist. One knows that an illusion *is* merely an illusion—one knows that both lines in the Müller-Lyer illusion[1] are really the same length—and yet one still succumbs to the illusion: one sees them as different. Delusions, on the other hand, are notoriously not normally relieved by any rational procedures. The very act of appreciating that an inference is fallacious usually frees one from its hold, and one appreciates that one has been deceived. And yet, like some optical illusions in which perspective spontaneously reverses (e.g. the Necker cube), we have come across cases in which insight into fallaciousness seems to fluctuate; and like most pathological delusions, we have encountered cases in which the subjects seem to reveal a stubborn resistance to enlightenment. Such cases, however, which only occur in more difficult problems, are relatively infrequent.

Since the advent of digital computers, it has become intellectually respectable to talk about what is assumed to be going on within an organism, and to do so in a way which is not just numerical. One implication of our book is that a theory of thinking will be both quantitative and qualitative. Hence some of the techniques used in programming computers are likely to be useful to the cognitive theorist. Indeed, Miller, Galanter and Pribram (1960) speak of *plans* for guiding behaviour as an analogy with the way in which programs control computers.

[1] The Müller-Lyer illusion, extensively studied by psychologists, consists of two lines of equal length with converging arrowheads on the ends of one line, and diverging arrowheads on the ends of the other line.

The advantage of such an approach is that it forces the research worker to be precise and consistent about his ideas, and secondly (with the aid of flow diagrams) it enables highly complex and inter-related theoretical assumptions to be represented so that they can be intuitively understood. Some of our ideas, of course, are not sufficiently complex to require expression in this way. And, indeed, we do not wish to claim that all human behaviour and experience can best be understood and explained within this framework. Other ways of theorizing may be developed in the future, but at the moment this language seems the best at our disposal.

The origins of our investigation into reasoning are to be found in two studies of negation (Wason 1959, 1961). The word *negation* has, of course, several different senses. It has a technical meaning in psychoanalytic and in Marxist theory, as well as in the writings of existentialist philosophers and theologians. In ordinary usage too, we may say, 'he is a very negative person', 'the results were negative', or 'negative numbers were obtained'. But the negation which our studies examined was the simple one expressed by the word 'not'.

If it is an accident that our work began with these studies, it is a singularly appropriate one because negation is a fundamental concept in reasoning. It is logically primitive, in the sense that 'not' is the only simple logical constant which operates upon a single proposition,[1] as opposed to 'and' and 'or' which connect two propositions. It is also primitive because it is difficult to envisage a logic lacking negation. It would be like banishing the notion of truth and falsity, and of course, the notions of negation and of truth and falsity are inter-related. If, for example, the affirmative sentence, 'there is an essay on this desk' is false, then the negative sentence, 'there isn't an essay on this desk' is true. In general, if a sentence p is false then not-p is true, and if p is true then not-p is false.

The logical relation between negation and falsity is reflected in the linguistic operations involved in the basic conceptual skill of classifying objects into those which possess, and those which lack, a particular property. For instance, if we are searching for

[1] Throughout this book we use the terms, 'proposition', 'sentence' and 'statement', etc., in their everyday sense without regard to any philosophical or logical distinctions between them.

cards with the code letter 'D', we can ignore other letters and simply think in terms of 'D' and 'not D'. Such a skill lies at the root of all conceptual behaviour.

Since negation is so basic to thinking, it is hardly surprising that no known language lacks negative terms and that most languages seem to possess a variety of them. English is no exception. It contains a great variety of such terms which intuitively vary in their explicitness or degree of negativity. Explanatory order has been brought to this variety by the research of many linguists but especially that of Klima (1964), working in the context of generative grammar. It enables us to distinguish between *sentential* negation and *constituent* negation. Sentential negation is exemplified by the following two sentences:

John does not believe in God.

John hardly believes in God.

The negative import of the words 'not' and 'hardly' applies to the whole sentence. This is clearly brought out by considering that the 'tag phrase', 'and neither does Mary', can be added to either sentence. Constituent negation, on the other hand, is exemplified when the negative refers only to a constituent within the sentence rather than to the sentence as a whole. This may involve a word with a negative affix:

John *dis*believes in God.

John is *un*able to believe in God.

Or it may involve a word which is 'inherently' negative:

John *doubts* the existence of God.

John is *too* sensible to believe in God.

In these cases the appropriate tag is, 'and so does (is) Mary', which demonstrates that the sentence as a whole is not negated. It would clearly be ungrammatical to add a tag which would be appropriate to sentential negation, e.g. 'and neither does Mary'.

It was with simple sentential negation that our studies began, and we were unaware of the distinction between different kinds of negation when we started the experimental work. Nobody had previously investigated the ease with which such sentences are understood. A computer could presumably be programmed to respond just as quickly to not-p as to p, but were human beings programmed in this way? Our first experiment (Wason, 1959) attempted to find out.

In this exploratory experiment (and in all subsequent experiments described in this book unless stated otherwise) the subjects were drawn from a population of university students. The material, which made up the task, consisted of a 'situation', which was assumed to represent a non-linguistic state of affairs: a square divided into four numbered quarters with a different coloured disc in each. Below it appeared an affirmative or negative sentence about the location of the discs in two quarters, and above it appeared a printed instruction to make the sentence agree with the situation, i.e. make it true; or to make it conflict with the situation, i.e. make it false. Four basic experimental conditions are produced by combining the two forms of sentence and the two forms of instruction: true affirmatives (TA), false affirmatives (FA), true negatives (TN) and false negatives (FN). Figure 1 illustrates the task for the true affirmative and false negative conditions. As shown in the figure, the subjects accomplished the task by encircling the appropriate colour words in the test sentence with a pencil. Twenty-four subjects were exposed to six examples of each of the four experimental conditions (permuted in 24 different orders), making a total of 24 trials. The colours, and the quarters specified in the test sentences, were varied at random from trial to trial. The time taken to perform the task at each trial was measured with a stop-watch, and any errors were recorded.

The average times to complete the task under each condition, and the corresponding errors, out of a maximum of 144 (in parentheses), were as follows: true affirmatives (TA) = 8·99 sec. (4), false affirmatives (FA) = 11·09 sec. (6), true negatives (TN) = 12·58 sec. (8), false negatives (FN) = 15·17 sec. (29). At each of the six presentations of the conditions the response times were, in fact, reliably differentiated in this order.[1] It is, of course, not surprising that TA should be the easiest and FN the hardest because the latter contains two negative components, 'false' and 'not both', and the former contains none:

---

[1] Unless otherwise stated all the results reported in this book are statistically significant.

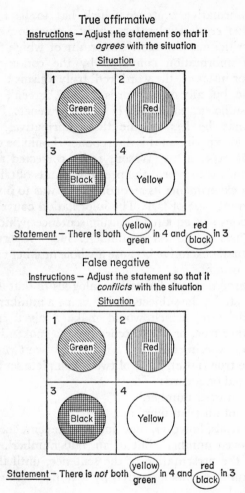

Figure 1. The original negation task. Examples of two of the experimental conditions (Wason, 1959)

conceptually they would seem to be at opposite extremes, even though they are logically equivalent and the correct response to them is the same. What is much more interesting is that TN appears to be consistently harder than FA. A sentence containing 'not', which has to be made true, gives more trouble than an affirmative sentence which has to be made false.

This rather crude exploratory study is open to a number of technical criticisms, the most important of which is that the amount of information conveyed by the conditions is not equated. For instance, the word 'red' truly affirms the presence of a red disc, but any of the words, 'black', 'green', or 'yellow' would be sufficient to negate truly its presence. In real life negatives may be less specific than affirmatives, but in a psychological experiment this discrepancy should be controlled.

A simpler experiment (Wason, 1961) corrected this defect. Its main aim was to repeat the previous results obtained in the exploratory experiment; its secondary aim was to investigate a rather different type of task. The information conveyed by all four conditions was equated by using sentences which referred to the evenness or oddness of numbers. Such properties are, of course, mutually exclusive because a whole number can be only either even or odd.

In the *construction task*, formally analogous to that used in the exploratory study, the subjects had to name a number (between 2 and 9 inclusive) which would make a given incomplete sentence either true, or false, according to a spoken instruction made by the experimenter, i.e. 'This time I want you to make the sentence true (false).' One of two incomplete sentences was then presented on a card:

'. . . is an even number.'

'. . , is not an even number.'

On half the trials, however, these incomplete sentences referred, not to an 'even number', but to an 'odd number'. The time taken from the presentation of the sentence, until the subject spoke the number, was measured by a stop-watch, and errors were recorded.

In the *evaluation task* the subjects had to say whether a complete sentence was true or false by uttering one, or the other, of these words. As in the construction task there were four basic conditions, illustrated by the following sentences:

TA   'Twenty-four is an even number.'
FA   'Thirty-nine is an even number.'
TN   'Fifty-seven is not an even number.'
FN   'Ninety-two is not an even number.'

Once again, the predicate 'odd', instead of 'even', was substituted on half the trials. For both types of task the design of the experiment, and the serial ordering of the conditions, was identical to that used in the exploratory experiment, i.e. six

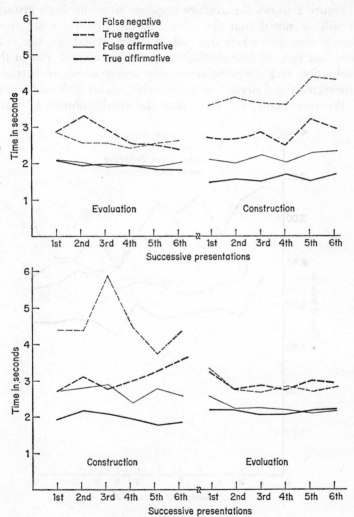

Figure 2. The binary negation task. Average response times of successive presentations (Wason, 1961)

presentations of each of the four conditions. However, one group of 24 subjects performed the construction task first of all, immediately followed by the evaluation task, and a second group performed them in the opposite order.

Figure 2 shows the average response times for both groups. It will be noted that the effects of the conditions are most clearly revealed when the task is done second. In the construction task all four conditions are differentiated, but in the evaluation task differentiation only seems to occur between affirmatives and negatives; truth value makes little difference.

We now know, however, that the results obtained in the

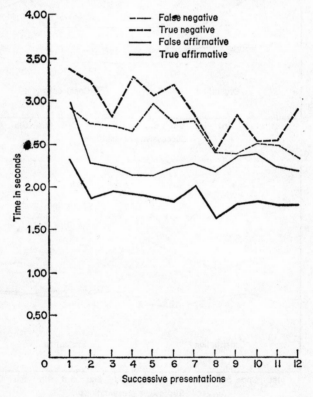

Figure 3. Average response times (evaluation) under conditions of very sensitive timing, showing the interaction between the form of a sentence and its truth value (Wason and Jones, 1963)

evaluation task are slightly misleading, probably because of the stop-watch timing. In fact, there is an interaction between the syntactic form of the sentence and its truth value. The correct order from easiest to hardest is: TA, FA, FN, TN. Expressed in simple terms, this means that the effect of falsity operates in the opposite way, depending on whether the sentence to be evaluated is affirmative or negative. It is most clearly shown, over a period of 48 trials (12 presentations of each of the four conditions) in Figure 3 which is taken from an experiment to be discussed subsequently (Wason and Jones, 1963).

This interaction has been highly corroborated (McMahon, 1963; Gough, 1965; Slobin, 1966). Interestingly enough, the total errors in the present experiment do reflect the interaction in the evaluation task, but not in the construction task where they are correlated with the response times (see Table 1).

TABLE 1 *Total number of errors made in the two tasks (n = 288 for each condition)*

	TA	FA	TN	FN
Construction task	13	28	46	77
Evaluation task	4	11	32	18

We shall return to a consideration of this result when one explanation for it has been postulated. First let us consider the results which are common to both types of task.

It is evident that negative sentences are harder than affirmative ones to grasp, both in terms of the time taken to understand them and the errors involved in so doing; that this is unaffected by practice over a period of 48 trials; and that negation contributes more to the difficulty than falsity. Why should this be so? It was the introspections of the subjects which were most revealing.

Even in the exploratory study (Wason, 1959) some subjects hinted at the reasons, e.g. 'There is something more awkward about having a negative in a statement than in an instruction. One tends always to see a statement as "there is" rather than "there is not".' But in the present experiment about half the subjects were much more explicit, and they all reported doing the same thing: *they converted a negative sentence into an affirmative one before responding to it.* In the evaluation task this was done in one of two ways: (1) mental deletion of the word 'not', evaluation of the resulting affirmative as true or false, and reversal of the answer; (2) conversion of 'not odd' into 'even' and 'not even' into 'odd'. It will be argued that the first of these artificial decision procedures would be sufficient to explain the interaction between syntactic form and truth value: false affirmatives harder than true affirmatives, but true negatives harder than false negatives.

The explanation rests upon two assumptions. The first is that a semantic mismatch (lack of correspondence) between a sentence and its reference takes an increment of time to process. The second is that a syntactic mismatch (the presence of a negative) takes a longer time to process because it depends on the mental deletion of the negative from the sentence. If these two assumptions are made, the order of the response times to the conditions follow. In TA there is neither kind of mismatch, and hence it should be the easiest. In FA there is just a semantic mismatch, and hence it should be the next easiest. In FN there is also just one mismatch, but it is a syntactic one, and hence should be harder. Finally, TN involves both a syntactic and a semantic mismatch, e.g. when the negative is deleted from, '5 is not an even number', a semantic mismatch remains to be processed. Hence, it should be the most difficult. If the reader finds this account rather intricate, an informal description of the four conditions should provide an intuitive understanding of the processing which is assumed to be involved in the evaluation task:

TA = a truth
FA = a falsehood
FN = denial of a truth
TN = denial of a falsehood

This should enable the reader to appreciate that in this task it is TN (and not FN) which constitutes a 'double negative'. More recent experiments (Young and Chase, unpublished) have required the subjects to carry out these and other conversions in accordance with explicit instructions. Their results confirm our analysis and more formal presentations of these strategies, based upon information-processing models devised (independently) by Clark (1972) and Trabasso, Rollins and Shaughnessy (1971).

The other way of making a negative sentence affirmative in form, i.e. conversion of 'not even' into 'odd' and 'not odd' into 'even', which we observed, would obviously not be expected to yield the interaction, and it could only be used when the sentences are binary. 'Not odd' is synonymous with 'even', but 'not red' has no affirmative synonym. Indeed, Clark (1972) refers, with some justification, to these conversions as the 'cheating' model of negation (as opposed to what he calls the 'true' model of negation which we have analysed), presumably because such conversions would be hardly likely to occur in a real-life context. He attributes the failure of the interaction to be manifested in the response times in our evaluation tasks to the fact that about half the articulate subjects reported using this method. Our own interpretation was that the failure was due to insensitive timing, and the frequency of errors gave some support to this suggestion. Not only did the errors reflect the interaction, but nearly twice as many occurred on TN (32) compared with FN (18).

In the construction task the interaction did not occur for the rather obvious reason that FN (rather than TN) is a 'double negative': an incomplete negative sentence has to be made false. But here, too, the decision procedures had the same effect of rendering a negative (or false) sentence into an affirmative one. The typical procedure was, for example, to remember that the instruction had been to make the sentence false, then select a digit which would make it true, and then add or subtract unity from the digit before uttering it. Exactly the same procedure was followed if the sentence was negative. Thus, suppose the instruction was, 'This time I want you to make the sentence false', and the sentence was, '. . . is not an odd number', the following extraordinary operations were apparently followed. (1) Selection of '7' because the sentence specifies an odd number; (2) Add unity because the instructions had been to make the sentence false—hence the digit becomes '8'; (3) Add unity to it again because the sentence is negative—hence the digit becomes '9' which is correct. This algorithm is infallible, but its serial and highly artificial character was completely unpredicted, and it must be admitted that there is something very 'computer-like' about it. One would not have imagined that a human being, in the process of understanding language, would work like this.

But if operations such as these are used, then it is hardly surprising that negative sentences take longer to evaluate or construct. There is little doubt that they do occur, but we may ask why do they occur, and just what grounds support the assumptions we have made to explain the interaction in the evaluation task. In the simplest terms, there would appear to be no logical necessity to prevent us verifying that a blue stimulus is not red, in a direct fashion. Clark (1969a) invokes what he calls the 'principle of congruence'. 'Subjects cannot retrieve linguistic information from memory unless the representation of the information sought is completely congruent with the representation of the question asked of this information.' And apart from our own experiments, the introspections of a philosopher (Russell, 1948) seem to corroborate this principle. 'When I say truly "this is not blue" there is, on the subjective side, consideration of "this is blue", followed by rejection, while on the objective side there is some colour differing from blue.'

But one may still press the matter further, and ask why negation apparently makes us behave like this. One reason may be that there is presumably an under-valuation of denials (as opposed to negative imperatives) in early learning about the world. It is no good telling a child that a dog isn't a cat; he must learn what a dog *is*; he must learn the name for this new object, or set of objects. Thus, in the early years, outside the psychological laboratory, the negative instance of one concept is labelled so that it becomes a positive instance of another concept. In general, it is little use knowing what something is not unless that helps to eliminate possibilities about what it is. One would imagine that denials would only be used in these cases when frequent confusions occurred in a child's mind because of an apparent similarity between two different things. Thus the utilisation of negative information is a relatively mature process because it implies a store of positive information which can be used as a standard against which to assess it. This assumption, in itself, might be sufficient to account for the fact that in our tasks a human being seems to behave like a computer programmed with an extra step for dealing with negatives.

A more recent hypothesis is that negation involves a greater number of grammatical transformations (in 'transformational grammar') than do affirmatives, and that for this reason a negative sentence takes longer to process than an affirmative one. This hypothesis was tested by George Miller and his associates at Harvard in the early 1960s. They found that in simple 'matching tasks', in which the appropriate negative sentence had to be located in a list, the time taken to do this was longer than when the given affirmative sentence had to be located. But they also found that the passive transformation, which is syntactically more complex than the negative, took even longer (Miller, 1962; Miller and McKean, 1964). Thus the differences found in our experiments could be due to the fact that the negative transformation is more complex than the affirmative one. However, matching tasks of this kind involve only the syntax, and not the meaning of the sentences. When the semantics of the sentences were involved, in tasks similar to our evaluation tasks, the previous results for affirmatives and negatives were replicated, but a much smaller difference in time was observed between active and passive sentences (McMahon, 1963; Gough, 1965; Slobin, 1966). It became evident that the difference in meaning between a negative sentence and its correlative affirmative contributes to the difference in latency over and above any syntactic difference between them. As Miller has put it: '. . . These results seem to favor an interpretation of Wason's results that stressed the importance of the semantic aspects of negation. . . . We conclude, therefore, that the syntactic conversion from negative to affirmative [in the matching tasks] was probably accomplished with all the speed of a highly skilled, unreflective act, whereas the reversal of the semantic interpretation was a slower, conscious, deliberate, not-highly-practised cognitive operation . . .' (Miller and McNeill, 1969).

A third reason for the difficulty of negatives in our experiments may be that explicit negatives involving the word 'not' (and its abbreviations) occur relatively infrequently in spontaneous speech (Goldman Eisler and Cohen, 1969). But it is admitted that such an argument would be circular: negatives could occur less frequently just because they give rise to difficulties. The methodological point made by Goldman Eisler and Cohen is that it is invalid to compare the times taken to understand affirmatives and negatives because of their differential frequency. This point, however, is indifferent to the investigation of the relation between the syntax and semantics of negation. The frequency argument would not predict the unexpected finding that false affirmatives take longer than true affirmatives, but true negatives take longer than false negatives in evaluation tasks. Similarly, it would be indifferent to an investigation of the effects of context on negatives which will concern us in a subsequent chapter.

Our discussion so far has suggested three possible reasons why negative sentences are more difficult to grasp than affirmative sentences: the fact that positive information is acquired first in early learning; the fact that negatives may be regarded as grammatical transformations from more basic structures; and the fact that negatives apparently occur much less frequently in spontaneous speech. But a further, less tangible reason impressed itself on us in the very first experiment. It will be discussed in the next chapter.

In the exploratory experiment (Wason, 1959) there was some introspective support for the supposition that negatives may be more difficult to handle than affirmatives because they had acquired an unpleasant connotation through their association with prohibitives (e.g. 'don't do that!') during the course of maturation. The subjects said things like, 'I don't like "not"— it's a horrid word', 'The capital letters of "not" always frighten one', ' "Not" gave me a sort of tremor half-way through'. Indeed, Roger Brown (1966) has suggested, in his analysis of the literary styles of Emerson and Thoreau, that the use of negatives in conjunction with the first person singular is an index of aggressiveness. In his view, it is aggressive for Thoreau to write: 'I would not have any one adopt *my* mode of living on any account.' The rationale for Brown's interpretation is that such a sentence implies the existence of another mind that holds to the affirmative form of the proposition being negated.

There is some empirical support for the emotional connotation hypothesis. In Hebrew there are two words for 'not': 'lo', which is used in all contexts including the prohibitive, and 'eyño', which is used only as a denial. Eifermann (1961) repeated our 1961 binary experiment, using two different groups of Israeli subjects for the two kinds of negative. On an evaluation task she found longer response times, and more errors, associated with 'lo' than with 'eyño'.[1] This result suggests that the connotative factors linked with prohibition may be partly responsible for the difficulty of handling negative sentences.

[1] H. H. Clark (1972) points out that the identical affirmative sentences (associated with the two types of negative) differed in response time, and that this invalidates Eifermann's conclusions.

Eifermann points out, however, that an alternative explanation could be based on the different syntactic structures of the two negative sentences. The result, incidentally, provides a further argument against any frequency interpretation of the difficulty of negation because 'lo' is more frequent in Hebrew speech than 'eyño'.

Eifermann's experiment inspired a study by Wason and Jones (1963) which attempted to abstract the denotative meaning of the negative from any possible emotional connotations. The use which the word 'not' performs in a simple denial is solely to reverse the truth of the correlative affirmative sentence. In fact, it would be difficult for psychologists to dispute this claim without engaging in vague, metaphysical speculations.

In the experiment the subjects first of all learnt by trial and error that the presence of a particular 'nonsense syllable' (e.g. DAX) in a sentence functioned to deny that a given number was even. Similarly, they learnt that the presence of another non-sense syllable (e.g. MED) functioned to affirm that a given number was even. They acquired this knowledge by putting a tick (signifying 'true'), or a cross (signifying 'false'), against sentences of this kind presented in a list; and they were corrected if their response was wrong. For example, suppose the experimenter had designated DAX as the assertion sign, and MED as the denial sign, then the first four sentences in the list, with the appropriate responses, might be as follows:

'7 MED an even number' : √
'4 MED an even number' : ×
'8 DAX an even number' : √
'3 DAX an even number' : ×

After they had learnt such a list consisting of 24 sentences, the subjects were exposed to 48 sentences containing these non-sense syllables which they had to evaluate by pressing a key marked with a tick (true), or a key marked with a cross (false). The subjects' responses terminated an automatic timing mechanism, and they were corrected whenever they were wrong.

A second group of subjects were exposed to the corresponding English sentences, containing the words 'is' and 'not'. Since the nonsense syllables should lack the emotional connotation of words, it was predicted that the difference in the time taken to evaluate sentences, in which they were substituted for 'is' and 'not', would be smaller than the corresponding difference for the English sentences. The four experimental conditions, TA, FA, TN, FN, were permuted as in the previous experiments, making a total of 12 presentations of each.

The prediction was clearly confirmed. But what was more interesting was its trend over the duration of the task. Figure 4 shows the extent to which TA and TN sentences were responded to faster, as a function of whether they were expressed as

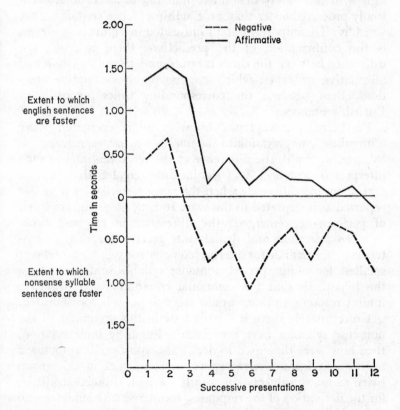

Figure 4. The extent to which affirmative and negative sentences are evaluated faster as a function of whether they are expressed in English or by a nonsense syllable (Wason and Jones, 1963)

English, or nonsense syllable, sentences. (The FA and FN sentences were omitted because of the interaction between syntactic form and truth value discussed in the previous chapter.) The striking point is that the response to the nonsense syllable sentences signifying denial is faster than to the English negative sentences from the third presentation until the last one. But the response to the nonsense syllable sentences signifying affirmation only becomes faster than that to the English affirmative sentences at the very last presentation. The latter difference was not predicted. It suggests that even with affirmative sentences, a sign with the purely denotative function of assertion is eventually processed faster than an English sentence containing the word 'is'. The important point illustrated in Figure 4, however, is the confirmation of the prediction: there is much less difference between the times taken to understand negative and affirmative sentences, which exercise purely denotative functions, than between the corresponding times for ordinary English sentences.

Furthermore, it was found that when subjects reported giving a linguistic interpretation to the nonsense syllables, e.g. MED = 'is', DAX = 'isn't', the difference in the response times to such interpreted sentences was significantly greater than to the corresponding difference when the nonsense syllables were not reported as interpreted in this way. In fact, three distinct levels of performance emerged: the difference in response times between assertions and denials was greatest for English sentences; intermediate for interpreted nonsense syllable sentences; smallest for uninterpreted nonsense syllable sentences. Thus the hypothesis that the emotional connotations of negatives inhibit response to them would seem to be well corroborated.

Unfortunately there is a basic flaw in this argument. If the nonsense syllables were not given a linguistic interpretation, then how were they used to derive the appropriate responses? Subsequent introspective reports revealed that in this group twice as many subjects apparently devised artificial strategies for the derivation of the responses, compared with subjects who reported interpreting the nonsense syllables linguistically. In fact, they coded the sentences by means of algorithms, or decision procedures, e.g. 'If an even number and DAX, or an

odd number and MED, then press "true", but otherwise "false".'
It is quite clear that such procedures have no resemblance
whatsoever to the functions of assertion and denial. These
subjects really do seem to behave like our hypothetical computer, and it might be expected that such strategies would
always be developed if the experiment goes on long enough.
All that is really interesting about the present experiment is
that the subjects, who were given the English sentences, showed
hardly any tendency (on their own admission) to develop such
strategies, and their response times showed objectively how this
failure slowed them down on the negatives. The experiment
shows the recalcitrance of the word 'not' to become a constituent in an artificial coding procedure, which would have
largely circumvented its difficulties, but the confirmation of the
prediction does not warrant the conclusion that the denotative
and connotative aspects of negation have been separated, and
shown to have different effects. The initial assumption was that
such aspects of meaning can be differentiated by the preliminary conditioning of a neutral sign to a function which it is
subsequently supposed to perform. This disregards the fact,
however, that negation is a linguistic concept which has no
strict meaning outside language. And this fact is exemplified by
the present results which show that such extra-linguistic signs
either become interpreted, or else incorporated into highly
artificial decision procedures which completely mask their intended functions in a sentence.

A series of experiments by Sheila Jones perhaps provides
more convincing evidence for the emotional connotation hypothesis. She compared, not simply the evaluation of affirmative
and negative sentences, but the effects of affirmatively and
negatively expressed instructions for a motor task. The move
from independent statements to instructions constitutes an
important step forward in the investigation of negation. In her
first study (Jones, 1966a) the material consisted of a long list of
digits from 1 to 8, arranged in a random order, and the subjects
(children) were given either the affirmative instruction, 'Mark
the numbers 1, 3, 4, 6, 7', or the negative instruction, 'Mark
all the numbers except 2, 5, 8.' It will readily be seen that both
instructions denote the identical responses.

C

The results were surprising. In spite of the fact that the subjects using affirmative instructions had to monitor five different digits, they performed the task faster than subjects using the negative instructions who had to monitor only three different digits. The errors were also revealing. An error can occur on either a digit mentioned in the instructions, or on one not mentioned. Under the affirmative instructions there was no difference in the relative frequency of these two types of error. But under the negative instructions there were relatively far more errors made on digits mentioned in the instructions, i.e. 'false positives' (marking a digit which should not be marked) than on digits unmentioned, i.e. 'omissions' (failing to mark a digit which should be marked). This occurred even though the probability of making the former type of error was smaller than making the second type. It is interesting to note that this potent effect of items actually mentioned in a sentence is a recurring feature of nearly all the experiments described in this book; in fact, it turns out to be one of its central themes. This experiment by Jones was the first to show the effect of a negative ('except') other than the word 'not'.

A subsequent experiment (Jones, 1968a) was a logical successor to the previous one in that it compared directly the effects of 'except', and the effects of 'not', in similar instructions. The two main conditions were:

    (a) 'Do not mark the numbers 2, 5, 8, mark all the rest.'
    (b) 'Mark all the numbers except 2, 5, 8.'

In addition, two other forms of instruction were used which inverted the order of the clauses for control purposes. The results showed clearly that the response times to the instructions containing the word 'except' were clearly differentiated as faster, over all the stages of the motor task, compared with the response times to the instructions containing the word 'not'. The order of the two clauses within the instructions, however, had no effect.

Thus, as in the experiment discussed earlier (Wason and Jones, 1963), Jones has shown three distinct levels of performance: an affirmatively expressed instruction is easiest, a negative instruction expressed with 'except' is of intermediate difficulty, and a negative instruction expressed with the word 'not' is hardest. She interprets these findings as being consistent with the emotional connotation hypothesis first tested by Eifermann (1961). However, there is a possible alternative explanation. The two sorts of negation are distinguished by Klima's (1964) criterion. The instruction with 'not' is a clear case of sentential negation because it permits a number of different sorts of diagnostic tags, e.g.

'Do not mark 2, 5, 8, and don't mark 9 *either.*'
'Do not mark 2, 5, 8, *not even* once.'

However, the instruction with 'except' is a case of constituent negation because such tags would be ungrammatical, e.g.

'Mark all the numbers except 2, 5, 8, and don't mark 9 either.'
'Mark all the numbers except 2, 5, 8, not even once.'

It is accordingly possible that the instruction with 'except' is easier because the negative does not apply to the whole sentence. This alternative explanation was, in fact, first proposed by Clark (1972), but on rather different grounds. He distinguishes the *scope* of the two negatives, not on the basis of Klima's syntactic tests, but on the basis of his own analysis of the underlying meaning of the two sentences.

It appears that the 'scope of the negative' and the emotional factor lead to the same predictions. For example, let us consider 'implicit negatives'. Intuitively, they are words which have a negative import, but tend not to involve the word 'not', e.g. 'impossible' rather than 'not possible', 'unsuitable' rather than 'not suitable', etc. But as we saw in Chapter 2, such negatives are cases of constituent negation. They usually have a smaller scope than explicit negatives. However, they also clearly involve less emotional connotations because they do not contain the word 'not'. Hence, both theories predict that implicit negatives will be easier to understand, and this is exactly what Clark and his associates have discovered in a number of elegant experiments (Clark, 1972). To cite just one example, Clark and Young (in preparation) examined the times taken to evaluate sentences such as 'The plus is absent' and 'The plus isn't present', in relation to the presence or absence of a plus sign in a picture. Even though such pairs of sentences are semantically equivalent, the implicit negative, 'absent', was evaluated faster than the explicit negative, 'isn't present'.

There may, however, be some indirect support for the emotional hypothesis in the work of Ben Reich (1970). He used an ingenious sentence completion task, in which the subjects were presented with 'sentence stems', i.e. words or phrases, and instructed to use them to complete a sentence in any way they liked. They were timed from the presentation until they *started* to speak.

The most remarkable, and well corroborated, result was that the sentence stem, 'I hate . . . because . . .', took considerably longer time to complete (on average 4·5 sec.) than the sentence stem, 'I love . . . because . . .'. Interestingly enough, when negatives were added to these stems, i.e. 'I don't hate . . . because . . .', and 'I don't love . . . because . . .', the difference in time was reversed, and the difference itself reduced, but the average response times increased from 8·2 sec. to 15·7 sec. This result, however, is not relevant to the emotional factor. On the other hand, there was no significant difference in the times taken to complete the following two sentence stems, 'He hates . . . because . . .', and 'He loves . . . because . . .'.

Thus it would seem that if a verb ('hate'), which can be assumed to arouse 'negative affect', is associated with the first person singular, then it tends to inhibit the completion of the sentence. With our work on negation, however, a similar effect is postulated regardless of reference. Hence, in order to infer the operation of similar affective processes, one must assume that the emotional connotations of 'not' are sufficiently strong to be indifferent to the reference of negation. But as we saw from the introspections in our very first study (Wason, 1959), this may indeed be the case: some subjects reported being disturbed by the word 'not', even when it referred to the disposition of coloured discs in a square.

However, the salient relation between Reich's work and our own, apart from the general difficulty of negative constructions, is that a particular word ('hate', 'not') may inhibit response for putative emotional reasons in a formal laboratory task. There are obviously many differences between his task and those which we have used, and the correspondence between

them is intended to be merely suggestive rather than con-
clusive. More pertinent evidence is to be found in our chapter
on the pathology of reasoning.

It may be concluded from all the experiments which we have
considered up to this point that at least three factors may cause
difficulty in grasping negative expressions. The difficulty of
negation may be an over-determined phenomenon. First, an
extra mental operation seems to be performed in the act of
understanding them. Second, an emotional connotation, derived from their association with prohibitives, may at least
momentarily inhibit response to them. Third, their scope, in
terms of whether they are sentential or constituent, may affect
their grasp as a function of the specificity of their reference.

Of these factors, the first one—the extra mental operation—
is, beyond question, the most pervasive, the most detectable by
the subjects, and the most highly corroborated. But the extraordinary thing is that in real life, we do not feel (*pace* Bertrand
Russell) that we are performing an extra mental operation, and
especially not one which lasts for at least half a second, when
we encounter a negative sentence. Have we all made a ghastly
mistake in our research, and wasted everyone's time? Perhaps
the experiments do not truly represent what goes on in real
life. This is a charge which is frequently directed at psychological experiments. But there is a special sense in which it
applies to the experiments under consideration.

Suppose someone, on arriving punctually at work, says, 'The train wasn't late this morning.' It is probable that this remark would have been made only when the train is known to be frequently (or invariably) late. The denial functions to correct the preconception, which the listeners could reasonably be expected to possess, that the train is notoriously unpunctual. In fact, if the remark were to be made, when the train is invariably punctual, it would be equally true—but pointless.

This example illustrates a variable, which had been overlooked in all previous studies of negation, and which may well have accounted for the tendency to change negatives into affirmatives before responding to them. Stated formally, a denial generally (not invariably) functions in language to correct the preconception which it denies. It is a characteristic of everyday language, as opposed to formal logic, that it makes great use of preconceptions. This suggests that if our 1961 experiment had first established an interest, or expectation, in the evenness of numbers, the results might have been very different. A 'thought experiment' illustrates the point. Compare the time it takes to check the truth of the following two sentences:

(1) '8 is even and 7 is not even.'
(2) '7 is not even.'

Sentence (1) sounds natural and easy to understand without any discernible extra mental operations—it has a context; but (2) sounds unnatural because, in the absence of a context, there is no apparent reason to make such a statement at all.

The first study (Wason, 1965) attempted to assess the relative effects of two different contexts on the understanding of negative sentences. Both seemed, *a priori,* plausible contexts of denial. The first was formulated as the *exceptionality hypothesis* as follows. 'Given a set of similar stimuli, x^1, x^2 . . . x^n, and a stimulus y, which is perceived to differ from these, it is more plausible to assert that y is not x, than to assert that x^1 is not y.' In more concrete terms, the statement to a child, 'A whale is not a fish', is plausible because a whale might be mistaken for a very large fish. But the statement, 'A sardine is not a mammal', is implausible because, although it is true, the supposition which it denies is remote. Similarly, in adult discourse, the statement, 'A spider is not an insect', is very plausible because many people labour under the misconception that spiders are insects. The present exploratory experiment attempted to simulate this exceptionality context in abstract material.

The experiment was actually conducted by Susan Carey. One group of 24 subjects was exposed to a series of cards, on each of which appeared eight numbered circles (see Figure 5). There were always either seven blue circles and one red one,

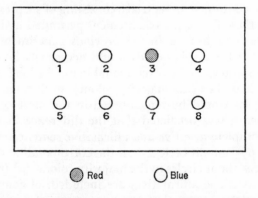

Red   Blue

Figure 5. Example of stimulus material used to test the exceptionality hypothesis. Since the whole array has to be remembered, circle 3 is coded as an exceptional item with reference to a residual class (Wason, 1965)

or seven red circles and one blue one; and the position of the one different circle varied from card to card. As each card was exposed, the subject had to describe it aloud so that he could remember it. These descriptions always took the form of, 'Circle No. 3 is blue and the rest are red', or 'All circles are red except for No. 3 which is blue.' The card was then removed, and one of the following four types of statement was exposed at each trial. The subject's task was to complete the sentence, by pressing a key marked RED, or a key marked BLUE, which stopped an automatic timing device.

'Circle No. 3 (for example) is —.'
(An affirmative statement about the 'odd man out', i.e. a 'different affirmative', DA.)

'Circle No. 3 is not —.'
(A negative statement about the 'odd man out', i.e. a 'different negative', DN.)

'Circle No. 6 (for example) is —.'
(An affirmative statement about any circle in the majority colour, i.e. a 'similar affirmative', SA.)

'Circle No. 2 (for example) is not —.'
(A negative statement about any circle in the majority colour, i.e. a 'similar negative', SN.)

The task continued for 24 trials, consisting of six presentations of each of these four types of statement permuted in a different way for each subject, as in the previous experiments. It was assumed that the display cards would necessarily be coded by the subjects in terms of an exceptional item (the 'odd man out') and a residual class (the majority colour), so that the colour of all the circles would be remembered in the most economical way. Hence it was predicted that the difference in the times taken to complete negative and affirmative sentences about the 'odd man out' would be less than the corresponding difference for sentences about circles in the majority colour, i.e. (DN − DA) < (SN − SA). The affirmatives are included, of course, solely as a control to ensure that there is no specific effect about referring to the 'odd man out', regardless of whether the sentence is affirmative or negative.

The prediction was confirmed at a high level of statistical significance. It was evidently easier to negate the exceptional item in terms of the property which makes it an exception than to negate an unexceptional item in terms of the property of the exceptional item.

The other context, which it was assumed would facilitate the grasp of a negative sentence, was formulated as the *ratio hypothesis* as follows: 'Given two sets of stimuli, which differ in magnitude, it is more plausible to deny that the smaller set possesses a property of the larger set than to deny the converse.' This hypothesis was based on the intuitive feeling that, for example, it is more natural to say, 'A quarter of this square is not red', than to say, 'Three quarters of this square is not blue.'

Another group of 24 subjects was exposed to the same series of cards, with the difference that they were not numbered. The nature of the task, and the prediction made, were the same as in the exceptionality hypothesis group. But the difference was that the subjects had to remember only the colour, and not the location, of the 'odd man out', and the colour of the other circles. Thus the cards were coded as either, 'Seven circles are blue (red) and one is red (blue)', or 'One circle is red (blue) and seven are blue (red).' The test sentences were as follows:

'Exactly one circle is —.'
(An affirmative statement about the 'odd man out', DA.)

'Exactly one circle is not —'.
(A negative statement about the 'odd man out', DN.)

'Exactly seven circles are —.'
(An affirmative statement about the circles in the majority colour, SA.)

'Exactly seven circles are not —.'
(A negative statement about the circles in the majority colour, SN.)

The prediction was not confirmed, nor was there the slightest evidence in its favour. Thus one context of denial (exceptionality), which seemed *a priori* likely to affect the grasp of negation, did so affect it; but another context (ratio), which seemed equally likely to affect it, did not do so. One unpredicted finding throws considerable light on this discrepancy. When only the affirmative and negative response times to the 'odd man out' (DA and DN) are compared under each context, it was found that over the entire task the response times to the two affirmatives were almost indistinguishable, and had the same average value of 1·60 sec. But the response times to the two negatives were strikingly different: 1·96 sec. under the exceptionality context, and 2·51 sec. under the ratio context. Thus negating a property of the exceptional item took on average, o·30 sec. longer than affirming it. But negating a property of the smaller class took, on average, o·91 sec. longer than affirming it. It is a reasonable inference that this difference, together with the confirmation of the exceptionality hypothesis, is due to the initial coding of the display cards under the two experimental conditions. In the exceptionality context the 'odd man out' is intrinsically related to the residual class which makes it an exception, e.g. 'Circle No. 5 is red and the rest are blue.' In the ratio context, on the other hand, the red and blue stimuli are merely partitioned into two independent classes of differing magnitude, e.g. 'Seven circles are red and one is blue.' It may then be inferred (rather speculatively) that the independence of the two classes in the initial coding of the cards in the ratio context may be the crucial factor which inhibits response to a subsequent negative sentence.[1] Under the exceptionality context the relation between the exception and the residual class is interdependent—there is a quality of 'oneness and otherness' about it—and this could facilitate response to a subsequent appropriate negative. Donaldson (1970), using children as subjects, has failed to confirm the exceptionality hypothesis; but, as she admits, there was no evidence that the stimuli were being coded in a way which a test of the hypothesis requires.

Judith Greene (1970a, b) had the insight that the effect of negation should be investigated as an effect between two sentences rather than between a sentence and the subjects' coding of a physical state of affairs. In her exploratory experiment the subjects had to judge whether two abstract sentences, printed on a card, had the same, or a different meaning. Her hypothesis was that the 'natural function' of a negative is to 'signal a change in meaning', and that it is exerting an unnatural function when it preserves meaning. This comes close

[1] Wales and Grieve (1969) argue that the ratio hypothesis should have been confirmed, but that artefacts in the experiment prevented its confirmation. See also Greene and Wason (1970). Clark (1971) and Just and Carpenter (1972) argue that it was quite correctly not confirmed, for reasons other than we have cited.

to our own formulation that negatives are usually used to deny preconceptions. (We may also anticipate the future discussion by observing that it follows directly from Greene's hypothesis that all 'true negatives' used in the previous experiments have been exerting an unnatural function.)

In the experiment the two sentences referred to variables, x and y, which the subjects were told to imagine represented any two different numbers. Consider the following pair of sentences which exemplifies 'natural' negation:

(1) 'x exceeds y.'
(2) 'x does not exceed y.'

These two sentences have a *different* meaning, whatever two numbers are (consistently) substituted for the variables. But now consider the following pair which exemplifies 'unnatural' negation:

(1) 'y exceeds x.'
(2) 'x does not exceed y.'

It is much harder to see that this pair of sentences has the *same* meaning. Appropriate controls were introduced to show that the *opposite* effect occurred when pairs of affirmative sentences were used in other grammatical transformations. It is harder to see that the following pair have a *different* meaning:

(1) 'y exceeds x.'
(2) 'y is exceeded by x.'

than that the following pair have the *same* meaning:

(1) 'x exceeds y.'
(2) 'y is exceeded by x.'

The subjects' task was simply to sort packs of 'natural' negatives (differing in meaning) and 'unnatural' negatives (preserving meaning), presented as sentence pairs, into two boxes, labelled respectively DIFFERENT and SAME. The 'natural' packs also contained affirmative pairs which preserved meaning, and the 'unnatural' packs affirmative pairs which changed meaning. In her exploratory experiment the 'natural' packs of cards were sorted much faster than the 'unnatural' packs; there was a difference of 35·9 sec., and the times for all the subjects were in the same direction. However, subsequent experiments showed that the effect was primarily due to the difference between the two kinds of negative rather than to the affirmatives. Similar results were obtained when meaningful material was substituted for the variables, e.g. 'Men outnumber women', 'Men do not outnumber women', etc. Further experimental checks also revealed that the order in which the variables x and y were mentioned within the sentence had no specific effect. Given the sentence, 'x equals y', it was as easy to determine that both 'x does not equal y', and 'y does not equal x', differed in meaning from it. The semantics of the sentences appeared to be crucial.

If the natural function of a negative is to deny a preconception, then the order in which the two sentences occurred on the card should be important. Surprisingly, Greene found that this had no effect. However, it seems very likely that this is because the subjects focused on the affirmative sentence first of all—a hypothesis which is corroborated by an experiment (Johnson-Laird and Tridgell, 1972) on the effect of negative premises in a deductive inference (see Chapter 5).

Greene's studies illuminate an important point which we hinted at previously. In real life negatives are nearly always false. This sounds silly but in fact it is sense. When I say, 'The train was not late this morning', it may indeed be true that the train was not late. But my utterance is *false in relation to the preconception that the train was late*; it falsifies the expectation of the people to whom my remark is addressed. The appropriate psychological criterion for assessing a negative is not its truth or falsity in relation to a state of affairs, but its relation to the preconception which it denies. Thus, Greene's 'natural' negatives deny the affirmative sentences associated with them; her 'unnatural' negatives do not do so. The affirmative takes the place of the preconception which might occur in a real life situation. Consistent with this account is our explanation in Chapter 2 of the fact that false negatives are easier to evaluate than true negatives.

If we introspect on Greene's 'natural negatives', and on the 'thought experiment' described at the beginning of this chapter, we do not notice any extra mental operation involved in understanding them. Hence, it might seem that the pronounced tendency to transform negatives into affirmatives, which was such a characteristic of the early context-free experiments, was merely an artefact of the conditions imposed on the subjects. But this conclusion would be a tempting over-simplification. In everyday life, negation may involve an extra operation which goes unnoticed because the interpretative step has already been done in grasping the preconception which is denied. When reading a book, talking, or arguing, there is no need to transform a negative sentence into an affirmative one: the affirmative has already been made, explicitly or implicitly. It is interesting to note that the process may break down when too many negatives occur together, because it is then difficult to keep track of the corresponding preconception for each, e.g. 'Unless you don't approve of saying no, you won't refuse' (Miller, 1951, p. 132). The same confusion is even apparent in the common type of idiomatic remark which does not mean what it is meant to mean: 'He's not a bad lecturer—quite the opposite in fact.'

All the experiments considered so far have been basically chronometric, i.e. concerned with the time taken to evaluate, construct, or complete negative sentences. In this respect they could be regarded as rather limited. In addition, they have all been concerned with responses which are either right or wrong. If similar effects could be observed in other types of task they would corroborate our interpretations. Accordingly, we decided to relax the contraints imposed on the subjects so that the responses could be assessed, not in terms of their correctness, but in terms of whether they were 'appropriate', according to criteria which we have already discussed. In the first study (Johnson-Laird, 1967), the subjects were instructed to create the context in which a negative sentence might have been uttered, i.e. indirectly, they have to supply the appropriate preconception. The task was to represent two statements by two drawings, in such a way that the drawings could be matched correctly with the statements by another person. In fact, the statements were (logically) synonymous. Two rectangles had to be coloured, with only red and blue crayons available, in order to depict a situation which might have been seen, when each of the following sentences had been uttered:

(1) 'The left hand end of the strip is red.'
(2) 'The left hand end of the strip is not blue.'

It was predicted that there would be more blue, and less red, in the drawing corresponding to (2) than to (1) because in (2) 'blueness' is both emphasized and negated. This prediction was confirmed, 13 out of the 16 subjects conforming to it. Thus, even in a very simple task it is possible to elicit an appropriate context for a denial.

A rather different approach was adopted by Elizabeth Cornish (1971) who was concerned with the interpretation of a denial under systematic variations in the stimuli. Her subjects had to complete the sentence, 'The circle is not all —', by pressing a key marked RED, or a key marked BLUE, as soon as a circle was exposed. The relative extent of these two colours was systematically varied under four different stimulus conditions. But, of course, in every case, both the response 'blue', and the response 'red', would be logically correct.

However, it was predicted that more 'blue' responses would be made when there was more blue than red in the circle, and secondly, that the number of such responses would systematically increase as a function of the relative amount of blue represented in the circle. There was overwhelming support for the first prediction, and considerable confirmation for the second one. Thus, Cornish was able to demonstrate that a sentence, referring to 'not all' of a property, tended to be completed in terms of that property, as an increasing function of its dominance. The more this property is dominant, the stronger the preconception that the circle is 'all blue', and hence the greater the tendency to deny that the discrepant (red) area is blue.

It would be possible to take such experiments to extreme lengths. For instance, imagine two rows (A and B) of four numbered squares. In A all the squares are blue except the third one which is red. In B all the squares are red. Now, suppose someone has said, 'The third square isn't blue', and the task is to infer whether the person was looking at row A or row B, when he made that remark. The remark is equally true of both rows, but it seems extremely likely that all the subjects would say 'A' (which contains mainly blue squares) rather than 'B' (which contains only red squares). The experiment might well be worth carrying out with young children, but it is described here only as a 'thought experiment' to illustrate the force of a preconception in relation to negation with maximal clarity. It is intended to stress the importance of this variable, in the investigation of negation, over and above syntactic and semantic variables, concerned with truth and falsity.

In summary, our experiments suggest that negation does involve an extra step, or mental operation, and that when the negative lacks a preconception, such a step tends to be deliberately and consciously performed. It is as if the affirmative preconception has to be recovered before the meaning of the negative can be grasped. This makes a human being behave like a computer programmed with an extra step for negation. On the other hand, in everyday life this extra step goes unnoticed because the preconception has already been processed as part of the context of the utterance. Other variables which were tentatively suggested as affecting the process of understanding were (a) the possible emotional connotations of negative terms, and (b) the scope of negation as sentential or constituent. This problem of the difficulty of negatives is by no means exhausted by the research reported in these three chapters. We now turn to the role which negation plays in reasoning about simple propositions.

Denial in
Propositional Reasoning

The most basic forms of inference in daily life are those which depend purely on the relations between propositions. For example, a scientist might argue: 'If Newton's theory is correct, then the velocity of light varies according to the velocity of its source. The velocity of light doesn't vary . . ., so Newton's theory isn't correct.' Such arguments utilize a fairly elementary logical system which, together with negation, involves the combination of the clauses expressing propositions by such connectives as *and*, *or*, and *if . . . then*. Since, as we have seen, negation is fraught with psychological problems, it is reasonable to suppose that it will also affect the difficulty of making inferences. However, before we examine this question, it is necessary to decide upon some criteria for what will count as valid, and invalid, inference. With many skills it is a simple matter to set up criteria for successful performance, but with reasoning it is less straightforward. The obvious guide is formal logic. Hence, it was logic, and the propositional calculus in particular, to which we turned in the first instance.

The advantage of a formal calculus is that it brings order to a great variety of inferences, and that it allows the specific content of an inference to be ignored. When the scientist in our example argues about the velocity of light, he is making exactly the same sort of inference that occurs in the following more prosaic example: 'If the water is on at the mains, then this tap works. But this tap doesn't work, so the water isn't on at the mains.' Substituting the letter p for the proposition, 'The water is on at the mains', and the letter q for the proposition, 'This tap works', the example can be symbolized as, 'If p then q; but not-q; so not-p.' This lays bare its logical form; and a similar pair of substitutions reveals that the inference about the velocity of light is formally identical. The essential logical point about such inferences is that validity depends purely upon the position of the propositions within their framework of logical connectives. Hence, when the internal structure of propositions has no bearing on an argument, the chances are that its validity may be assessed by reference to the propositional calculus. Once the form of the inference has been ascertained there are simple mechanical procedures which will reveal whether it is valid. Tentatively armed with the calculus as a guide to performance, we may now pose the fundamental question: are people naturally adept at reasoning with propositions?

The answer seems at first to suggest that they are surprisingly good. A number of studies have been reported which make this claim. A typical study, conducted by Shirley Hill (1961) (cited in Suppes, 1965), examined children's ability to reason. A whole battery of problems was used, and each of them consisted of two or three premises, spoken aloud to the child, followed by a question concerning the conclusion to be drawn. For example, 'If that boy is John's brother, then he is ten years old. That boy is not ten years old. Is he John's brother?' The problems concerned sensible everyday matters, and Hill took care to ensure that the question itself provided no clue to the correct answer.

The remarkable feature of Hill's results is how well the children actually performed. With problems of the same form as the example, even six-year-olds gave 74 per cent correct answers, and eight-year-olds gave 84 per cent correct answers. If they had been guessing, one would expect on average only 50 per cent correct answers. The one factor which emerged as a potent source of difficulty was the introduction of additional negatives into the premises. Generally speaking, this caused more trouble than the introduction of a third premise which necessitated two inferential steps to obtain the correct answer. However, negatives introduced in this way are likely to lack a natural context and to bring with them the difficulties we anticipated.

There are other studies which also confirm that children possess a considerable degree of logical competence. However,

D

the stage in their development at which such ability generally emerges is more controversial. Piaget, who pioneered the study of children's thought, suggests that complete competence with propositions is not attained until early adolescence. Hill's results point to a slightly earlier age. But, regardless of such discrepancies, it is obvious that adults ought to have few difficulties in reasoning with propositions. No one, of course, would be surprised by a demonstration that adults sometimes make mistakes or that certain problems are just too difficult to be solved. Few of us are likely to get very far in drawing a conclusion from the following set of premises:

If he goes to a party, he does not brush his hair.
To look fascinating it is necessary to be tidy.
If he is an opium eater, then he has no self-command.
If he brushes his hair, he looks fascinating.
He wears white kid gloves only if he goes to a party.
Having no self-command is sufficient to make one look untidy.

This problem, devised by Lewis Carroll, defeats us not so much because of the complexity of the logical procedures it demands, but because of the sheer number of such operations we have to perform and to remember. Given time, and a paper and pencil, we are competent to solve it. Obviously, then, our basic question must be reformulated. The point at issue is whether the ordinary, intelligent individual is capable of making each and every one of the basic inferences from which such problems are constructed, and, of course, of refraining from fallacies which resemble them.

Of all the inferences which might be said to be basic, the foremost candidate is one of the following sort:

If the object is rectangular, then it is blue.   If p then q.
The object is rectangular. p
Therefore the object is blue. $\therefore q$.

This is a valid inference and, to introduce some useful nomenclature, we shall call it after its classical name, *modus ponens*. It is a fundamental pattern of inference in that it is difficult to see how it might be derived from some deeper underlying logical principle. As Lewis Carroll himself showed, it is rather difficult to prove to a sceptic that it is valid, because most proofs turn out to involve the very principle it exemplifies.

There is a related pattern of valid inference which has the following form:

> If the object is rectangular, then it is blue.   If p then q.
> The object is not blue.   Not-q
> Therefore the object is not rectangular. $\therefore$ not-p.

As befits a more complex inference involving negatives, we shall give it a more complex name: *modus tollendo tollens.*

Bearing a strong similarity to these two valid forms of inference, there are two fallacious forms:

> If the object is rectangular, then it is blue.   If p then q.
> The object is blue. q
> Therefore the object is rectangular. $\therefore$ p.

This is invalid because the conditional premise does not imply that *only* rectangles are blue, i.e. it does not imply its converse, 'if the object is blue, then it is rectangular'. The inference is known as the fallacy of *affirming the consequent*.

The second fallacy, involving negatives, has the form:

> If the object is rectangular, then it is blue.   If p then q.
> The object is not rectangular.   Not-p
> Therefore the object is not blue. $\therefore$ not-q.

Once again, the conditional does not imply that only rectangles are blue, and the inference is invalid. It is known as the fallacy of *denying the antecedent*.

The fallacies are named after their second premise, and not the conclusion that is invalidly drawn. Thus, affirming the consequent refers to the fact that the consequent (q) of the conditional (if p then q) is also a premise. Some thinkers, notably Polya (1954), have argued that although they are technically invalid, they are nevertheless plausible inferences. They often do lead from true premises to a true conclusion, e.g. 'If it's good, then it's expensive. It's expensive. Therefore (probably) it's good.' The problem is to determine whether people appreciate the need for the parenthesized word, 'probably', or whether they think the inference is genuinely valid.

To discover how adults reacted to such problems, Diana Shapiro gave two versions of each of the fallacies and two versions of each of the valid inferences to a group of 20 students. The order of presentation of the eight problems was carefully counterbalanced; and their content was fairly abstract, very much on the lines of the examples above, so as to preclude the drawing of merely factual conclusions. The subjects' task was to read the problem and to decide whether or not the inference was valid.

The total number of errors that were made in evaluating the four types of inference were as follows: *Modus ponens* 2, *Modus tollendo tollens* 21, Affirming the consequent 8, and Denying the antecedent 10.

It is surprising how many errors were made in comparison with Hill's children. The subjects certainly show a susceptibility to the fallacies, and a reliable difficulty in appreciating that *modus tollendo tollens* is valid. This may be due to the relatively abstract nature of the material.

The contrast between performance with the two valid inferences suggests that while *modus ponens* is a fundamental inferential pattern, *modus tollendo tollens* is certainly not one. Of course, there is often more than one way of evaluating an inference. An individual may possess the particular rule among his repertoire of basic inferences or, given sufficient practice with the type of inference, he may come to learn the pattern of the premises and conclusion, and thus acquire a new rule of inference. With *modus tollendo tollens*, the most sophisticated procedure short of actually possessing the rule is probably to translate the conditional into some other more amenable expression. Thus, a subject may translate, 'if the object is rectangular, then it is blue', into 'only blue objects are rectangular'. The second premise asserts that the object is not blue. Hence, it follows that it cannot be rectangular. An individual trained in logic might even translate the conditional into its so-called 'contrapositive', namely, 'if the object is not blue, then it is not rectangular'. And from this restatement the inference is very easy to make.

In fact, the subjects' poor performance suggests that they adopted no such procedures. If they adopted any genuinely inferential procedures, it seems most likely that they tackled the deduction by a *reductio ad absurdum*. The reasoner, in effect, says to himself: 'Suppose the object *is* rectangular. Then it follows from the conditional premise that it is blue. But the second premise asserts that it isn't blue. This is absurd: the object can't be both blue and not blue. Thus my original supposition leads to a contradictory state of affairs, and must be false, i.e. the object is not rectangular.' It may be, however, that some subjects merely attempted to guess the answer, or, in a slightly more sophisticated way, they might have argued that since the consequent of the conditional is negated by the second premise, the natural conclusion is one that maintains parity by negating the antecedent of the conditional. This is really a sort of aesthetic gamble. The conclusion 'feels right'— it has the right sort of 'atmosphere'—because it completes a symmetrical pattern with the premises.

The trouble with these approaches is that, with the exception of guessing the answer, they all yield the correct solution— something which cannot be said for Shapiro's subjects. Did her subjects, then, attempt to guess the solution to the *modus tollendo tollens* problem? This seems most unlikely; they evidently did not do so for the other problems; and they did appear to be trying to infer their conclusions. It seems probable that they made a genuine attempt to evaluate the inference, but for some reason were led into error. And the most obvious reason is the presence of the negative. It will be remembered that a negative sentence seems to require an additional step in its interpretation, unless this is to some extent counterbalanced by the occurrence of the sentence in an appropriate context. Such a context allows the preconception to be grasped before the negative sentence is encountered. This suggests that when a negative occurs in a deductive argument its location will be crucial. It will be appropriate when it negates a previous proposition of the argument; it will be inappropriate when it comes 'out of the blue' and makes no reference to any previous proposition. The reader may care to carry out the following deductions which illustrate the point. Given the following premises, what can be inferred about John?

Either John is intelligent or else he is rich.

John is not rich.

And what can be inferred from the following premises?

Either John is intelligent or else he is not rich.

John is rich.

Some people think, at least at first, that nothing follows from the second problem, or that one can infer that John is not intelligent. The answer is, in fact, the same for both problems: John is intelligent. But the second deduction is harder to make. Problems of both sorts were given to 24 undergraduates in an experiment which we recently conducted (Johnson-Laird and Jeremy Tridgell, 1972). On average, the first sort of problem took 4·5 sec. to solve whereas the second problem took 8·4 sec.

Such findings are, of course, compatible with our hypothesis about the difficulty of understanding negatives. The negative in the first problem denies a statement which has already been encountered in a premise, whereas the negative in the second problem lacks such a context. Doubtless there is some truth in this explanation. But the question is whether anything more is involved other than the difficulty of understanding the premises. Perhaps the real trouble occurs, not during the interpretation of premises, but during the process of making the inference itself.

This alternative introduces a rather different sort of explanation. In the first and easier deduction, the premise that *John is not rich* contradicts an affirmative proposition. The subject has to argue: John is not rich, so it is false that he is rich; hence the other part of the disjunction is true, and John is intelligent. But in the second and harder deduction, the premise that *John is rich* contradicts a negative proposition. The subject has to argue: John is rich, *so it is false that he is not rich*; hence the other part of the disjunction is true. This argument contains the denial of an already negative statement—a step which is a sort of 'double negative' and which does not occur in the first inference.

The two explanations are similar, yet there are grounds for believing that it is the 'double negative' hypothesis, rather than the 'interpretative' hypothesis, which is correct. A third type of inference was investigated in the experiment. This involved premises of the form:

Either John is intelligent or else he is rich.
John is poor.

Such problems proved to be of intermediate difficulty. Their solution took on average 6·1 sec. There is no evidence to suggest that an implicit negative, 'John is poor', is harder than an explicit negative, 'John is not rich.' Indeed, there is evidence to the contrary (see the study by Clark and Young which we described in Chapter 3). Hence it seems unlikely that this third problem was harder than the first one because of some difficulty in interpreting the premises. The explanation seems to be that it is easier to grasp that a negative denies an affirmative than to grasp that an affirmative denies a negative.

Let us return to the effects of negation upon *modus tollendo tollens* and try to determine whether the 'double negative' principle is relevant here. The effects of negatives have been systematically investigated by Jonathan Evans (1972a), working with both *modus tollendo tollens*, and the fallacy of affirming the consequent. He constructed four versions of each type of inference as a function of the number of negatives introduced into the conditional premise. Hence, a typical problem was:

> If the letter is not 'A', then the number is '3'. $\neq \bar{A}, 3$
> The number is not '3'.

The task was to choose which of three possible conclusions was correct:

> The letter is 'A'.
> The letter is not 'A'.
> Nothing can be inferred concerning 'A'.

The most striking result with the valid inferences was that when the antecedent of the conditional was negated, as in the example above, a large number of subjects mistakenly assumed that no definite conclusion could be drawn. Such mistakes occurred in 61 per cent of the inferences as opposed of 17 per cent of the inferences with unnegated antecedents. However, whether or not the consequent was negated had little effect upon performance.

This certainly confirms that the location of the negative is crucial. It might again be argued that this is because of the importance of context on interpreting the negative. However, a negated antecedent and a negated consequent appear to be equally lacking in a plausible context. Can the 'double negative' hypothesis provide any better explanation? The answer is that it can provided that it is assumed that the deduction is made by a *reductio ad absurdum*. This is plausible because, as we argued earlier, the *reductio* seems to be the least sophisticated procedure for making the inference, as opposed to relying upon guesswork. What it entails is that the subject first assumes that the antecedent of the conditional ('The letter is not "A" ') is true. This enables him to infer that the consequent is true ('The number is "3" '). However, this contradicts the second and categorical premise ('The number is not "3" '). Hence the initial assumption is false and must be rejected. It is this final step that is critical. When the antecedent of the conditional is a negative, it involves *denying* a negative; but when the antecedent is affirmative it involves a simple and straightforward denial of an affirmative. However, it is immaterial whether or not the consequent is a negative, because at no stage is it necessary to deny the consequent. The results seem to be satisfactorily explained in terms of the 'double negative' principle although Evans himself (Evans, 1972a) prefers an explanation in terms of the difficulty of seeing how a negative could be made 'more false' by contradiction, and by a possible reluctance to think that one can reason soundly to a conclusion from an assumption of falsity.

If our argument is correct, then the difficulty of an actual *reductio ad absurdum* should be affected by whether the assumption from which it derives is affirmative or negative. Since the assumption leads to a contradiction, it has ultimately to be denied, hence the inference should be more difficult when the assumption is a negative than when it is an affirmative. This was exactly what was found in another experiment by Evans (1972b). He presented both forms of problem to 24 students in the guise of stories. The critical premises of the first were:

> You must either go to the pictures tonight, or not go for a walk tomorrow (but not both).
> If you go to the pictures tonight you must not go for a walk tomorrow.

What follows from these premises? At first sight, one might suppose that no conclusion can be derived. But, suppose for the sake of argument, that you go to the pictures tonight, then it follows, from the first premise, that it is false that you don't go for a walk tomorrow, and, from the second premise, that it is true that you don't go for a walk tomorrow. Clearly, the assumption leads to a contradiction and must be false. Hence, you do not go to the pictures tonight. The second problem had similar premises except that they led to the denial of a negative assumption ('you must not go to the pictures tonight').

The main result of the experiment was that the first sort of problem was easier than the second sort, and that more *reductio* arguments were used in its solution: nine for the first problem, as opposed to only two for the second problem. The subjects' introspective reports, and their written justifications of their answers, confirmed that the main source of trouble was not in making the assumptions, or in deriving the contradiction, but in denying the negative assumptions. Quite often a subject would infer that 'you can't not go to the pictures', but then fail to realize that this implies an affirmative. It is interesting that subjects with no training in formal logic spontaneously adopted the *reductio* form of inference. It is quite possible that their logical competence could be without this particular form of argument. It is by no means essential—indeed, the Intuitionist school of logicians have abandoned it because it establishes truths in an indirect fashion rather than in a direct and constructive way.

In view of these studies, we sought more direct evidence that the difficulty in such arguments lies, not in making a negative assumption, but in denying it. In an experiment conducted by Diana Shapiro one group of eight subjects had to write down what followed from premises such as:

If Mary doesn't stay sober, then she doesn't keep on her diet.

Either Mary keeps on her diet or else she gets depressed.

All that the subject has to do is to make the hypothetical, but negative, assumption that the antecedent is true ('Mary does not stay sober'), from which it follows that the consequent is true ('She doesn't keep on her diet'). It is then a simple matter to infer that she gets depressed; and, since the inference rests upon a hypothesis, to conclude, 'If Mary does not stay sober, then she gets depressed.' The subject's fundamental problem, of course, is to select a fruitful proposition to put forward as a hypothesis in order to get the deduction in motion.

A second group of eight subjects did not have to make the negative assumption: it was given as an additional categorical premise, e.g.

If Mary doesn't stay sober, then she doesn't keep on her diet.

Either Mary keeps on her diet or else she gets depressed.

Mary doesn't stay sober.

Both groups of subjects received two versions of the inference involving a different content.

The total number of logically correct answers (out of a maximum of 16) was 14 for the direct inference and 13 for the hypothetical inference. Thus it would seem that there is no particular difficulty attached to making a negative assumption. (There were, however, other differences between the two groups which will be taken up in the next chapter.)

In all the experiments considered so far in this chapter we have been concerned with the sources of difficulty connected with making valid inferences from negative propositions or assumptions. It is something of a digression from our main theme, but it is of some interest, to examine the effects of positive and negative information when an inference would be invalid. Here the achievement is to refrain from making an inference. The task is different from those considered previously, and it is not strictly concerned with propositional reasoning at all, but it takes us naturally into the topic of fallacies which we consider subsequently. In addition, the experiment is worth describing because (in one form of the task) it seems to exert an almost hypnotic power over some people who try it. The idea, which arose out of a discussion with A. R. Jonckheere, is quite simple. The subject is presented with four symbols: a blue diamond, a yellow diamond, a blue circle and a yellow circle (see Figure 6). When the problem is posed in positive terms the instructions are as follows:

'I am thinking of one of those colours and one of those shapes. If a symbol has either the colour I am thinking about, or the shape I am thinking about, or both, then I *accept* it, but otherwise I *reject* it. I *accept* the blue diamond. Does anything follow about my acceptance, or rejection, of the other symbols?'

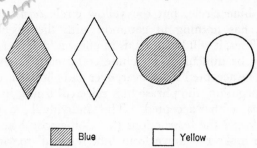

Figure 6. Material used in 'Acceptance', 'Rejection' experiment

A number of informal studies suggest that individuals are likely to reason in the following way. 'I can't say anything about the yellow diamond (because there is a diamond in the accepted symbol) nor about the blue circle (because there is blue in the accepted symbol), but the yellow circle has nothing in common with the blue diamond. Therefore it must be rejected.' This is a characteristic and instructive mistake. The positive instance (blue diamond) is evidently wrongly identified with the colour and shape which the experimenter is assumed to have in mind. In fact, all that can be inferred is that the experimenter is not thinking about 'yellow and circle'. But it does not follow from this that the yellow circle must be rejected. It would obviously be acceptable if the experimenter were thinking about 'yellow and diamond', or 'blue and circle'. In disjunctive concept attainment tasks this error is known as the 'common-element fallacy' (Bruner, Goodnow and Austin, 1956, p. 168).

Let us now consider the identical problem posed in implicit negative terms. The instructions are:

'I am thinking of one of those colours and one of those shapes. If a symbol has either the colour I am thinking about, or the shape I am thinking about, or both, then I *reject* it, but otherwise I *accept* it. I *reject* the blue diamond. Does anything follow about my rejection, or acceptance, of the other symbols?'

When the individual tackles this version, he is likely to reason erroneously, like the individuals given the positive version, as follows. 'I can't say anything about the yellow diamond, nor about the blue circle, but the yellow circle *cannot be rejected* because it has nothing in common with the rejected blue diamond.' This, it will be noted, is in effect a 'double negative', and it may be difficult to conclude consistently: 'The yellow circle must be accepted'. However, over and above the difficulty of double negation, the phrase 'not rejected' is not, in general, synonymous with 'accepted.' The individual may, quite plausibly, forget the instructions ('. . . otherwise I accept it'), and fail to make the move from 'not rejected' to 'accepted'. Hence, it seems likely that no inference will be made about the yellow circle. On the other hand, in the positive version of the problem, 'not accept' does seem synonymous with 'reject'. For example, the sentence, 'I don't accept that argument', suggests that the argument is rejected. But the sentence, 'I don't reject that argument', strongly suggests a suspension of judgement, rather than acceptance.

Let us see what happened in the experiment. In collaboration with Sheila Jones, we tested 54 15-year-old children, presenting the problems in the guise of a plausible story. Half the subjects were given the positive version, and the other half the negative version. Under the positive version 60 per cent of the subjects made the invalid inference, equivalent to the 'rejection of the yellow circle', but under the negative version only four per cent made the invalid inference, equivalent to the 'acceptance of the yellow circle'. These results tended to substantiate our hypothetical analysis of the thought processes involved in the two versions of the problem.

It should be stressed, however, that in the negative version the subjects' achievement is not especially meritorious. In fact, they were almost certainly correct for the wrong reasons. They tended to refrain from making an invalid inference, not through any logical acumen, but either because of (a) the difficulty of 'double negation', which we have found to be so pervasive in other tasks, or (b) through an apparent asymmetry between positive and negative terms. A discussion of this latter factor, however, would take us a long way from the theme of this chapter. What is more interesting is that the positive problem tempts the majority of the subjects into an interesting, and deceptive fallacious inference. And this takes us naturally into the main topic of the next chapter, when we shall consider fallacies of a simpler and more basic kind.

What emerges from this chapter is that, apart from the acknowledged difficulty of understanding negatives, there is a special difficulty which arises when they occur in deductive arguments. As a general rule, there is no particular problem when they deny affirmative propositions—an explicit negative may, in fact, be easier than an implicit negative, but when a negative is itself denied by an affirmative, it becomes difficult to keep track of the argument. And the most parsimonious explanation for this seems to be the difficulty of 'double negation'.

It is hardly surprising that negation created difficulty in the
process of deduction. But why should subjects in Shapiro's first
experiment, or in Wason's (1964) study which will be described
presently, have succumbed to the fallacy of affirming the
consequent? The argument is of the form:

If p then q.

q

∴ p.

and clearly does not involve negation. One explanation is that
they illicitly convert the conditional premise to *if* q *then* p.
The conclusion then follows validly by a simple *modus ponens*
inference.

Likewise, the mere presence of negation does not explain
the tendency to commit the fallacy of denial of the antecedent.
The argument is of the form:

If p then q.

Not-p

∴ not-q.

The simplest explanation is that the conditional premise is
illicitly taken to imply its obverse, *if not*-p *then not*-q. The
conclusion then again follows by a simple *modus ponens*.

Of course, it might be claimed that certain individuals
actually possess direct rules of inference corresponding to these
two fallacies. In the light of the propositional calculus, these
unfortunate individuals would have to be classed as irrational.
Indeed, if there are people whose deductive competence included such 'plausible' rules of inference, as Polya terms them,
then it is clear that the calculus can no longer be used as a
criterion against which to measure logical performance. Hence.

it seemed to us at the time that the illicit conversion and obversion of premises was the more likely hypothesis. The question was: what aspects of performance led to the illicit conversions, and what should we manipulate in order to lead our subjects into the path of temptation? Obviously, we could introduce problems which were very complex. But, unfortunately, this might tempt them to abandon reason in favour of guesswork. What was really required were problems that did not engender any conscious sense of their difficulty, problems that would engage the individual's rational attention without seeming to lie outside his ability.

Our first idea, working with Shapiro, was to devise a way which would produce more revealing evaluations of the two fallacies. We decided to use material which had a more familiar 'everyday' quality to it, and to ask the subject to evaluate *two* inferences from the same premises at the same time. By ensuring that one of them was valid and the other invalid, we would be able to assess the relative ease of the two sorts of deduction. Our prediction was that when the valid deduction was easy, few fallacies would be committed; but when it was difficult, there would be a greater tendency for the illicit conversion to be made and hence a greater tendency for the fallacies to be committed.

Two basic types of problem were used in the experiment. The first type had the following form:

> Rembrandt's work is known to every artist.
> Everyone who knows Rembrandt's work appreciates its beauty.
> John knows Rembrandt's work.
> Therefore (1) John appreciates the beauty of Rembrandt's work.
> (2) John is an artist.

Superficially, it seems as though the complex premises are no longer in the form of conditional sentences. However, they do have a conditional form because the underlying logic of the first premise corresponds to, 'If an individual is an artist, then he knows Rembrandt's work', and likewise the second premise corresponds to, 'If an individual knows Rembrandt's work, then he appreciates its beauty.' It should now be clear that the first conclusion follows validly from the premises, whereas the second conclusion does not. *Modus ponens* is contrasted with the fallacy of affirming the consequent. The second type of problem had the form:

> Rembrandt's work is known to every artist.
> Everyone who knows Rembrandt's work appreciates its beauty.
> John does not know Rembrandt's work.
> Therefore (1) John does not appreciate the beauty of Rembrandt's work.
>   (2) John is not an artist.

Here, the first conclusion is invalid and the second conclusion valid, and the contrast is between *modus tollendo tollens* and the fallacy of denying the antecedent.

The results of the experiment were very surprising: hardly any errors were made. This confirmed that few if any individuals actually possess rules of inference corresponding to the fallacies. But the task was logically more complex than Shapiro's straightforward investigation, and the subjects came from the same population of university students. Why, then, were no fallacies committed? It seems likely that this is because of the nature of the materials. Shapiro had used relatively abstract material, e.g. 'If an object is blue, then it is rectangular', whereas in the present study we used more familiar everyday material.

Despite this setback, it still seemed worth pursuing the idea that cognitive difficulty would influence the tendency to commit fallacies. But the task would have to be made harder. One relevant factor is whether the subject is required to evaluate a given inference or actually to make an inference. Evaluation merely requires him to test the logical relation between the premises and the conclusion. Both ends of the inference are quite specific, and he can work both forwards and backwards between them. In *making* an inference, however, the subject has to draw his own conclusion. He is bound to concentrate upon the premises, and should he wish to work backwards from the conclusion he must first advance one of his own. The chances of guessing the answer correctly are thus considerably reduced. In pursuing our problem, the natural strategy seemed to be to get subjects to draw their own conclusions. The one potential difficulty was that different people express themselves in different ways, even when they are saying the same thing, and it might be awkward to evaluate and to score their responses. The simple way to obviate this problem would be to devise a task where the responses were automatically constrained. This we were able to do in the next experiment, which was carried out in collaboration with Graham Gibbs.

The subjects were asked to imagine that there were three pigeon-holes arranged vertically—a top one, a middle one, and a bottom one—and three objects 'A', 'B', and 'C', which had to be assigned each to their correct pigeon-hole. The subjects were given three true statements concerning the positions of the objects, and their task was to write down the order of arrangement on the basis of this information. This problem requires an inference to be made, while it ensures that responses are sufficiently constrained to prevent difficulties in their evaluation.

The task allowed us to combine a valid and an invalid inference within a problem, and hence to determine whether the likelihood of the fallacy depends upon the ease of making the valid inference. We decided to concentrate upon the fallacy of affirming the consequent because this is free of the further complexities of negation. Since the earlier results had established that *modus tollendo tollens* is more difficult than *modus ponens*, it was predicted that subjects would be more susceptible to the fallacy when it was associated with the former than with the latter.

The prediction was tested by using two types of problem. The first consisted of premises in the following form:

(1) If 'A' is at the top, then 'B' is in the middle.
(2) If 'C' is in the middle, then 'A' is at the top.
(3) 'A' is at the top.

Any determinate order of the objects must start from the simple categorical assertion that 'A' is at the top. The valid inference, *modus ponens*, is made by combining this information with premise (1) to infer the order:

E

```
┌───┐
│ A │
├───┤
│ B │
├───┤
│ C │
└───┘
```

The fallacy of affirming the consequent is made when the categorical premise is combined with premise (2) to infer the order:

```
┌───┐
│ A │
├───┤
│ C │
├───┤
│ B │
└───┘
```

This is fallacious because, as we have remarked, a conditional does not necessarily imply the truth of its converse.

The second type of problem consisted of premises of the following type:

(1) If 'B' is at the bottom, then 'A' is in the middle.
(2) If 'C' is in the middle, then 'A' is at the top.
(3) 'A' is at the top.

The fallacy, and its corresponding arrangement of objects, are exactly the same as before. The valid inference, *modus tollendo tollens*, involves premise (1); and it is necessary to argue that since 'A' is not in the middle, 'B' is not at the bottom. This yields the order:

```
┌───┐
│ A │
├───┤
│ B │
├───┤
│ C │
└───┘
```

It was necessary only to test a small number of subjects in order to establish a greater susceptibility to the fallacy in the second type of problem. Each subject was given eight versions of both types in order to counterbalance such variables as whether the categorical premise referred to the item at the top or the item at the bottom. On average, 4·5 problems of the first type were correctly solved, whereas only 1·6 problems of the second type were correctly solved. This difference was reflected in the individual results of seven out of the eight students who were tested—the odd man out only got one problem right, and that towards the end of the experiment.

These results confirmed our hypothesis: when a seemingly difficult or insoluble problem can be solved by assuming that a conditional does imply its converse, then subjects are prepared to do so. Once this illicit conversion has been made, a simple *modus ponens* can quite correctly be performed and the order of the objects inferred. It is interesting to note that A. Mazzocco (reported by Legrenzi, 1970) has also found that statements of the form, 'All red objects are square', are assumed erroneously to imply, 'All square objects are red', when this helps to ease the mental difficulty of a problem. Are there any other factors likely to induce subjects to make an illicit conversion?

Paolo Legrenzi (1970) has argued that a conditional is more likely to be taken to imply its converse in what he calls a 'strictly binary' situation. This means a situation in which the subject realizes that the antecedent of the conditional refers to one of only two possible events, and that the consequent refers to one of only two possible events. An example of such a situation is provided by the experimental materials which Legrenzi himself used to investigate the hypothesis. A ball ran down a channel on a table either to the right or else to the left. When it reached the bottom of the channel, either a red light came on, or else a green light came on. The subjects were asked to classify these various contingencies, which were plainly strictly binary, with respect to a statement of the form, 'If the ball rolls to the left, then the green light comes on.' The classifications of 22 out of the 30 subjects who were tested showed that they had interpreted the conditional as though it implied its converse. Thus, for example, when the ball rolled to the right and the green light came on, the trial was considered to be incompatible with the rule.

What is particularly interesting about this study is that several investigators in the Piagetian tradition (e.g. Matalon, 1962; Peel, 1967) have suggested that children are prone to making illicit conversions until they reach the age of reason (or 'level of formal operations'). However, the experimental situations giving rise to this conclusion have often been of a strictly binary nature. Hence, we were pleased when Peter Thompson offered to investigate the way in which children interpreted conditional statements, and we designed an experiment in which a strictly binary situation was compared with a non-binary situation. The children were in three different age groups: 5–6 years, $7\frac{1}{2}$–$8\frac{1}{2}$ years, and 10–11 years; and there were 12 subjects in each age group.

The children were presented with the conditional rule, 'If the switch is down, then the light is on', together with a simple switch and light circuit. When there is a single light and a single switch, it seems natural to believe that the switch completely determines the state of the light. It was for this reason that, in a separate condition, we introduced *two* switches. In the first, the strictly binary condition, the children almost invariably took the conditional to imply its converse; and, incidentally, even the youngest of them appreciated that when the light was off the switch would be up. However, as we had expected, the presence of two switches disrupted the illicit conversion of the conditional. We had predicted that when they were asked, 'What can you say about the (relevant) switch, when the light is on?', they would now say words to the effect that nothing could be inferred about its state. This would be because they had appreciated that the other switch might also be involved in controlling the light. Contrary to our expectation, however, the children did not perform in this more mature fashion. Instead, they tended to develop a number of idiosyncratic hypotheses about how the two switches might work in tandem, e.g. when one is up, the other must be down, and to answer the question about the hidden (relevant) switch partly on the basis of the position of the visible (irrelevant) switch. They were less certain about how to answer the questions put to them, and produced a greater variety of answers than in the strictly binary situation. Nevertheless, the tendency to assume the converse of the statement was broken, even though it was not replaced by any one dominant or cohesive interpretation.

There is a further factor likely to influence the interpretation of conditional statements; and, due perhaps to our predisposition towards formal logic, and towards using the propositional calculus as a criterion for performance, it was some time before we appreciated it. The actual content of the antecedent and the consequent of the conditional effects what it is understood to mean. For example, a conditional such as, 'If you clear up your toys, you can go to the pictures' is likely to be taken to imply, 'If you don't clear up your toys, you can't go to the pictures.' Indeed, for many parents (and children) the obverse is merely a more forceful way of spelling out the dire consequences of failing to fulfil the antecedent of the original conditional. But the original conditional most certainly does not imply its converse, i.e. 'If you can go to the pictures, you clear up your toys.' Other conditionals, however, seem to imply both their converse and obverse. For example, 'If you are over 18, then you are eligible to vote' suggests both that 'If you're eligible to vote, then you're over 18' and that 'If you are not over 18, then you are not eligible to vote.'

Unfortunately, the definitive criteria for deciding just what is implied by a conditional have yet to be discovered—if indeed there are any. However, we have found two rules of thumb to be quite useful guides. The interpretation in which both converse and obverse are implied tends to demand a conditional which, if its components are affirmative, is the statement of some sort of generalization, or is a statement which rests upon a generalization, e.g. 'If John is Mary's brother, then Mary is John's sister.' In such cases, there is a tendency for the antecedent and consequent to be in the same mood and the same tense. Our second rule, we were pleased to discover, was anticipated by Galen, the second century (A.D.) physician and logician. Of conditionals with negated antecedents such as 'If it is not day, then it is night' he wrote that they are 'called a "conditional" by those who pay attention only to the sounds, but a disjunction by those who pay attention to the nature of what is meant' (quoted by Mates, 1961). Thus, for example, 'If it isn't John, then it's John's brother' is synonymous with

'Either it's John or it's John's brother.' The converse and obverse of such conditionals are clearly implied ('If it's John's brother, then it isn't John', 'If it's John, then it isn't his brother'). In other words, there is something special about negating the antecedent of a conditional: it yields a statement different from the rest of the species.

This observation may throw some light on an interesting finding in Jonathan Evans' (1972a) study of conditionals. The reader will recall that when the antecedent of a conditional premise was negated, subjects found certain deductions difficult to make correctly. In the case of valid deductions, we explained this result in terms of the 'double negative' hypothesis. However, in other cases, the deductions were fallacies:

If the letter is not an 'A', then the number is a '3'.
The number is a '3'.
Therefore: the letter is not an 'A'.

The subjects were very prone to accept the conclusion as valid. The error is not simply due to the introduction of a negative, because negating the consequent did not produce it. It is therefore natural to suppose that it is the negation of the antecedent which renders the conditional more susceptible to illicit conversion. The reason for this would seem to be that such a conditional is interpreted as a disguised disjunction. In everyday life, context would completely clarify whether or not the conditional is to be treated as a disjunction. In the experimental situation, however, such a conditional is ambiguous. It thus seems quite arbitrary as to whether its conversion should be treated as illicit.

We have examined several factors which are likely to lead to the conversion of conditionals: the use of abstract material, the difficulty of the task, situations which are strictly binary, and the negation of the antecedent. It is natural to enquire whether there is any variable which can exert a remedial effect and lead to the spontaneous correction of the error. In fact, a very potent source of correction has been discovered (Wason, 1964).

The subjects in this experiment were given an incomplete rule, for example, 'Any employee aged — years, or more, will receive a salary of at least £1,900 a year.' This was followed by the ages and salaries of ten employees, making a series of ten trials. On each trial the subjects had to say what they could infer about the limits of the critical age. On the first trial, for instance, the information might be that *an employee receiving £1,500 is aged 25*. It follows quite validly that the critical age omitted from the rule must be more than 25, because any individual of at least the critical age receives a salary of £1,900, or more. On the second trial, the information might be that *an employee receiving £2,000 is aged 27*. The fallacy, here, is to infer that the critical age cannot be more than 27. It could very well be, for the simple reason that the rule does not imply its converse, and hence someone under the critical age could receive more than £1,900. The rule merely asserts that anyone of, or over, the critical age will receive at least this amount.

It is possible to reason fallaciously and yet to arrive at a conclusion which happens to be true. The fallacy of affirming the consequent is, as Polya (1954) stressed, no exception to this principle and this was exploited in the experiment. The rule was sufficiently complicated to cause 20 out of the 30 subjects who were given it to commit the fallacy. But the experiment was arranged so that the invalid conclusions were, at first, quite consistent with the valid conclusions inferred on the alternate trials. They were true although they were invalidly obtained. Thus, a typical series of four trials, with the subject's conclusions, might run as follows:

(1) Receives £1,500 Aged 25 Hence the critical age must be more than 25 (Valid)

(2) Receives £3,000 Aged 40 Hence the critical age cannot be more than 40 (Invalid)

(3) Receives £1,800 Aged 27 Hence the critical age must be more than 27 (Valid)

(4) Receives £2,300 Aged 35 Hence the critical age cannot be more than 35 (Invalid)

On the fifth trial, however, the treatment of the subjects diverged. One group continued to receive material where the invalid and valid inferences yielded compatible conclusions. The other group encountered conflicting information. For example, on the fifth trial they might be given:

(5) Receives £1,500 Aged 37

The valid conclusion from this information is that the critical age must be more than 37, and this is incompatible with the previous inference that it cannot be more than 35. It is worth noting that the valid inference contradicted a previously made fallacious inference but was consistent with subsequent fallacious inferences. Thus there was no direct impediment to continuing to commit the fallacy, and their relinquishment must have been due to insight into the illicit nature of the conversion.

Two further quite separate groups of subjects were treated in identical fashion except that their fallacious inferences were cases of denying the antecedent (and thus of making an illicit obversion of the conditional).

What happened was that those groups who received the conflicting material, and were thus led to contradict themselves, henceforth showed a reliable tendency to withhold the fallacious inference; and once having withheld it no subject subsequently relapsed into error. On the other hand, the groups who received the compatible information tended to persist in committing the fallacy. Of course, not all the subjects committed the fallacies in the first place: exactly half of the 60 subjects tested proved to be susceptible to them, with ten subjects denying the antecedent and 20 subjects affirming the consequent. The numbers of these subjects, who at some stage learnt, or did not learn, to withhold the fallacious inference are given in Table 2 as a function of whether they received the compatible or incompatible material.

TABLE 2 *The numbers of subjects withholding the fallacious inference as a function of whether or not they received compatible material*

	Compatible material	Incompatible material
Withholds fallacy at some subsequent stage	4	9
Continues to commit the fallacy	12	5

Although more subjects affirmed the consequent than denied the antecedent, there was little difference between the fallacies when it came to the effects of the contradiction upon them. Evidently, this forced the subjects to reconsider their interpretation of the conditional, and presumably brought home to them the fact that they had behaved in a way which, though sometimes plausible in ordinary life, was logically unwarranted. They had assumed that the rule implied its converse, or obverse, and now they were forced to see that it did not.

In this chapter, we have established that the individual's grasp of the logic of propositions is not quite so secure as might have been supposed. However, if individuals are irrational, the evidence so far suggests that this is not because they possess faulty rules of inference, but because they sometimes make unwarranted interpretations of conditional statements. We have argued that some conditionals in ordinary discourse do legitimately imply their converses (or obverses). It is not yet possible to lay down any definite criteria, but according to two rough guides such conditionals include those which state some generalization, and those, involving negated antecedents, which are disguised disjunctions. However, a purely situational variable—the presence of strictly binary conditions—also exerts an influence. The reader may by now have hit upon the most obvious explanation why such a situation is likely to lead to illicit conversion and obversion. It produces a natural temptation to make a causal interpretation of the conditional, and to assume that the antecedent event, p, is the unique cause of the consequent event, q. Hence when p does not occur, the cause of q is absent, and q will not occur; and when q does occur, it is legitimate to infer that its cause, p, must have occurred.

This 'set' was evidently disrupted in the experiment with children by the introduction of an alternative cause (i.e. the second switch); and it is arguable that it would have been broken in Legrenzi's experiment if, for example, a light sometimes came on without the ball rolling down either channel. The topic of illicit conversion is by no means exhausted, but in the meantime we shall turn to another aspect of 'causal' thinking in the following chapter.

incompetence

Our doubts about the propositional calculus as a useful yard-stick for logical performance had been growing for some time before we appreciated what was staring us in the face. People are not very much concerned with, or governed by, systems of thought which merely interrelate the truth or falsity of pro-positions. They have inferential concerns, other than the purely *truth-functional* relations, which may inhere within a complex web of inter-related propositions. Often these concerns reflect a practical or causal approach to the problem. The fact that such matters enter into the thinking of an individual is, of course, no evidence that he cannot make strictly formal or truth-functional deductions. It seems that people can make such deductions, but they are perhaps an exception outside the laboratory. Our present concern is accordingly with the contrast between these modes of 'practical' and 'pure' reason. The terms have been appropriated from philosophy, but what they mean for psychological purposes is closer to their common connotations, as we shall see.

The evidence to support the limited role of truth-functional thought falls into two categories. First, there are findings on the sheer difficulty of thinking in this way—a difficulty which would not arise if we were naturally equipped for such per-formance. Second, there is evidence showing how the individual departs from the strict canons of truth-functional thought, and the sort of considerations which enter into his deliberations when he does so.

What finally brought home to us the problems of purely logical thought was the result of an experiment (Johnson-Laird and Penny Hayes, unpublished), which was designed for quite another purpose.

At the time, considerable interest had been aroused by an information-processing model of the way in which individuals form new concepts out of old. The details of this model, devised by Hunt (1962) need not detain us: it assumes that subjects 'focus' on what are presented as positive instances of the concept. The point of a concept attainment task (described more fully in Chapter 16) is that the subject is exposed to positive and negative instances of the concept (or 'idea') which the experimenter has in mind. His task is to discover this concept, and demonstrate that he has discovered it, by anticipating correctly whether further instances are positive, or negative, or by defining the concept in his own words. These two criteria are not necessarily attained at the same time: usually the ability to make correct anticipations precedes the ability to define the concept. However, the ability to identify members of a class seems to be a more 'objective' criterion than the ability to describe it—an important factor when psychology was dominated by the positivist ethos of Behaviourism—and it is certainly more directly amenable to statistical analysis.

The fact that the behavioural criterion takes temporal precedence over the definitional criterion seems to signify that the role of language is subsidiary to the basic process of acquisition. It is also true that some concepts are virtually ineffable: those, for instance, which underlie the ability to recognise a good claret, a fragment of Mozart, or the literary style of a particular author. With such skills, partly perceptual and partly conceptual, there is no substitute for experience—for encountering a series of positive and negative 'instances', and common sense tells us that it is futile to dwell too much upon their verbal definitions. Such concepts are likely to exert a strong and perhaps unacknowledged influence over our behaviour. Michael Polyani (1958) has suggested that some may be so implicit, so ineffable, that an individual might be unaware that he possessed them. This certainly coincides with the view of psychotherapy which sees its goal as teaching the patient to put into words, and hence to face up to, covert feelings and wishes which were originally acquired prelinguistically (cf. Dollard and Miller, 1950). But there are just as many concepts which are acquired, not by encountering a series of positive and negative instances, but by verbal definition. The bulk of our education rests upon this principle and it seems so obvious as to be hardly worth saying. If a concept can be defined at all, it can usually be defined clearly enough to be communicated; otherwise all one can do is to point to exemplars of it.

What this argument establishes is that the standard psychological investigation of concept-attainment is a mixed metaphor. It uses a technique appropriate for ineffable concepts with materials which are all too easy to describe: the gruelling presentation of a series of positive and negative instances of concepts that can be defined in a couple of words. 'So what?' the reader may be tempted to ask, especially if he happens to be a psychologist. Well, there is the general point, which will assume an increasing importance in this book, that the content of the problem is often a most pertinent variable in reasoning tasks. But, more specifically, this analysis of concept-attainment suggested to us that what ought to be studied was the *communicability*, rather than the attainability, of the sorts of concepts customarily investigated by psychologists. The relevance of Hunt's information-processing model was, first, that he had made the provocative statement that putting a concept into words once it had been 'behaviourally attained' was a trivial problem; and, second, that the model applied to a variety of logical types of concept. Concepts which involve the logical combinations of pre-existing concepts are particularly suitable for communicating by verbal definition, e.g. a 'warehouse class of building' is defined in the London Building Acts as 'a warehouse, a manufacturing building, a brewery, a distillery, *or* any other public building exceeding 150 thousand cubic feet which is *neither* a public *nor* a domestic building'. We accordingly set out to investigate the relative ease of describing different sorts of concept.

The basic task was a sort of minimal concept-attainment, but very little learning was involved because the concept was spelt out in the form of a simple and systematic table of positive and negative instances. All that the subject had to do was to express in his own words the appropriate concept, or rule, represented by the table. The task might therefore be described as one of 'concept description'.

To provide an appropriate context for their exercise, the subjects were told to imagine that they were going to be given some secret information about the way a chemical compound could be manufactured. Their job was to study this information and to write down as economical a formulation of it as they could.

The problems always involved four chemicals, two of them were denoted by letters (e.g. 'T' and 'U') and the other two by numbers (e.g. '6' and '7'). The information, concerning which combinations yielded the desired compound, was presented in a tabular form. Thus, a typical problem was:

T	6	O
T	7	I
U	6	O
U	7	I

where 'I' indicates that a combination yields the desired compound, and 'O' indicates that a combination does not yield the desired compound. All that the subject has to do is to write down a description of how the compound could be manufactured. In this rather simple practice problem, the subject might write, 'Any chemical with "7" '; but since he was told that there was an imaginary recipient of the message who possessed a similar table except that it lacked the 'I's and the 'O's, it was quite permissible to write just '7'. However, one variable that we were naturally interested in was the effect of negation; and in order to compel the subjects to use negatives, there was a general rule that only the chemicals at the head of the table could be explicitly mentioned in descriptions. Thus, the solution to the example would have to be, 'not-6'.

In order to get the feel of the problem, the reader may care to try to describe the following table, bearing in mind that only '9' and 'R' can be explicitly mentioned in the description:

9	R	O
9	S	I
10	R	I
10	S	O

Most people appreciate that this can be described as, '9 and not-R, or not-9 and R'; relatively few people, apart from those trained in logic, are able to produce the more elegant, 'either 9 or else R, but not both'.

There is a close connection between the logic of these sorts of concepts and the propositional calculus; and, of course, this is hardly surprising because it must be the essence of a communicable concept that propositions can be put together to characterize it. However, at the time the experiment was performed, we were much more concerned with the relative difficulty of describing different sorts of concept than with any implication the experiment might have for propositional reasoning. Our basic assumptions were that concepts which were essentially conjunctive in form would be easier to formulate than concepts which were essentially disjunctive in form, and that whenever a component was negated there would be a slight increase in difficulty. A table which contains only one 'I' (and three 'o's') is essentially conjunctive since its most economic description will be of the form 'something-AND-something', e.g. 'T and not-6'. A table which contains three 'I's' (and one 'o') is essentially disjunctive since its most economic description will be of the form 'something-OR-something', e.g. 'T or 6 (or both)'. A table with two 'I's' (and two 'o's') is not either of these two essential forms, hence we suspected that they might be hardest to describe. Clearly, there are 16 possible tables which can be constructed. But only ten of them are relevant to testing these predictions. Two of the ten are trivial variants of others within the set. These were omitted from the experimental materials, as were simple conjunction and its mirror-image (obtained by converting 'I's' to 'o's' and 'o's' to 'I's'). The remaining six types of concept, which were used in the experiment, are summarized in Table 3. They consist of

TABLE 3 *The six types of concept used in the experiment*

	T OR 6	not-T AND not-6	not-T OR 6	T AND not-6	T OR 6 but not both	T AND 6 OR neither
T 6	1	0	1	0	0	1
T 7	1	0	0	1	1	0
U 6	1	0	1	0	1	0
U 7	0	1	1	0	0	1

three sorts of concept together with their respective mirror-images, or negatives.

In order to allow for the likely differences in the ways in which different individuals would describe the concepts, each of the 24 subjects described all six of them in different counter-balanced orders. The numbers and letters used to represent the chemicals were varied from one problem to the next.

It proved possible to rank order each subject's description in terms of their accuracy and economy[1], and the average ranks for the concepts are shown in Figure 7. The general increase in the difficulty of describing the concepts is a very reliable one and it conforms to the predictions. The two conjunctive

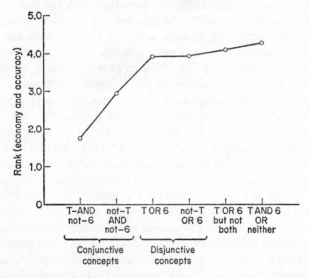

Figure 7. The average ranks (for accuracy and economy) of the six types of concept

[1] The descriptions were ranked according to the following principles:
  (a) accurate descriptions were ranked higher than inaccurate ones; and ambiguous descriptions with one interpretation which is accurate were given an intermediate ranking.
  (b) within these categories, descriptions were ranked according to the number of occurrences of letters and numbers referring to chemicals, e.g. 'T or 6 (or both)' was ranked higher than 'T with 6 or not-6, or not-T with 6'.

concepts are easiest, followed by the two disjunctive concepts, and the two concepts which involve both a conjunctive and a disjunctive relation are hardest of all. The order within the first pair can be accounted for by the extra negation needed to describe, 'not-T and not-6', as opposed to, 'T and not-6'.

The order of difficulty conforms to the order obtained when subjects have to *learn* concepts in the conventional manner; and a variety of different theories have been proposed to explain this order (cf. Haygood and Bourne, 1965), ranging from the familiarity of the form of concept in daily life to the efficacy of Hunt's 'focusing' strategy.

What was really striking about the subjects' performance, however, was the great difficulty they had with the task. All of them were able to describe the simplest conjunctive concept in economical terms like 'T with any but 6'. But with the disjunctive concepts only about half the subjects produced economical descriptions like 'All except T and not-6' or 'not a T without 6'. The remainder of the subjects produced list-like descriptions enumerating each line of the table separately in what logicians call 'disjunctive normal form', e.g. 'T and 6, not-T and 6, not-T and not-6', 'T and not-T with 6, not-T with not-6'. Such descriptions were almost universal for the two hardest concepts. The first was described as 'either T or else 6' by only two subjects, though a further four subjects did manage, 'T and 6 but not both together'; the second was described as 'T and 6 or neither' by only one subject. Obviously, there was a very strong tendency to approach a problem by focusing on the positive contingencies in the table, as Hunt had proposed; and this led to subjects spelling out each positive line separately. Only a very few individuals realized that it could be more economical to describe the solitary negative instance of a disjunctive concept, and then to negate that description, e.g. 'not (T and not-6)'.

It may be difficult to appreciate just how hard the task is unless one has observed an intelligent student struggling to express, say, a disjunctive concept and, after two minutes, producing some tortuous expression listing each of the positive contingencies. But it was this aspect of performance, together with the general dearth of the verbal formulae used by logicians to express tabular information, that suggested that the problem might be alien to the normal patterns of thought of the educated adult. Perhaps Hunt had been a little too glib in declaring that no great problem was involved in describing concepts once they were attained; perhaps the logically naive individual does not naturally think in a logically pure and truth-functional manner.

This hypothesis was put to a more direct test in an experiment involving hypothetical reasoning. The essential idea was to compare deductive performance with two different, though logically equivalent, formulations of a problem. The underlying *logic* of a conditional statement such as, 'If prices increase, the firm goes bankrupt' is also expressed in the statement, 'Prices increase only if the firm goes bankrupt.' There is a distinct difference in meaning between these statements, yet they are logically and truth-functionally equivalent: they are falsified only by the occurrence of a price increase without the firm going bankrupt. Where they differ is in their temporal or causal connotations. The first statement suggests that the increase of prices will cause, or at least precede, the firm's bankruptcy; whereas the second statement suggests that the firm's continuing solvency exerts a causal check on the increase of prices.

Although logicians have recently shown an increasing interest in the logic of temporal and causal expressions[1], the standard systems of logic, such as the propositional calculus, are quite free of such concerns. Practical inference, however, seems unlikely to escape from them. Hence, we felt that an individual's ability to make a strictly deductive inference might be impaired by misleading causal connotations in the material. Specifically, an inference from the following premises:

> If Mary does not stay sober, then she doesn't keep on her diet.

> Either Mary keeps on her diet or else she gets depressed.

would be relatively easy (as we saw in Chapter 5) because the necessary hypothetical assumption corresponds to the *causal* antecedent of the conditional. It would be easy to assume that Mary does not stay sober, because this is an obvious causal assumption. It follows, of course, that she doesn't keep on her

---

[1] See Rescher (1968) for a useful chapter and bibliography on 'chronological' logic.

diet (from the first premise), and hence she gets depressed (from the second premise). The inference that can accordingly be drawn is:

'If Mary does not stay sober, then she gets depressed.'

However, if the premises are in the following guise the inference should be relatively difficult:

Mary does not stay sober only if she doesn't keep on her diet.

Either Mary keeps on her diet or else she gets depressed. The first premise has the same logic as before but it now suggests that keeping to her diet enables Mary to maintain sobriety. There will be a natural tendency to base the inference on the causal antecedent, i.e. to assume that Mary doesn't keep on her diet. But this time the causal assumption is not the logical key to the problem. It leads nowhere. The deduction, in fact, depends upon making the same assumption as in the first problem, and leads to the same conclusion, 'If Mary does not stay sober, then she gets depressed.'

In the experiment (Johnson-Laird and Shapiro, unpublished), eight subjects were given four problems with the straightforward conditional premises, and a further eight subjects were given four equivalent problems with the 'only if' premises. On average, the first group made 1·25 correct inferences, whereas the second group made only 0·4 correct inferences. Furthermore, disregarding whether or not an inference was correct, there were reliably more *conditional* conclusions in the first group (on average, 2·37) than in the second group (on average, 1·0). This suggests that the subjects presented with the 'only if' premises found it difficult to make any sort of hypothetical inference, let alone the correct one.

The experiment confirmed our view that the individual tends naturally to think in a causal fashion, and that if this tendency is set into opposition with the logical requirements of an inference, it is extremely difficult for the correct deduction to be drawn. The propensity for causal and temporal thinking was also borne out by the actual words in which the subjects expressed their conclusions. They would conclude, for instance, 'If Mary does not stay sober, then she will get depressed', implying a temporal connection between the two events, or

'Mary gets depressed from drinking', implying a causal connection between them.

Practical deduction, involving temporal and causal considerations, is obviously going to depend to a considerable extent upon the content of the problem. It will occur if the material concerns sensible everyday matters; it will not occur if the material is abstruse or abstract. However, we suspected that it might also be influenced by a more logical property of inferences, namely, whether or not they were hypothetical in form. In daily life, hypotheses are seldom of a purely logical nature, they are much more often causal in form. We therefore predicted that temporal, modal, or even explicitly causal, conclusions should be more likely to occur in a hypothetical deduction, where it is necessary to make an assumption, than in a direct deduction, where it is not necessary to make an assumption.

In a previous experiment described in Chapter 5, the reader will recollect that there was no difference in logical difficulty between the hypothetical inference and the direct inference where the assumption was given as a simple categorical premise. The two groups did differ, however, in the frequency with which they drew temporal, modal, or causal conclusions. The subjects who were given two hypothetical inferences produced an average of 1·9 such conclusions; the subjects who were given two direct inferences produced an average of only 0·9 such conclusions.

The difficulty of truth-functional thinking had originally been suggested by the results of the 'tabular' experiment (Johnson-Laird and Hayes, unpublished). This involved relatively abstract material, in the guise of combinations of chemicals, about which it was difficult to make any practical assumptions. (Indeed, the few subjects who knew something about chemistry found the conception of it embodied in the experiment slightly absurd.) Hence the subjects were forced to try to think in a purely deductive way, and showed a striking lack of facility at so doing. The two experiments on hypothetical reasoning, however, involved pre-eminently practical material and it was observed, in the first of them, that when the habitual pattern of practical thought ran counter to the deductive task, the subjects found it almost impossible to infer the correct conclusion. In the second of these experiments, there was, of course, no such conflict. The subjects performed with considerable logical accuracy but their protocols clearly revealed that, when the deductive requirements of a problem forced them to make an assumption, this was often couched in a causal or extra-logical form. These findings made us wonder how the logically naive individual would cope with the 'tabular' task if the material consisted of sensible everyday propositions. Would there now be signs, not only of difficulty in thinking in a truth-functional way, but also of practical patterns of inference?

An experiment (Johnson-Laird and Shapiro, unpublished), was conducted to try to find out. It utilized a very similar design to the previous study, but the tabular information involved simple assertions:

The musicians are good	The programme is boring	
True	True	1
True	False	1
False	True	1
False	False	0

The subjects were instructed to treat the table as the outcome of a series of observations, with a '1' indicating that a particular contingency had been found to occur, whereas a '0' indicated that it had never been found to occur. Thus, for example, the third row of the table indicates that on at least one occasion the musicians had not been good (i.e. 'The musicians are good' was false), and the programme had been boring (i.e. 'The programme is boring' was true). The task was to produce an accurate and economic description of the information summarized in the table.

The connection between the logic of these sorts of tables and the propositional calculus is very close. Indeed, the logical connections of the calculus are often defined by means of such tables. The final column of the table, instead of concerning what had been observed, defines the truth, or falsity, of the proposition as a whole. For example, the disjunctive connective, usually symbolized by 'v', may be defined by the following 'truth table':

p	q	$(p \; v \; q)$
True	True	True
True	False	True
False	True	True
False	False	False

This means that when any two propositions are combined disjunctively the resulting statement is true when at least one of the two propositions is true. The resemblance between this and the table used in the experiment is obvious; and one economical description of the experimental table would indeed be: 'The musicians are good OR the programme is boring.'

A new variable was introduced in this experiment to try to manipulate the extent to which practical, as opposed to pure, thinking occurred. This was the degree to which the two assertions in each table were related to one another. When they were directly related, we argued, the individual's practical mode of reasoning should be engaged. However, when they were unrelated, the task would seem to be more abstract, and the individual would be unable to indulge so easily in practical thought. It was predicted that the difference would emerge in three ways. First, the logical accuracy of the descriptions should be greater for the unrelated material than for the related material. Second, the descriptions should take less time to formulate for the unrelated material than for the related material. This would be because with the unrelated material the subjects would be concerned only with the truth functional nature of the table, and not with extra-logical considerations. Third, there would be a greater tendency for practical and causal factors to emerge in the descriptions of the related material. These would manifest themselves in a variety of ways, e.g. the use of temporal or modal auxiliary verbs, the use of causal connectives such as *because*, the tendency for one assertion to be embedded within the other in the descriptions. In short, the actual wording of the two given assertions is likely to be changed to a greater extent in the descriptions of the related material so as to bring out the causal assumptions underlying the subjects' thinking.

The relatedness of the material was manipulated by changing just one word in the pair of assertions. For example, the related material included the assertions, 'The vase falls on to the floor' and 'The glass cracks'; the corresponding assertions for the unrelated condition were, 'The vase falls on to the floor' and 'The glass melts.' It is intuitively obvious that the first pair of sentences are related, or at least relatable, in a way in which the second pair are not. But it is curiously difficult to specify in formal terms wherein the distinction resides. In such cases, the psychologist often has recourse to operational tests, so we might, for example, have given our material to an independent panel of judges and asked them to corroborate our judgements. This seemed to us a slightly absurd exercise, with the results a fore-gone conclusion. However, the reader may judge for himself: the rest of the material consisted of the following items, where the word in brackets occurred in the unrelated material in place of the word it follows:

It is raining.	The girl is soaked (prejudiced).
The lungs are congested.	The patient smokes (reads).
The engine requires oil.	The pump (telephone) is faulty.
The liquid freezes.	The temperature (product) is zero.
The verdict is fair.	The decision (bill) is correct.
The operator is over-worked.	Mistakes (eclipses) occur.
The man sleeps.	The bed (fruit) is soft.

We tested 24 undergraduates altogether, and half of them received the related material and the other half received the unrelated material. Each of them did eight different types of truth table, and these consisted of the six types used in the first 'tabular' experiment and, in addition, simple conjunction and its negation. The lexical content of the problems, of course, was also varied by using the eight pairs of assertions. The order of presenting the lexical material was held constant while the order of the types of concept was counterbalanced.

It was obvious from the most superficial analysis of the results that the task was a difficult one. It was even harder than the previous 'truth-table' experiment, and produced descriptions of a rather different type. Only 48 per cent of the descriptions were definitely correct, 20 per cent were definitely incorrect, and the remaining 32 per cent were ambiguous, but with at least one interpretation which was correct. There was no reliable difference between the 'related' and 'unrelated' groups in terms of either the accuracy or the economy of their descriptions. Hence the first prediction was not confirmed. However, there was a very reliable difference in the times that the two groups took to formulate their descriptions. The average time per description for the 'related' group was 3 min. 25 sec., and the average time for the 'unrelated' group was 1 min. 59 sec. This difference was reflected in the times for each type of truth-table. Hence the second prediction was confirmed.

As we had expected, a variety of changes in the wording of the original assertions was made, and it was possible to distinguish four main qualitative categories of description:

(1) Logically pure: these were descriptions which merely attempted to make a logical statement of the information, e.g. 'Either the engine requires oil or the pump is not faulty, but not both', 'The lungs are congested and the patient does not read.'

(2) Temporal: these descriptions established a temporal relation between the two events, e.g. 'The liquid freezes when the temperature is not zero', 'The man sleeps only when the fruit is not soft.'

(3) Frequential: these descriptions explicitly introduced the notion of the frequency of events, e.g. 'The girl is less frequently prejudiced when it is raining than when it is not', 'The engine always requires oil, and the pump is usually faulty.'

(4) Causal: these descriptions asserted, or denied, a causal connection between the events, e.g. 'If the liquid freezes at all the temperature *must* be zero', 'An incorrect decision does not lead to a fair verdict as does a correct one sometimes.' A special sub-category of causal descriptions were those where, as the result either of embedding one of the assertions within the other, or of some grosser metamorphosis, only a single unified event was specified, e.g. 'The girl does not go out in the rain', as a description

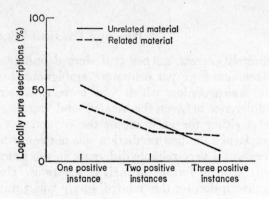

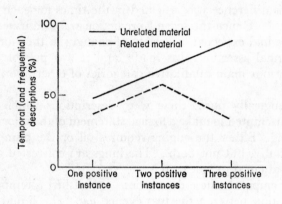

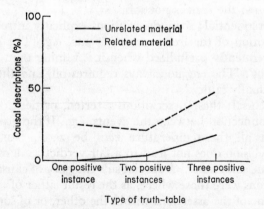

Type of truth–table

Figure 8. Percentages of the different categories of description as a function of the type of material and the type of truth-table

of the table corresponding to 'It is raining and the girl is not soaked.'

It will be noted that these four categories of description are not mutually exclusive. Hence, for purposes of classification a description was assigned to the most 'practical' category which it exemplified, e.g. a description which was both causal and frequential would be assigned to the causal category.

The relative frequencies of the four types of description appeared to be influenced by both the type of table, and by whether the assertions were related or unrelated. Three of the tables are essentially 'conjunctive' in that they contain just one positive contingency; a further three are essentially 'disjunctive' since they contain three positive contingencies; and the remaining two contain two positive instances. Figure 8 shows the percentage of logically pure, temporal or frequential, and causal descriptions as a function of the number of positive instances in the truth-table and the type of material.

What seems to have happened is that as the number of positive instances in the truth-table increases, so the number of logically pure descriptions decreases. In the case of the related material, this decline is compensated for by an increase of causal descriptions; and in the case of the unrelated material it is compensated for by an increase in temporal and frequential descriptions. This difference between the two sorts of material is also reflected in the descriptions of truth-tables with only one positive instance: causal descriptions occur more often with the related material than with the unrelated material; temporal and frequential descriptions occur more often with the un-related material than with the related material.

An irresistible impression emerges that, even with fully-fledged assertions, individuals do not naturally engage in truth-functional thought. They are always ready to leave the logical requirements of the task behind and try to establish some meaningful connection between events. If the events cannot be directly related, the best that can be done is to establish some temporal connection between them. But where the events do seem to be related to one another, the subjects will spend a considerable amount of time attempting to derive a satisfactory causal model of them. In contrast to the first 'tabular' experiment, there were few descriptions which consisted of an exhaustive list of the positive contingencies. Instead there were many descriptions of the form, 'when such-and-such happens, so-and-so occurs', or 'such-and-such occurs only when so-and-so happens'. The sole concession to logical accuracy in these statements was the introduction of negatives where appropriate. This bias towards temporal connectives extended even to simple conjunction where nearly half the subjects utilized *when* rather than the logically adequate *and*. The difference between *when* and *if* is largely a matter of certainty, as opposed to uncertainty, about the events concerned. But in either case, it is necessary to assume that one of the two statements in the truth-table is temporally, or causally, prior to the other. A truth-table that is correctly described by, 'It is raining and the girl is soaked', naturally elicits a description of the form, 'When it rains the girl is soaked', rather than, 'When the girl is soaked it rains.'

The lack of any difference in logical accuracy between the two groups now seems so obvious that we are beginning to wonder why it was ever predicted. The fact that sentences were related introduced no actual conflict between practical considerations and the logical requirements of the task. It simply elicited an attempt to find a practical interpretation of the truth-table—a phenomenon which is reflected, both in the actual wording of the descriptions, and in the greater length of time taken to produce them.

In an elegant series of experiments, Michotte (1963) demonstrated that an individual watching certain simple events such as a stimulus moving across the visual field and touching another, which itself begins to move, naturally and involuntarily perceives that the first stimulus *causes* the second to move. This interpretation is hard to resist, provided that the stimulus-events lie within certain constraints governing their timing. Doubtless, it has an adaptive value. The world becomes a more orderly and predictable place if its events are spontaneously organized into a causal matrix. It is hardly surprising, then, that causal assumptions should be so salient a feature of practical deductions. Presumably, they facilitate the activity of drawing inferences in the outside world; certainly, it would be a foolish individual who sought only logical grounds in order to anticipate reality. But of course within the laboratory— granted the psychologist's excessive preoccupation with pure deduction, a causal assumption may be as unwarranted as a causal perception of the stimuli in Michotte's experiments. It can also seriously interfere with the task in hand, as for example in the experiment on hypothetical reasoning, where what was causally appropriate turned out to be logically inappropriate.

It should, nevertheless, be emphasized that a person's normal mode of deductive thought is best exhibited in tasks with familiar everyday material. The individual wants to understand events and to reason about them. He lives in a world in which he perceives a causal flux. He speaks a language whose internal organization reflects a considerable degree of logical coherence. Hence, when he makes inferences of a practical nature, he is prepared to make assumptions about causal or temporal re- lationships. He is particularly concerned with what the premises *mean*, in the widest sense, and he performs a considerable amount of logical 'work' through the exercise of his linguistic skills, e.g. the ability to paraphrase. But, in addition to these extralogical activities, he also carries out certain purely logical operations. There is a deductive component to his thought. And it is a grave mistake to assume that one only gains a clear conception of its operation in problems purged of any practical concern. The ordinary mortal passes into a looking-glass world when confronted by a problem which is abstract, or symbolic, in nature. In this world people talk to him of making deductions which are valid in virtue of logic alone, and of the distinction between true conclusions and valid inferences. These ideas are perplexing, not because they are contrary to his practice, but because they are wholly alien to his habitual patterns of thought. Naturally, he proceeds in a very tentative manner, staying close to the information given to him, and attempting to reason in formal terms, even to the extent of making explicit matches between the surface forms of expressions. But he is undoubtedly handicapped, both by being unable to exercise his intuitions about the real world, and by being cut off from any natural recourse to those semantic skills which are normally integrated with his deductive powers. Far from isolating his true logical ability, it seems that one might as well hope to discern it in an individual surgically deprived of his linguistic ability.

The distinction between pure and practical reasoning has been recognized from the time of Aristotle, and its existence has seldom been disputed. But the exact nature of the distinction has proved to be elusive, perhaps because it is only recently that empirical investigations into actual thought have been undertaken. The various views that have been held on the subject may be divided, for the sake of simplicity, into two opposing schools of thought. The first school argues that practical reasoning proceeds by rather different rules of inference from those of pure reasoning (which are known only to the enlightened). In particular, a number of forms of inference that are strictly speaking invalid have become sanctioned in everyday life because they often lead to true conclusions. This point of view was perfectly expressed to one of the authors by his tutor in logic. 'The inferences of daily life,' he would remark dryly, 'are invariably trivial and usually invalid.'

The second school of thought argues that the distinction between the two sorts of reasoning should be put another way. It is not so much a distinction in the *way* the individual reasons, but more in *what* he reasons upon. The practical reasoner makes logically unwarranted assumptions, ignores premises explicitly given to him, and generally, as Mary Henle (1962) so succinctly puts it, refuses to accept the logical task. But once he gets down to drawing inferences, he is governed by exactly the same rules as are to be found in pure logic. Historically, such a view is naturally associated with the idea that the laws of logic are also the laws of thought. As to the fallacies which undoubtedly occur, they are the result not of deduction, which is something that an individual does on his own behalf, but of argumentation and rhetoric, which is aimed at securing the adherence of others.

We are now in a position to propose a third and perhaps more comprehensive point of view, to which both these schools of thought contribute.

Practical thought is the habitual pattern, and it depends

upon a number of underlying abilities, which are not so much illogical, but rather beyond the scope of current logic to characterize adequately. However, there is within this underlying competence a purely deductive component. At most, one catches a glimpse of how this component works—sometimes in practical tasks, sometimes in abstract tasks. They manifest an intermittent ground-swell on which are imposed the perturbations of causal thought, illicit conversions, and other interpretative errors when thought is placed under strain. It is our next task to represent the outlines of this ground-swell, to delineate the processes involved in the purely deductive component.

8   The Deductive Component

*'If it was so, it might be; and if it
were so, it would be: but as it isn't, it
ain't. That's logic.'*   TWEEDLEDEE

Logic has developed into a deliberate and self-conscious attempt
to construct formal systems in which formulae may be transformed into new formulae according to certain rules governing
the manipulation of symbols. The utility of such systems, as
opposed to their intrinsic logical interest, depends upon the
feasibility of interpreting them in a way which is relevant to
actual problems. Although many systems have a considerable
utility for mathematicians and computer programmers, it is a
strange fact that they have little value for practical problems
of deduction. It is probably no longer sensible to ask whether
the laws of logic are the laws of thought, because logic is no
longer a monolithic body of doctrine. There are many varieties
of logic. What one can ask is whether there is any particular
logical system which provides a useful model of human thought.
We began by assuming that the propositional calculus might
serve as a criterion for logical ability. But the careful reader
will have sensed our growing disenchantment with this notion.
Much of the individual's thinking lies outside the realm of the
calculus, indeed outside any established branch of formal logic,
since it concerns questions of causality. Yet the system of
practical inference does contain a purely deductive component,
and a few of its characteristics have been demonstrated, e.g. it
lacks a rule of inference corresponding directly to *modus tollendo
tollens*. Perhaps this component might be truly modelled by a
version of the propositional calculus? It would, indeed, be an
aesthetically pleasing coincidence if thought turned out to be
structured in this way. The claim has been forcefully urged for
many years by Jean Piaget; and since so distinguished a psychologist has defended this view, it is necessary to give it a close
scrutiny.

A critical property of the propositional calculus is that it is bivalent, i.e. any statement within it is either true or false. This is an apparently innocent stipulation to which many people would raise no objection. Yet it leads to a decisive impasse in the use of the calculus as a model of the deductive component of thought. In particular, it leads to difficulties with conditional statements, which play so central a role in ordinary reasoning. Often enough, a conditional is a virtual warrant for an inference. It tells us what conclusion we may infer from the truth of its antecedent; and, when it comes to arguing with propositions, the few other rules of inference the individual possesses seem to be closely related to this fundamental pattern. But the logical analysis of the conditional has always created controversy—'the very crows on the roof caw about the meaning of conditionals' is an early Stoic counterpart to Tweedledee's dictum. The present issue is simple: how is the logic of the ordinary conditional statement to be represented within the propositional calculus?

The calculus contains a logical connective known as 'material implication' which is defined in the following way. One proposition materially implies another when it cannot be the case that the first is true and the second is false. An obvious example occurs when one statement logically implies another. Indeed, we often say, 'if so-and-so, then (it follows) that such-and-such', using a conditional to express the implication. It is thus plausible to suppose that the underlying logic of the conditional may correspond to material implication—a supposition which is central to Piaget's argument (cf. Beth and Piaget, 1966, p. 181). Let us examine this idea in more detail.

Suppose that the following conditional is true: If John loved Mary, then he married her. It is legitimate to ask what may now be inferred about the truth or falsity of its antecedent and consequent. Obviously, the conditional does not legislate about whether John did in fact love Mary. If he did not love her, then it is consistent with him marrying her (perhaps for her money), or not marrying her. In other words, of the four possible contingencies that could have occurred, three are quite compatible with the truth of the conditional, and only one—John loved Mary and did *not* marry her—is incompatible with it. This information, of course, can be summarized in a truth-table:

John loved Mary	He married her	If John loved Mary, then he married her (as material implication)
True	True	True
True	False	False
False	True	True
False	False	True

It seems on this analysis that the logic of the conditional might correspond to that of material implication. But consider what happens when, instead of working from the truth of the conditional to the truth or falsity of its components, we work in the opposite direction, from the truth or falsity of the components to the truth of the conditional. Is it not strange that provided John did not love Mary, the conditional is true? Or that provided he married her, the conditional is true? (In other words, a false antecedent or a true consequent ensures that the conditional is true.) Certainly, in ordinary life we do not argue in this way. The following bizarre inference, for example, would be quite valid if the conditional behaved like material implication:

If John loved Mary, then he married Mary.

If John loved June, then he married June.

Therefore, if John loved Mary he married June, *or* if John loved June he married Mary.

The validity of this argument is easy to see provided one remembers the peculiarities of material implication[1].

Such arguments so obviously fly in the face of common sense that the reader may now wonder whether *any* conditionals possess the logic of material implication. In fact, there are a few which do perhaps possess its logic. The most notable examples

[1] The argument goes as follows: Either John loved Mary, or else he did not love her. (1) Suppose John loved Mary. It follows from the first premise that he married her. Hence the second conditional in the conclusion is true because its consequent is true. The conclusion as a whole is accordingly true because one of its two disjunctive components is true. (2) Suppose John did not love Mary. It follows that the first conditional in the conclusion is true because its antecedent is false. The conclusion as a whole is therefore true.

are those conditionals with negated antecedents which, as we have seen, function as covert disjunctions. Certain of them allow that both components of the disjunction could be true, e.g. 'If *The Ancient Mariner* isn't by Coleridge, then it's by Wordsworth.' Such a conditional is true, of course, if its antecedent is false (the poem *is* by Coleridge), or if its consequent is true (the poem is by Wordsworth). But the majority of conditionals are clearly not of this form, and material implication is, in general, an unsatisfactory model for them.

There is just one other way of accommodating conditionals, and, should this fail too, the affinity between the calculus and the deductive component of thought collapses. This involves another logical connective, known as 'material equivalence', which has the following truth-table:

John loved Mary	He married her	If John loved Mary, then he married her (as material equivalence)
True	True	True
True	False	False
False	True	False
False	False	True

Unfortunately, this has decidedly too forceful consequences for the conditional. It is the truth-table of one which implies both its converse and its obverse. While it is true that some conditionals have such properties (cf. pp. 61–2), this is not true for the majority of them. Indeed, our example, 'If John loved Mary, then he married her', would not normally be taken to imply either, 'If John married Mary, then he loved her', or 'If John did not love Mary, then he did not marry her.'

Because we have already seen the absurd results that follow from treating conditionals as material implications, it is clear that they cannot be reconciled with the propositional calculus. Hence, mature deductive powers, whatever else they may be, are not founded upon an implicit grasp of the calculus. What is evidently required is a quite different conception of logical ability, and a quite different concept of the logic of the ordinary conditional.

One of the major divergencies between formal logic and

G

ordinary discourse concerns the role of presuppositions. Many statements in everyday language presuppose some state of affairs and, if this presupposition is unfulfilled, the statement is neither true nor false. It is simply null and void. This insight was expressed by Strawson (1950), who seems to have been the first to appreciate it, by the following argument. If someone asserts, 'All my children are asleep', and it transpires that he has no children, the assertion would hardly be said to be false, for this would suggest that not all of his children were asleep. On the contrary, his listeners would be baffled and wonder what on earth he meant: his statement would be devoid of a truth value. The determination of the presuppositions of a statement is an intricate task of linguistic analysis. But, in the case of the conditional the task is much simpler: the antecedent is an explicit statement of a presupposition. Hence, as Quine (1952) remarked, the ordinary conditional is a conditional assertion rather than the assertion of a conditional. When the presupposition stated by its antecedent turns out to be unfulfilled, no assertion is made: it is not treated as true and it is not treated as false. It is irrelevant. When it transpires that John did not love Mary, the statement about his marriage to her is empty: it is as though it had never been made.

On this presuppositional analysis, the conditional has an incomplete or 'defective' truth-table: no value is specified for those cases where the antecedent is false:

John loved Mary	He married her	If John loved Mary, then he married her ('defective' truth table)
True	True	True
True	False	False
False	True	Void
False	False	Void

It was our conviction that this interpretation of the conditional provides its commonest employment in ordinary usage; and we set out to test this hypothesis in an experiment (Johnson-Laird and Tagart, 1969). Since the task was very simple, the material could deliberately be made rather abstract in nature, and so prevent it suggesting any particular interpretation of the conditional. The subjects were accordingly presented with statements such as, 'If there is a letter "A" on the left-hand side of the card, then there is a number "3" on the right-hand side.' Their task was to sort through a pack of cards, depicting various combinations of symbols, and to place each card into one of three categories:

(1) Cards truthfully described by the statement.
(2) Cards falsely described by the statement.
(3) Cards to which the statement was irrelevant.

The majority of the subjects, 19 out of the 24 who were tested, classified the cards according to the 'defective' truth-table that we expected. Whenever a card falsified the antecedent—and there were a variety of ways in which this occurred because the situation was *not* a strictly binary one[1]—it was considered to be irrelevant to the truth value of the statement as a whole.

Did we put words into our subjects' mouths by introducing the third category of cards to which the statement was irrelevant? It seems not; because they studiously avoided this category in a second condition of the experiment. The statement here was disjunctive in form, e.g. 'There isn't a letter "A" on the left-hand side of the card, or there is a number "3" on the right-hand side, or both.' The underlying logic of this statement was intended to correspond to that of material implication, and this is how it most frequently was classified by the subjects. They seldom considered a card to be 'irrelevant', even when it seemed that the negative clause in the statement had led them into error[2].

At the time this experiment was performed, we suspected that the 'defective' truth-table of the conditional was somehow associated with the word *if*, since, as Tweedledee might have said, it is such an 'iffish' word. However, a third condition of the experiment quickly dispelled us of our illusions. The state-

[1] When the situation *is* strictly binary, the conditional tends to be evaluated in accordance with the truth-table of material equivalence (Legrenzi, 1970).
[2] This result has been strongly corroborated by Evans (1971c), in which the category, 'irrelevant', in relation to conditional statements, was not made explicit to the subjects but inferred by the experimenter as a residual class.

ment was of the form, 'There is never a letter "A" on the left-hand side of the card without there being a number "3" on the right-hand side.' This was treated in an almost identical fashion to the conditional. With hindsight, it seems obvious that there are several ways to make a conditional assertion, e.g. 'Cards that have "A" on their left-hand side have "3" on their right-hand side', 'Only cards with "3" on their right-hand side have "A" on their left-hand side.' The conditional retains its dominant character in the play of natural reasoning, but *if* is by no means the sole way of expressing it.

It is evident that a conditional may possess the logic of material implication, material equivalence, or the 'defective' truth-table. It is not a creature of a constant hue, but chameleon-like, takes on the colour of its surroundings: *its meaning is determined to some extent by the very propositions it connects*. This property yields a final argument against the propositional calculus as a model of the deductive component. A connective in the calculus can be used with any arbitrary pair of propositions, since the sole aim is to relate the truth values of statements. Hence, a statement such as, 'If elephants are pink, then $2 + 2 = 4$', is entirely acceptable, construed as material implication. Not surprisingly, such sentences are considered to be rather odd by those unfamiliar with the idiosyncracies of the calculus. And, indeed, they *are* odd, since they violate the principles governing the cohesion of discourse. The nature of these principles is little understood—they probably involve more than purely linguistic factors. Yet, it is clear that conditionals must be cohesive precisely because they are not merely used to convey truth-functional relations between their components. They are, in fact, used to establish particular semantic relations, such as causal connection or logical implication, and it is from these relations that their truth-functional properties arise. This is borne out by Matalon's (1962) finding that, in evaluating non-cohesive statements, like the example above, subjects looked above all for a link between the antecedent and consequent. We also saw how salient this phenomenon was in practical inference (cf. pp. 77–82). The clearest case of the use of conditionals to express a semantic relation is provided by those which are 'counterfactual'. For instance, the conditional,

'If John had married Mary, he would have come to hate her', presupposes that he neither married her, nor came to hate her. A truth-functional analysis of this statement would be meaningless, since it is clear from the start that antecedent and consequent are false. The principle function of the statement is to communicate the *connection* between two hypothetical events.

To summarize our argument so far: we have established that the deductive component of thought cannot be adequately characterized by the propositional calculus. This is because the calculus possesses at least two properties which run counter to ordinary reasoning: it is bivalent and it is truth-functional. A third factor is implicit in our argument. The calculus analyses propositions in terms of their logical form, ignoring their specific content, but we have established that the meaning of component propositions may decisively influence the interpretation of everyday conditionals.

In fact, it is clear that no conventional notion of logical form is viable for the analysis of ordinary deduction. Consider any arbitrary calculus within which *modus ponens* is a valid inference. It will contain a rule to the effect that arguments of the form, 'If p then q; p therefore q', are valid. It is unlikely that any arguments of this form are actually invalid in everyday life. A number of them, however, are strangely vacuous, e.g. 'If you want the money, it's in the tea-pot. You want the money. Therefore, it's in the tea-pot.' This is an empty inference because it is clear that the conditional is no real conditional, but a disguised assertion that the money is in the tea-pot. On the other hand, there are inferences which are essentially of the *modus ponens* form, but which fail to fulfil the strict formal characteristics of the rule, e.g. 'If I keep animals in my flat, then I'm liable to eviction. I keep an alligator in my bath, therefore I'm liable to eviction.' The native speaker of English appreciates that 'an alligator in my bath' is a special case of 'an animal in my flat', and it is unnecessary to have separate premises to establish this point. Certain inferences, of course, depend solely on semantic relations, e.g.

Vegetation is killed by this chemical spray.

Therefore, flowers are killed by this chemical spray

and are, presumably, carried out solely by recourse to the individual's linguistic ability.

A curious phenomenon came to light in an experiment involving such inferences (Johnson-Laird and Graham Gibbs, unpublished). The closer the relationship between the crucial items, in valid inferences, the faster the deduction. Thus inferences such as the one above were evaluated faster than ones such as:

Vegetation is killed by this chemical spray.

Therefore, roses are killed by this chemical spray.

This aspect of the results is entirely plausible, since in passing from *vegetation* to *roses* the route may be by way of the intermediate item *flowers* (cf. Collins and Quillian, 1969). However, with invalid inferences constructed by transposing the crucial items, e.g.

Roses are killed by this chemical spray.

Therefore, vegetation is killed by this chemical spray.

exactly the opposite results were obtained. The closer the two items, the longer it took to evaluate the inference. Whatever the explanation of this surprising switch in difficulty from valid to invalid deductions, it is clear that essentially it concerns the organization and retrieval of information from semantic memory. This strengthens our contention that the only viable notion of logical form, for the analysis of everyday inference, is one which takes the *meaning* of statements as fundamental rather than the purely superficial disposition of words within the premises. This applies even where arguments make no reference to temporal or causal matters: it applies to the purely deductive component of the inferential machinery.

If the propositional calculus is an inadequate model, how is the deductive component of reasoning to be characterized? Our results permit us only to make the merest sketch of some of its more likely properties. Systems of logic are often formalized so as to have the minimum number of rules of inference. The usual formalization of the propositional calculus, for example, involves a number of axioms, but only two rules of inference. These suffice to derive every valid theorem from the axioms. The deductive component of ordinary thought, however, is likely to contain a relatively large number of rules of inference, but few if any axioms. The reason for this is clear: natural thought is primarily concerned with moving from one proposition to another, rather than with deriving logical truths.

There seem to be three main sorts of rules of natural inference. First, there are rules which are simply consequences of the individual's linguistic ability. These account for a variety of immediate inferences from one statement to another. Some of these inferences involve relations between individual words like *vegetation, flowers* and *roses*; others involve equivalent formulations of logical connectives, e.g. 'It isn't snowing or sleeting', is equivalent to, 'It's neither snowing nor sleeting.'

Second, there are the major rules of inference, e.g. *modus ponens*, the disjunctive rule (*p* or *q*; not-*p*; therefore *q*), and a number of other purely logical principles. For example, although an individual's command of his language will tell him when two statements contradict one another, it will not tell him that at least one of the assumptions from which a contradiction is derived must be rejected, nor will it tell him that an assumption may be made in a deduction. These principles, which underlie the *reductio ad absurdum* are major rules of inference.

Third, there are auxiliary rules of inference. Consider the following inference: If John has a ticket or is accompanied by a member, he will be admitted; he is accompanied by a member; therefore, he will be admitted. At first glance, it appears to be just another case of *modus ponens*. However, its validity depends upon the fact that, 'He is accompanied by a member', immediately implies, 'John has a ticket or is accompanied by a member.' This is so obvious that one hardly notices it. Yet it is a very necessary precursor to the main inference. The way in which these sorts of immediate inference are handled in a formal calculus is to include a rule to the effect that any proposition, *p*, logically implies the disjunction of that proposition with any other proposition, i.e. *p* or *q*. But such a rule is no part of ordinary deductive competence. It suggests that the individual passes readily from an assertion such as 'I like bananas', to the disjunction of this with any arbitrary assertion, e.g. 'I like bananas, or Hitler is dead.' This may be logically impeccable, but it is absurd. Of course people say absurd things, but they do not make deductions in this way. Nor do they make other similar deductions in a direct way, e.g. the inference from p AND q to p. The essential characteristic of these sorts of deduction is that they are *auxiliaries*: they occur only as a part of other major inferences, e.g. *modus ponens*, and they have no independent status.

The picture which emerges from these last few chapters is of the intelligent but logically naive individual possessing a considerable degree of deductive competence. But his inferential powers may be upset or disturbed by a number of factors. He is liable to have difficulty with negation, especially if it proves necessary to negate an already negative expression. This seems to be essentially a problem of keeping track of information rather than the result of a basic flaw in the inferential machinery. He is also liable to have difficulty in interpreting conditional statements, especially if they involve abstract material, and he may assume, perhaps illicitly, that they imply their converses. Again, this is probably not ascribable to 'bad logic', but to the absence of the normal semantic cues to the interpretation. When the individual's deductive ability is undisturbed by such factors, it is nevertheless clear that it is not adequately characterized by the propositional calculus. The divergence centres on the role of presuppositions in ordinary discourse, and on the alien nature of purely truth-functional relations. It should not be assumed, however, that a model dealing solely with propositional thinking covers the full range of the individual's ability.

9

Meaning and Imagery
in Relational Inferences[1]

Propositional thinking depends essentially upon the connections between propositions. But this analysis breaks down in a fundamental way with certain quite simple inferences. Consider, for example, the following sort of argument:

John is taller than James
James is taller than William
Therefore, John is taller than William.

Clearly, the validity of the inference depends upon the *relation* of the items both within and between the sentences. It is no longer useful to take the proposition as the basic unit: it is necessary to analyse the internal structure of the proposition. This applies to a variety of different types of inference:

Beer contains hops
Hops contain sucrose
Therefore, beer contains sucrose.

Joyce is an ancestor of Evelyn
Vivian is a descendant of Evelyn
Therefore, Joyce is an ancestor of Vivian.

Ann followed John
Mary preceded John
Therefore, Ann followed Mary.

More complex inferences with a larger number of premises or a mixture of different relations can also be constructed:

John stood in the last local elections in Camden
Camden is a borough of London

[1] The reader may find this chapter rather technical. It may be skipped without loss of continuity. Much of the argument is based on Johnson-Laird, (1972).

London had its annual borough election on Tuesday
Therefore, John stood in the elections on Tuesday.

William is Susan's father
Arthur is William's brother
Alice is Arthur's daughter
Therefore, Susan and Alice are cousins.

However, the essential ability to make a relational inference is elicited by that special class of problems which have only two premises containing either the same comparative term or a comparative and its converse, e.g.

Ken is taller than Bill
Tom is shorter than Bill
Who is tallest?

These are known as 'three-term series' problems (or 'linear syllogisms').

The most important logical point about the answers to such problems is that they are not, strictly, valid deductions. They depend upon additional and unstated premises. To the ordinary intelligent individual, however, these premises are granted immediately by his knowledge of the language. For example, part of the meaning of *taller* is that it is transitive, i.e. if 'A is taller than B' and 'B is taller than C', then it follows that 'A is taller than C' regardless of what A, B and C denote. This is appreciated without conscious reflection just as it is appreciated that the relation of, say, *is the father of* is not transitive. Once again, a considerable portion of logical work is thus performed by knowledge of the language[1].

The fundamental problem in making a relational inference is to set up some internal representation of the premises, be it abstract or concrete, that will allow the relation between those items, not specifically linked in a premise, to be determined. A potential controversy about the process seems implicit in the earliest experimental observations. Störring, who introduced the problem into the laboratory, described a variety of methods

[1] It is worth mentioning that, for this reason, the following inference is quite valid in ordinary life: 'The teacher is *much* cleverer than Paul, and Dorothy is only slightly cleverer than Paul: so the teacher is cleverer than Dorothy.'

used by his subjects (cf. Woodworth, 1938). Some individuals evidently formed a mental diagram of the premises, representing it by a visual or kinaesthetic image. Others pondered upon the meaning of the premises and solved the problem in a purely verbal way.

Although series problems continued to be studied after Störring's pioneer efforts, e.g. by Burt (1919) and Piaget (1921, 1928), it was not until fairly recently that comprehensive proposals were made about the way they were solved. Broadly speaking, there are three alternative theories, which will be described in the order of their historical development. Two of them are currently claimed to make rival statements about the phenomena—one is an 'image' theory, the other a 'linguistic' theory. Our aim is to show, as is implicit in Störring's findings, that the parties to the controversy are both partly right and partly wrong.

The first definitive proposal about the *process* of inference in series problems was made by Ian Hunter (1957), in what we shall call the OPERATIONAL model. It takes as its starting point an idea which William James described as the fundamental principle of inference, namely, that with a linear series of the form $a > b > c > d$ . . . 'any number of intermediaries may be expunged without obliging us to alter anything in what remains written' (James, 1890, p. 646). Hunter assumes that the same principle applies to relational premises provided that they lead naturally on one from the other as in:

A is larger than B
B is larger than C.

In other words, the reasoner can simply delete the two occurrences of B and infer that 'A is larger than C'. However, says Hunter, where the premises are not arranged in this 'natural' order, certain cognitive OPERATIONS have to be performed in order to bring them into it. This is a psychological analogue of the traditional idea in logic of reducing an inference to a simpler form known to be valid. But, of course, in the present case the reduction is not necessarily a deliberate or conscious stratagem.

There are two main operations. First, a premise may have to be *converted*. This usually applies to the second premise because Hunter assumes that the first premise creates a 'set' for its interpretation. Thus, with a problem such as:

A is larger than B
c is smaller than B

the second premise has to be converted to 'B is larger than c' before the middle term can be expunged. Second, the premises themselves, and not their terms, may have to be *re-ordered*, when they do not naturally follow on one from the other. Such an operation is required in the case of:

B is smaller than A
c is smaller than B

in order to yield the 'natural' order: c is smaller than B, B is smaller than A. We have to imagine that the premises are cognitively rearranged so that in the mind's eye they *do* follow on from each other. Some combinations of premises require both operations to be performed, e.g.

B is smaller than A
B is larger than c

Here it is necessary to convert the second premise to 'c is smaller than B', and then to re-order the two premises. (The 'natural' order could also be obtained by going back to the first premise to convert it. This, Hunter claims, would also involve two operations: *reverting* to the first premise and *converting* it to 'A is larger than B'.)

In order to facilitate comparison with the subsequent models, we have attempted to express the model in information-processing terms, summarizing it in the flow diagram[1] of Figure 9.

According to the model, the individual sets up some internal representation of the first premise (0). He then checks to see whether the second premise involves the same relation (1), and, if it does not, he converts it (2). If the premises follow on

---

[1] Flow diagrams are a very useful way of describing the processing of information, and they are much used by computer programmers. We have followed the convention that a diamond shape is used to indicate a comparison or a question to which the answer is 'yes' or 'no', and that a rectangle is used to indicate a definite instruction to be carried out. Much of the credit for introducing this way of theorizing to psychology must go to Miller, Galanter and Pribram (1960).

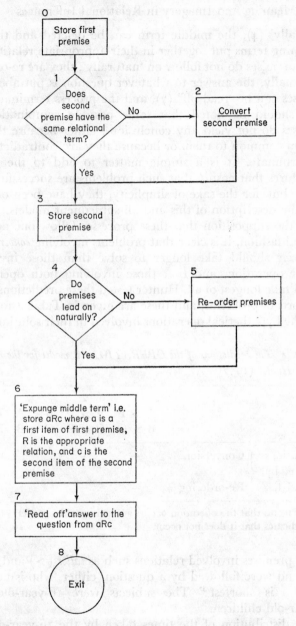

Figure 9. The OPERATIONAL model for the solution of three-term series problems (based on Hunter, 1957)

'naturally' (4), the middle term can be deleted and the two remaining terms put together in their appropriate relation (6). If the premises do not follow on 'naturally', they are re-ordered (5). Finally, the answer to whatever question is put about the premises can be 'read off' (7), and the process terminates (8).

(It should be noted that some possible combinations of premises do not yield any conclusions, either because there is no item common to them or because they are contradictory or indeterminate. It is a simple matter to add to the model procedures that ensure that such problems are successfully detected, but, for the sake of simplicity, they have been omitted from the description of this and all subsequent models.)

On the supposition that these processes follow one another in serial fashion, it is clear that problems involving *conversion* or *re-ordering* should take longer to solve than those involving neither operation, and that those involving both operations should take longest of all. Hunter tested these predictions using four sorts of problems, and these are given in Table 4 together with the hypothetical operations involved in their solution. The

TABLE 4 *The predictions of the OPERATIONAL model for the material used by Hunter (1957)*

		1 A > B B > C	2 A > B C < B	3 B < A C < B	4 B < A B > C
*Operations predicted by the model	Conversion	—	+	—	+
	Re-ordering	—	—	+	+

* + indicates that the operation occurs according to the model
  — indicates that it does not occur

actual premises involved relations such as *taller* (>) and *shorter* (<), and were followed by a question, either 'who is tallest?' or 'who is shortest?' The subjects were 16-year-old and 11-year-old children.

The distribution of the times taken by the 16-year-olds to solve the problems supported the model: type 1 problems were easier than types 2 and 3, and type 4 were hardest of all. Since type 2 problems were easier than type 3, Hunter argues that *conversion* is a simpler operation than *re-ordering*. Somewhat surprisingly, the 11-year-olds even found type 2 problems easier than type 1—a finding that Hunter attributes to an 'atmosphere' effect (cf. pp. 129–39 below).

A more recent proposal about the solution of series problems is due to De Soto, London, and Handel (1965). They suggest that the crucial step is the combination of the interpretations of premises into a unitary representation. This unitary representation consists of a visual image of a vertical or horizontal array in which the items are located in their appropriate position. The novel aspect of the IMAGE theory, however, is that the difficulty of a problem depends to some extent upon the sort of relational terms used in the premises. To illustrate the point, they recount an anecdote about a baseball fan who went to see two great players in an exhibition game. Unfortunately, both were having an 'off day'. Finally, the fan, unable to contain his anger, bellowed at one of them, 'I came to see which of you guys was better—instead, I'm seeing which is worse!'

Clearly, this is an insult, but why?—Isn't it the case that the two statements are equivalent? De Soto and his colleagues claim that they are not, because *better* refers to the 'good' end of the scale, whereas *worse* refers to the 'bad' end. The fan is implying that neither player is any good. It follows that if such comparatives are represented by a vertical array, items related by *better* will be at the top end and items related by *worse* will be at the bottom. Moreover, the items related by *better* will be inserted into the array working downwards, whereas those related by *worse* will be inserted working upwards.

The theory postulates that evaluative comparatives, even though they are not explicitly spatial, are indeed represented in this manner. Other comparatives such as *wider* and *narrower* call for a horizontal array, or else like *lighter* and *darker* seem to call for no consistent orientation. There are two principles governing the construction of arrays. First, there is a natural preference for constructing vertical arrays starting from the top and working downwards, and for constructing horizontal arrays working from left to right. It is unclear whether this is intended to be anything more than the principle governing occidental reading habits. Second, a premise is easier to represent in the array if its first item is an 'end-anchor', i.e. an item that occurs at one end of the final array rather than the middle item.

The evidence that De Soto obtained certainly seemed to support the principle that a premise would be easier to interpret when its items can be put into the array working downwards. A problem of the form:

A is better than B
B is better than C

was consistently easier than one of the form:

C is worse than B
B is worse than A.

Equivalent results were also obtained with *above–below* and *more–less* (see Handel, De Soto, and London, 1968). Such differences cannot be explained by Hunter's OPERATIONAL model because the premises follow on naturally from one another in both types of problem, but they can be explained in terms of the preferred direction of working. The principle is also claimed to apply to the order of the premises themselves as well as to the items within them. Hence, a problem such as:

A is better than B
C is worse than B

allows the array to be constructed working downwards, since it contains the 'best' item, A, in its first premise; whereas the problem with the same premises in the opposite order:

C is worse than B
A is better than B

requires the array to be constructed working upwards, since it contains the 'worst' item, C, in its first premise. This prediction, too, was confirmed experimentally.

Performance was consistent with the OPERATIONAL model only with those comparatives which did not automatically suggest one end of the array or the other, e.g. *darker–lighter*. Indeed, in these cases De Soto suggests that the first item of the first premise is assigned to the topmost (or leftmost) position of the array, and, if necessary, the second premise is converted so that the third item can be added to the array.

The second principle concerning 'end-anchoring' seems somewhat arbitrary. Why should problems be easier if their premises are end-anchored? Janellen Huttenlocher (1968) suggests that it is not the fact that the end-anchor is the first item that is crucial but rather that it is the grammatical (deep structure) subject of the sentence. She and her colleagues (Huttenlocher and Strauss, 1968; Huttenlocher, Eisenberg, and Strauss, 1968) discovered that when children have to arrange objects to fit such descriptions as 'The blue block is on top of the brown block', they find the task easier when the block to be moved corresponds to the subject of the sentence rather than to the object. If the adult's construction of imaginary arrays is similar to the child's construction of real arrays, the difficulty of a premise should depend on the grammatical status of the item that has to be fitted into the array. Hence, the principle of end-anchoring may be reformulated: it is easier to understand a premise that refers to an end item with its grammatical subject than with its grammatical object.

De Soto's principles, together with Huttenlocher's explication of end-anchoring, seem intuitively satisfactory until one attempts to put them into information-processing terms. It is then apparent that the two principles are confounded. This can best be demonstrated by considering the different ways in which a given three-term series can be expressed. Consider the following series: $A>B>C$. There are eight basic ways of formulating premises that will yield this series:

First premise: $A>B$ $B<A$ $B>C$ $C<B$
Second premise: $B>C$ $C<B$ $B>C$ $C<B$ $A>B$ $B<A$ $A>B$ $B<A$

Any one of these eight formulations is completely specified by describing its characteristics solely with respect to the first principle of the IMAGE theory, which concerns the direction of working. For example, if the premises are ordered so that the 'worst' item is in the first of them, and both of them involve working downwards, then the problem must be: 'B is better than C, A is better than B'. It follows that the IMAGE theory, as formulated by De Soto *et al.*, incorporates two principles which are not independent, i.e. (a) the principle governing the

H

direction of working, and (b) the principle governing end-anchoring.

Obviously, there are a number of ways in which the theory could be reformulated, sacrificing one or other principle with regard to the first or second premise. In attempting to put it into information-processing terms, a guiding cue was Huttenlocher's (1968) remark that subjects do not report making a spatial array for the second premise. Their goal is rather to determine the end-anchor and its position relative to the array representing the first premise. This version of the IMAGE theory is summarized in Figure 10.

What happens according to the model is that the individual

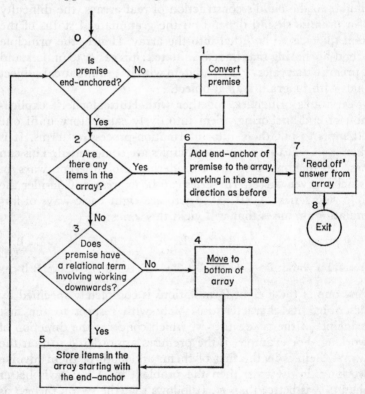

Figure 10. The IMAGE model for the solution of three-term series problems (based on De Soto *et al.*, 1965)

determines whether the first premise is end-anchored (o). This clearly involves considering its first item (or subject), and examining the second premise to see whether it also occurs there. For example, the first premise of the problem, 'B is better than C, A is better than B', is clearly not end-anchored since its first item, 'B', also occurs in the second premise. The model assumes that, in such cases, the premise is *converted* (1). It becomes 'C is worse than B' which clearly is end-anchored since C does not occur in the second premise, 'A is better than B'.

Since no items have previously been encoded (2), the by now end-anchored premise will be represented by an array constructed from the end-anchor either working downwards from the top (3, 5), or else upwards from the bottom (3, 4, 5), whichever is appropriate. Working upwards from the bottom is assumed to be more difficult and hence requires an additional operation (4). In encoding the second premise, there is again a search for the end-anchor (o, 1); but, since there are now items in the array (2), it is only necessary to add the end-anchor (6), *working in the same direction as before*. The answer may be 'read off' from the resulting array (7, 8).

It might be argued that when a premise is not end-anchored, the individual merely encodes its second item prior to its first item. This would be theoretically distinct from the present proposal, i.e. that the premise is converted, though it is difficult initially to see quite how the two ideas differ in practice. However, one subtle consequence of conversion is that when it is applied to the first premise, in order to locate the end-anchor, the direction of constructing the array is also necessarily changed. Hence, not all premises with *better* involve working downwards: those in which the first item is not an end-anchor will be converted to *worse* and will require the array to be constructed working upwards. This can hardly be said to conflict with De Soto's theory since it is precisely at this point that his theory incorporates two opposing principles.

The simplest way to evaluate the reformulated IMAGE model is to compare its predictions with the results obtained by De Soto *et al.* (1965) and Huttenlocher (1968). De Soto and his colleagues presented each combination of premises four times, once with each of the questions, 'Is A better than C?', 'Is C better than A?', 'Is A worse than C?', and 'Is C worse than A?', where 'A', 'B', and 'C', were in fact mens' first names. The subjects were allowed ten seconds in which to answer 'yes' or 'no', and the data consist of the percentage of correct answers over the four versions of each premise combination. Huttenlocher worked with the relations *taller* and *shorter* and used a rather different technique. After the first premise of the problem, the subject was asked both 'who is taller?' and 'who is shorter?' in a counterbalanced order. The second premise was presented, and finally the subject was asked either 'who is tallest?' or else 'who is shortest?' Two versions of each type of problem were given to the subjects, and the data consist of the times which elapsed from the presentation of the second premise until the subject responded. Such a technique is likely to minimize the contribution of the first premise to the difficulty of the problem, and this is clearly reflected in the results. Table 5 gives the results of both these experiments together with a summary of the predictions of the reformulated IMAGE model.

The model evidently gives a good account of the findings though it appears that the effects of the hypothetical operations are not necessarily linear.

The third and most recent approach to the problem is the LINGUISTIC theory developed by Herbert Clark (1969a, b). Clark argues that the process of deduction is virtually identical to the process of comprehension, and that difficulties in solving three-term series problems can be accounted for by three psycholinguistic principles.

The first is the principle of *lexical marking*, which asserts that certain comparatives are easier to understand and to remember than others. According to a linguistic analysis, so-called 'unmarked' comparatives, such as *better* and *taller*, can be used in a neutral way merely to convey the relative degrees of two items on a scale, whereas the converse 'marked' terms, *worse* and *shorter*, always convey in addition something about the absolute position of the items on the scale. Thus, for example, 'A is better than B' normally informs one only of the respective merits of A and B, but 'B is worse than A' also informs one that both A and B are towards the 'bad' end of the scale. The

TABLE 5 *The IMAGE model: predictions and results*

	A>B / C<B	A>B / B>C	C<B / A>B	C<B / B<A	B<A / C<B	B<A / B>C	B>C / A>B	B>C / B<A
1st premise / 2nd premise								
*Operations predicted by the model — Convert 1st premise	−	−	+	−	+	+	+	+
Work upwards	−	−	+	+	+	+	+	+
Convert 2nd premise	+	+	+	+	−	+	+	+
Percentage of correct answers (De Soto *et al.*, 1965)	61·8	60·5	57·0	42·5	50·0	41·5	52·8	38·3
Latencies (centisecs) (Huttenlocher, 1968)	141	155	142	161	142	157	135	157

* + indicates that the operation occurs according to the model
− indicates that it does not occur

asymmetry between such comparatives, in contradistinction to
De Soto's claim that they merely refer to different ends of the
absolute scale, is supported by several characteristics of unmarked comparatives. It is, for instance, quite acceptable to
assert: 'John and James are both very bad but John is slightly
better than Bill.' But it is somewhat deviant to assert: 'John
and James are both very good but John is slightly worse than
Bill.' Unmarked comparatives, as befits their neutral usage,
also tend to give their name to the scale as a whole, e.g. *length,
width, depth, height, heaviness, thickness, warmth.* The greater
psychological simplicity of unmarked comparatives is confirmed
by Donaldson and Wales (1970), who found that children tend
to understand them before they can understand marked comparatives, and by Clark and Card (1969), who found that they
are easier to remember than marked comparatives.

On the assumption that unmarked comparatives are taken
in their neutral sense—for on occasions they can be used in an
absolute way, it follows that they should be easier to work with
than marked comparatives, because they lack the additional
absolute information. This principle obviously accounts for the
same sort of phenomena as De Soto's notion of a preferred
direction for constructing the array. Both hypotheses predict
that

A is better than B
B is better than C

should be easier than

C is worse than B
B is worse than A

but for different reasons. Their predictions diverge, however,
for a new sort of premise introduced by Clark. These are the
so-called 'negative equatives' and they have the form, 'B isn't
as good as A' or 'A isn't as bad as B'. The first example involves
working up the array and should therefore be more difficult
than the second, according to the IMAGE theory. But the
LINGUISTIC theory makes the opposite prediction because the
first example contains the unmarked term 'good' whereas the
second contains the marked term 'bad'. (To anticipate some
results, it seems that the LINGUISTIC theory is right and the
IMAGE theory is wrong.)

The second psycholinguistic principle in Clark's theory has an interesting precursor in a 'clinical' observation made by Piaget (1921). Evidently a potent source of error in children's reasoning arises in the following way. Given the statement, 'Edith is better than Suzanne', the child is likely to argue that they are both good. When this is followed by the statement, 'Edith is worse than Lily', the child argues that *they* are both bad. Hence Suzanne is good, Lily is bad, and Edith is between the two. Of course this is nonsense, but it is close to the principle of *the primacy of functional relations* which Clark proposes for adult reasoning. He suggests that with a statement such as, 'Edith is worse than Lily', an individual can comprehend that Edith and Lily are bad faster than he can comprehend their relative degrees of badness. Clark justifies this intuitively plausible assumption on linguistic grounds. The *deep structure* or underlying representation of the statement is, Clark claims, roughly of the form: (Edith is bad) more than (Lily is bad), and the simple subject–predicate relations are easier to retrieve than the relation between the two clauses.

There is an addendum to this principle, and this too is related to an earlier observation. Margaret Donaldson (1963) noted that children often encode a premise such as 'Mary is taller than Martha' as 'Mary is the taller one'. (Both Burt (1919, p. 126) and Hunter (1957) suggest that on occasion young children may even encode it as 'Mary is the tallest one'.) The consequences of the abbreviated encoding depend upon the form of the second premise. If it is 'Ann is taller than Mary', it is a simple matter to infer that Ann is the tallest. But if it is 'Martha is taller than Ann', then there is no obvious series. As Clark points out, in appropriating the strategy, the subject must try to recover the whole first premise or back-track with the information that 'Martha is the taller one' to apply it to the first premise or revert to some other time-consuming strategy.

The principles of lexical marking and of the primacy of functional relations characterize the comprehension of premises. Let us attempt to express them in information-processing terms, before proceeding to the third principle, which governs answering the question. Although the theory is consistent, it fails to specify the complete process of solution. The most crucial omission, surprisingly, concerns what happens after the separate interpretations of the two premises. In principle, there seem to be three major possibilities: (a) after appropriate operations, the middle item can be simply expunged leaving the remaining items in their correct relation (e.g. Hunter's theory); (b) the information in the premises can be combined to form some sort of unified representation of the three items (e.g. De Soto's theory); and (c) the three items can be separately stored with some representation of their respective possession of the attribute in question.

The distinction between these approaches may seem abstruse, and perhaps it may be clarified by an analogy with a simple everyday problem. To determine the relative weights of three objects, they could be compared two at a time using a balance, and the middle item would clearly be heavier in one comparison and lighter in the other. Or they could be attached to three separate spring-balances, and the resulting spatial arrangement would clearly reflect their relative weights. Finally, their weights could be recorded using a conventional weighing machine. These three different methods correspond to the three possibilities for solving series problems. It seems that the spirit of Clark's theory, and in particular his principle of the primacy of functional relations, commits him to the 'weighing machine' approach. The reasoner stores each item separately according to the underlying information conveyed by the premise, and the 'weight' attached to the middle item is merely adjusted according to the information about it in the second premise. For example, the sentence 'A is better than B' would be represented by storing A *is more good* and B *is less good*. A further premise, 'C is worse than B', would be represented by C *is more bad* and B *is less bad*. This information would then be classified by amalgamating the item stored twice to read B *is middle* and by setting *more* to *most* (and *less* to *least*). Hence the final representation would be of the form: A *is most good*, B *is middle*, C *is most bad*. It should be borne in mind, of course, that the representations involving *bad*, or any marked item, will be more complex than those involving *good*, or any unmarked item, since according to the principle of lexical marking the marked terms contain an additional piece of information about absolute scale-values.

Figure 11 presents the first part of the LINGUISTIC model based on this interpretation of Clark's theory. It deals solely with the comprehension and representation of the premises; the solution of problems depends upon a further component to be described presently.

When a premise is presented, the first task is to analyse it linguistically. It is assumed that with negative equatives, the premise is transposed in order to eliminate the negation (0, 1). For example, a premise such as 'John isn't as tall as Bill' is transposed to 'Bill is taller than John'. This assumption goes beyond what Clark specifically claims, yet it is plausible since converting the premise to 'John is shorter than Bill' would introduce a marked comparative in place of the unmarked original. However, it could be claimed that negative equatives concentrate attention upon the item which comes second, and hence that the second item is merely stored before the first. Flores d'Arcais (1970) has suggested that there is this sort of re-focusing of attention in understanding such sentences as, 'Lambs are *less* ferocious than lions', which clearly resemble negative equatives. However, in this instance, it is immaterial which approach is adopted, since transposition, unlike conversion, does not change the comparative from marked to unmarked, or *vice versa*. But it does eliminate the negative and in this respect parallels the performance of many subjects attempting to remember negative equatives (cf. Clark and Card, 1969).

The model assumes that what the individual stores from the premises depends upon whether the comparative is marked or unmarked (2). Specifically, if the premise is of the form 'A is better than B', he stores the fact that A is *more good* (4). (This is not to be taken literally; all that is assumed is that A is symbolically represented as the 'better' item.) If the premise is 'A is worse than B', he stores the fact that A is *more bad* (3, 4). Since at this stage no premises have been previously stored (5), the other item mentioned in the premise is stored as being *less good* or *less bad*, whichever happens to apply (6).

The procedure for storing the second premise (7), is exactly the same for dealing with its first item (0, 1, 2, 3, 4). Suppose,

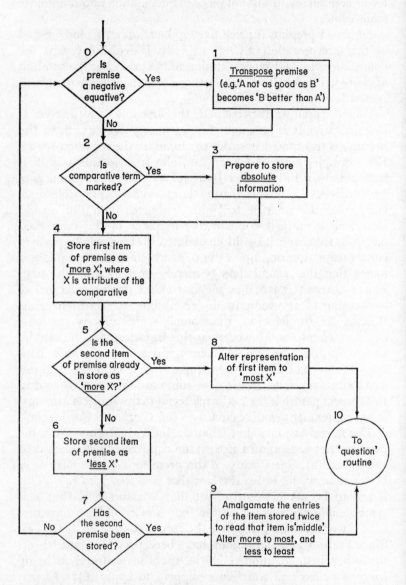

Figure 11. The LINGUISTIC model. Part 1: the comprehension of three-term series problems (based on Clark, 1969a, b)

however, the problem is of the form: 'B is better than C, A is better than B.' When A has been stored as *more good*, the model discovers that B (the second item of the second premise) has already been stored as *more good* (5), hence it is obvious that A is the best of the trio. This is represented in the model by storing A as *most good* (8). An exactly parallel process can occur with problems concerning *worse*. An obvious series has been found and the individual can now begin to deal with the specific question posed in the statement of the problem (10). But consider a problem of the form: 'A is better than B, B is better than C.' The only difference between this and the previous problem is in the order of the premises. But the difference is crucial. When B in the second premise has been stored as *more good* (4), the check (5) reveals that C (the second item in the premise) has not been previously stored as *more good*. Hence no obvious series emerges and in Clark's words it is necessary for the subject to 'backtrack' or to 'engage in some other time-consuming strategy'. In fact, it is assumed that he goes on to store C as *less good* (6). There are no further premises to be interpreted (7); and the individual has stored the following items:

A is *more good*
B is *less good*
B is *more good*
C is *less good*

How should he next proceed? It is, of course, at this point that Clark gives no specific answer, and that the 'weighing machine' approach was selected. The item which has been stored twice is located and the fact that it is the *middle* item recorded (9); and, in order to simplify the business of answering the question, any remaining occurrence of *more* is altered to *most*, and any remaining occurrence of *less* is altered to *least*.

This first part of the model gives a sufficient representation of the premises for the problem to be solved. It contains three decisive choice points (i.e. (0), (2) and (5)) which will affect the psychological difficulty of a problem. First, problems involving negative equatives will be harder because they necessitate an extra operation of transposition. Second, problems involving 'marked' comparatives such as *worse* will be harder because they require more information to be stored. Third, certain problems require information to be stored about both items of both premises. They will be harder than those which require only the first item of the second premise to be stored.

Although both Hunter (1957) and De Soto (Handel, De Soto, and London, 1968) reported that the nature of the question put to the subject about the premises exerts a significant effect upon performance, neither of them sought to integrate an explanation of the effect into their main theories. However, Hunter makes an interesting remark about the problem: 'B is shorter than A; C is shorter than B.' He writes (p. 244):

> 'In deriving a series from these premises, the writer was very much aware of finding that C interrupted the direction of the series and of bringing forward C as the shortest member of the series. This made it possible to answer straight away the question "who is shortest?" whereas the question "who is tallest?" required a further reconsidering of the two remaining terms to decide which was indeed the tallest. If this introspective evidence is generalized into a formal statement, it would be: the term which is contained only in that premise which has to be reorganized is isolated on the ground that it should come at one end or the other of the entire series.'

Hunter establishes that his results, especially with the 16-year-old children, tally with such an explanation.

Clark, on the other hand, assumes that the nature of the question has a profound effect on the subject's performance. His third principle is that the subject searches for information which is *congruent* with the form of the question. A premise of the form 'A is better than B' is represented by storing A is more good and B is less good. If one then asks, 'who is worse?', the question is incongruent with such a representation. It takes longer to answer even just about a single premise, as Clark (1969a) himself showed experimentally. In information-processing terms, there are two possible strategies in such a case: either the information stored with the items must be converted, or else the form of the question must be converted, with the goal being in both cases to make information and question congruent with one another. Clark makes the more parsimonious suggestion: he assumes that the question is converted from 'who is worse?' to 'who is least good?' It is now possible for a search to be made among the items for the one that is least good. This final part of the LINGUISTIC model is represented in Figure 12.

The model assumes that the reasoner first checks to determine

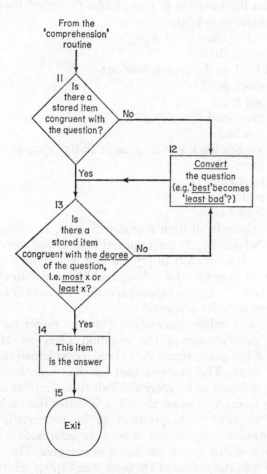

Figure 12. The LINGUISTIC model. Part 2: the question-answering routine (based on Clark, 1969a, b)

whether he has any information which is congruent with the question (11). If the question is 'who is worst?' but both premises contain the relation *better*, then this test will be failed, and the question will be converted (12) to 'who is least good?'; a similar conversion of 'who is best?' to 'who is least bad?' is made in the appropriate circumstances. Even if there is some information congruent in form to the question, it does not follow that the question is answerable. Consider, for example, the comprehension of the premises:

B is better than c

B is worse than A

This will lead to the representation:

B is more good

c is less good

B is more bad

A is less bad

The two entries for B will be amalgamated, etc., so that what is finally stored is:

c is least good

B is middle

A is least bad

Although there is an item stored with *good*, in answering the question 'who is best?' the required item is one stored as *most good*. There is no such item (13); and it is necessary to convert the question (12) to 'who is least bad?' in order to obtain the answer (14), 'A'. An analogous procedure is necessary to obtain the answer to 'who is worst?'

This rather subtle interaction between understanding the premises and answering the question gives an alternative account of the phenomena that De Soto explained in terms of end-anchoring. The problem that has just been analysed, for instance, is found to be more difficult to solve than one of the following form: 'c is worse than B, A is better than B.' The first problem requires both questions to be converted, but this second problem always has congruent information available because c is stored as *most bad* and A as *most good*. The difference is reflected in the results of De Soto *et al.* (1965), Huttenlocher (1968) and Clark (1969a, b) himself.

It should now be evident that the IMAGE theory and the

LINGUISTIC theory offer alternative explanations of the phenomena. For premises involving simple comparatives, the two
theories compete together, making the same prediction for
different reasons. Parallel to the IMAGE principle that it is easier
to work down the array, there is the LINGUISTIC principle that
unmarked comparative terms are simpler; and parallel to the
'end-anchoring' principle there is the principle of 'congruity'.
Not all pairs of antonymous comparatives yield problems
which differ empirically in their ease of solution, e.g. *lighter–
darker, fatter–thinner*. But even here the two theories are largely
in agreement. Such pairs tend not to elicit any 'directional
preference' according to De Soto; and, as Clark has observed,
they also tend to consist of terms which are *both* marked, and
therefore involve the same amount of information. In these
cases, Hunter's OPERATIONAL model also appears to characterize
performance quite adequately.

The theories do not always coincide in this fashion. The
IMAGE theory predicts that *to the left of* should be easier than
to the right of because it allows a horizontal array to be built up
in the natural and preferred direction, i.e. from left to right.
The LINGUISTIC theory presumably makes no such prediction
since both relations would seem to be marked. The evidence
(De Soto *et al.*, 1965) supports the IMAGE theory. However, it
is clear that *to the left of* provides a very special mnemonic that
its converse does not: the physical disposition of terms on the
printed page corresponds to the spatial locations described by
the statement. Subjects might quickly appreciate this fact and
exploit it in their inferential strategy. The IMAGE theory also
predicts that *shallower* should be easier than *deeper* because it
allows the array to be constructed working downwards. The
LINGUISTIC theory makes the opposite prediction because *deeper*
is unmarked whereas *shallower* is marked. In this case, the
results (Clark, 1969a) support the LINGUISTIC theory.

The most obvious confrontation between the two theories
seems to occur with the negative equative premises. On extra-
polating the IMAGE theory, problems involving the relation *not
as good as* should require the array to be constructed working
upwards. Hence they should be harder than those involving
the relation *not as bad as*. But exactly the opposite prediction is

made by the LINGUISTIC theory on the grounds of lexical marking. A similar conflict arises over the matter of end-anchoring.
A problem such as

A is not as bad as B

C is not as good as B

contains premises which are both end-anchored, i.e. the first
item is at one end of the array. But neither premise in:

B is not as good as A

B is not as bad as C

is end-anchored. Hence, on IMAGE theory, the first problem
should be easier than the second. A little reflection should
convince the reader that the LINGUISTIC theory makes the
opposite prediction on the grounds of congruity between
questions and premises. There is little doubt from the findings
of Clark (1969a, b) and Huttenlocher, Higgins, Milligan and
Kauffman (1970) that the predictions of the LINGUISTIC theory
are confirmed on both counts. But does this mean that the
IMAGE theory is eliminated?

The answer is not simple. Most investigators are agreed that
subjects may construct a mental picture of the premises. But
this in itself has little explanatory value. It is unlikely that all
individuals can, or do, construct images, or that all relational
problems can be represented in visual terms. The main function
of the imaginal aspect of performance may be as an aid to
memory. In blindfold chess, for example, some kind of visual
representation of the pieces seems to be vital in order to keep
track of the moves. But this representation no more determines
which move should be made than would the use of an actual
chessboard. Similarly, making an inference requires the
reasoner to construct an underlying representation of the premises. The process is probably similar to the one that occurs in
ordinary comprehension, which again may, or may not, involve
visual imagery. But regardless of the form of the representation,
the process of inference requires a number of steps in information-processing; and it is a specification of these processes, not
whether the representations are abstract symbols or concrete
images, which constitutes an explanation of the phenomena.

Quite apart from such explanatory considerations, several
studies have found less evidence for explicitly visual imagery

than was provided by De Soto's study. Sheila Jones (1970) studied her subjects' directional preferences by the ingenious expedient of giving them pencil and paper and allowing them to jot down the names mentioned in three-term series problems. Nearly three-quarters of her subjects wrote the names in systematic orders, usually prefering a vertical to a horizontal axis. The majority wrote down the names in the first premise in a preferred order (as De Soto predicts) and then added the third name to conform with the order. However, once a subject had decided upon an axis he seldom changed from it as a function of the relational terms. For example, subjects using the vertical axis did not tend to change to the horizontal to represent problems involving *lighter* and *darker*. This contrasts with De Soto's claim that certain relations require certain axes.

Yet it is a simple matter to restore the IMAGE theory, and to reconcile it with the LINGUISTIC theory. The principle that negative equatives are implicitly transposed (e.g. 'A is not as good as B' becomes 'B is better than A'), which makes good sense for the LINGUISTIC theory, makes equally good sense for the IMAGE theory. Indeed, Huttenlocher *et al.* (1970) have already invoked it in arguing for their general principle that overt tasks involving the movement of objects mirror the difficulties of covert conceptual tasks of an equivalent form.[1] If this transposition is made, then the manifest differences between the two theories disappear. A premise with *not as good as* still requires the array to be constructed working downwards though the order in which the items are inserted into it is reversed. Hence the principles of preferred direction of working and of lexical marking are reconciled. Similarly, a problem of the form, 'B is not as bad as C, B is not as good as A' seems at first glance to have premises that are not end-anchored. When

---

[1] Huttenlocher's claim that a transposition of another form may also occur, e.g. from 'A is not as high as B' to 'A is lower than B', is corroborated by Jones (1970). A number of factors seem to be involved in eliciting it. It seems to be more likely with unmarked comparatives, as one would expect from the principle of lexical marking. It may also have been encouraged by Huttenlocher's use of the questions, 'which is on the top?' and 'which is on the bottom?' They introduce a new sort of incongruity with the premises which may have suggested that the difference between *higher* and *lower* is less important than usual.

they are transposed, however, both are clearly end-anchored, and the principle of end-anchoring again coincides with the principle of congruity.

Although it is easy to reconcile the two theories, this may fail to do justice both to them and to the three-term series problem. But in order to see why, we must revert to our previous distinction between 'pure' and 'practical' reasoning. A 'practical' deduction involves the reasoner in reflection upon the full meaning and implications of the premises—indeed, he may go beyond them and begin to make causal assumptions. These deeper meanings of the material are ignored in making a 'pure' deduction. The real contrast between the competing theories does not concern the role of visual imagery or the 'primacy of functional relations'—both theories can be reformulated without them and without any loss in exploratory power. It lies in a more abstract distinction about the representation of premises. The IMAGE theory assumes that the two premises are combined into a unified representation of the three items; the LINGUISTIC theory assumes that information about the items is stored separately. This distinction may reflect the differences between a pure or practical approach to the problem.

We saw how the nature of the material—whether it was concrete or abstract, related or unrelated, categorical or hypothetical—could influence whether an individual thought in a pure or practical way. It is entirely feasible that with a series problem the inexperienced subject represents the premises in a unified form (with or without imagery) because this is likely to be the normal practical mode of dealing with the relational information. But by dint of sheer repetition this approach is likely to give way to a purer and more formal strategy geared to the specific constraints of the problem. It is unnecessary to form a unified representation to solve the problem, and the practised subject may well have learnt to store the minimum information which suffices—separate 'weights' on one or two of the items. In short, subjects seem likely to pass from an approach analogous to the IMAGE theory to one analogous to the LINGUISTIC theory.

The most convincing evidence for this sort of change comes from a study by David Wood (1969). He used series problem involving up to six premises and giving rise to many different types of array. All the premises involved the comparative term *taller*; and the question was always of the form 'who is taller x or y?' A typical problem was:

(1) D is taller than E
(2) C is taller than D
(3) A is taller than C
(4) A is taller than B
(5) B is taller than C
     Who is taller B or E?

The structure of such a problem can best be represented by what mathematicians call a 'Haas' diagram. The appropriate one is given in Figure 13. The items are represented in a vertical array according to their relative heights. The dotted line represents the question posed at the end of the premises.

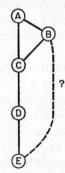

Figure 13. A Haas diagram of a five-term series problem

Wood predicted that subjects would initially solve such problems after the fashion of De Soto's IMAGE theory: they would build up an internal representation of the items in a structure which would presumably resemble the Haas diagram (though Wood uses a different sort of diagram). However, he suspected that with experience they would develop a more sophisticated strategy. Granted the constraint that the premises always involved the term *taller*, a subject seeking to determine whether B or E was the taller could scan the left and right hand sides of the premises looking for them. In the example above, B occurs on both sides, but E occurs only on the right side. It follows that provided the problem is determinate, B is the taller. There are, of course, a variety of such strategies; and the key point about them is that the reasoner at no time builds up a unified representation or mental picture of the array of items.

This development from a representational to a more economical non-representational strategy is consistent with our hypothesis about three-term series problems. But there is a snag. The reconciliation of the two theories has become an embarrassment, because if a subject passes from an approach analogous to the IMAGE theory to an approach analogous to the LINGUISTIC theory, surely one would expect their predictions to differ. Why, indeed, do they make such similar predictions? The most natural explanation rests upon one of Wood's findings.

He invented a simple but elegant test to determine the nature of his subjects' approach to the problems. After a subject had solved a certain number of conventional problems, he would be given a special test problem in which, having answered the main question, he would be asked a further unexpected question such as 'who is taller A or D?' These supplementary questions were so formed that they could be readily answered only by those subjects who had formed a unified representation of the premises. By varying the number of conventional problems encountered before the test problem, Wood was able to confirm that subjects began by using the representational strategy but rapidly abandoned it in favour of more specialized non-representational procedures. What was particularly striking was the rapidity of this development. No doubt this was aided by the uniform content of the problems. Nevertheless, it is surprising that the biggest drop in the ability to answer the supplementary question was from those subjects who had previously encountered two conventional problems to those who had previously encountered three.

This finding suggests that subjects in the more orthodox studies of *three*-term series problems are likely to have abandoned the representational strategy fairly rapidly. These studies have tested subjects repeatedly, and hence both the IMAGE theory and the LINGUISTIC theory have almost certainly been based upon the performance of fairly experienced subjects. No wonder that despite their divergent assumptions they have tended to converge upon the same empirical predictions. They are both likely to have miscalculated slightly, with IMAGE theory failing to be sufficiently 'naive' and LINGUISTIC theory failing to be sufficiently 'sophisticated'. Both are perhaps guilty of 'regression towards the mean', and our final task in this chapter is to offer some suggestion on how they might be reformulated to correct this bias.

It is extremely difficult to say how a unified representation is formed by an inexperienced individual. What is needed are studies concentrating on the subject's initial performance and perhaps abandoning the customary procedure of asking a specific question about the premises. This constrains the individual; and a more general question merely asking what follows from the premises might be more revealing about inferential strategy. Meanwhile, it is possible to make some tentative suggestions based on a number of small but interesting discrepancies in the results of the experiments in the literature.

First, it seems likely that Hunter's notion of a 'natural' order for premises is relevant, and that inexperienced subjects find it easier to represent premises in a unified form when they do follow one another naturally. For example, judging by the number of errors they made, the subjects tested by De Soto *et al.* (1965) seem to have been less experienced than those tested by Clark (1969b). De Soto's subjects found problems of the form 'A > B, B > C', easier than those of the form, 'B > C, A > B'; whereas Clark's subjects yielded the opposite results. The hypothesis is also corroborated by the finding (Handel *et al.*, 1968) that with only 20 problems to solve, those of the form 'A > B, B > C', were easier than those of the form, 'A > B, C < B'. This conflicts with the performance of Huttenlocher's (1968) and Clark's (1969a, b) more practised subjects. It also conflicts with the performance of the younger children tested by Hunter (1957), but is consistent with the performance of the older children.

Second, according to the LINGUISTIC theory, the nature of the question should have *no* effect on a problem of the form:

B < A
B > C

since the alternative questions are both incongruous with the representation of the items. However, Hunter's subjects found that 'who is best?' was reliably easier than 'who is worst?' There are a number of possible explanations for this finding. Hunter himself suggests that the subjects may *revert* to the first premise and *convert* it, and that the answer to the question is particularly salient when it is in a premise that has been operated upon in this way. It is also possible that congruity between question and the adjacent second premise is more important than that between question and the first premise.

Finally, it is likely that the principle of lexical marking applies to both naive and experienced subject alike. This seems more parsimonious than the notion of a preferred direction of working, since it seems to apply to language behaviour in general. (For example, marked comparatives are harder to remember than unmarked comparatives.) It would be premature to present an information-processing model of naive performance; but it is clear that it would differ from the IMAGE theory principally by incorporating an aspect of Hunter's OPERATIONAL theory and some sort of question-answering procedure.

The effect of practice is probably to induce a more 'mechanized' approach to the problem, which minimizes effort and which is appropriate to the particular constraints of the material. At the same time such an approach is likely to be less flexible and may make it harder to solve an unexpectedly novel type of problem. In characterizing the effect of practice upon drawing conclusions from problems involving five premises, Hunter (1957) drew attention to an important aspect of performance. He wrote:

'When the student first tackles such a problem, his activity is haphazard. He may combine a couple of premises, draw a part conclusion, leave it, combine a further pair of premises, draw a second part conclusion, and try to see if this can be combined with the first part conclusion. . . . But after solving a few more problems of this type, his performance is characteristically transformed. He largely ignores the order in which the premises are presented: he reads through the statements in search of that one of the two terms which are not repeated and which he will take as his starting point: and from this starting point, he considers each premise in such a sequence that the terms form a consecutive chain with identical terms juxtaposed.'

Likewise, the most natural modification in solving three-term series problems is to read the question *before* reading the premises. Of course, subjects may glance fleetingly at the premises to obtain a global impression of them, but it is suggested that their detailed interpretation will be guided by the nature of the question. The procedure resembles working backwards from the conclusion of an inference to its premises, and its great advantage is that it often renders it unnecessary to examine more than one premise in any detail. Where only one premise is congruent with the question, then this premise will be processed first; and once it has been interpreted and the item which is *more*-x stored (where x is the relevant attribute), there is a simple time-saving procedure. If the item does not occur in the other premise, it is the solution to the problem. Where both premises have the same comparative, there is likely to be a natural tendency to interpret them in a standard order. The same technique of establishing the item which is *more*-x, where x is congruent with the question, can be used; and it is only necessary to interpret the other premise if this item is also mentioned in it.

It is a simple matter to express this sort of model in information-processing terms. A more pertinent issue is whether there is any evidence to support it. Ironically, although in principle it entails less processing than the LINGUISTIC model, it yields exactly the same differential predictions for those problems which have been studied so far.

One of the chief difficulties with the proposal that one approach to a problem is succeeded by another is to account for the process of transition. It is necessary to invoke a higher-order conceptual skill responsible for generating new strategies out of old (cf. Miller, Galanter, and Pribram, 1960). Yet it is not too difficult to envisage how this might occur. Wood (1969), for instance, suggests that a record is kept of all the procedures used in tackling a problem, and its eventual outcome. Hence, if a certain procedure always leads ultimately to a particular outcome, other intervening procedures may be dropped as redundant. In this way, for instance, a subject might learn that it was unnecessary to interpret the second premise in any detail if the item which is *more*-x in the first premise does not occur in it. However, in addition to the relatively passive monitoring of processes, a more radical and active search mechanism may have to be postulated in order to account for genuine innovative changes in strategy, such as learning to read the question before the premises.

If the present analysis of series problems is correct, then two main conclusions may be drawn. First, it is a valuable exercise to attempt to express theories about problem-solving in information-processing terms. This may show up inconsistencies or points of vagueness or unclarity within them. Second, one of the most important, though neglected, independent variables in a cognitive task is the number of problems a subject is given to solve. Subjects think, not only in solving a problem, but also about how to solve it. They are likely to move from general and flexible procedures to more economical and specialized strategies. They are likely to start with simple practical procedures, perhaps involving an iconic representation (cf. Bruner, 1964), and then to adopt more formal procedures involving symbolic representation of the problem material. Hence, one can no longer ask how an individual solves a three-term series problem without asking when in his intellectual development *within the experiment* it was given to him.

10

Reasoning with Quantifiers: the Atmosphere Effect

To demonstrate the validity of a relational inference it is necessary to analyse the internal structure of its premises. This procedure, which distinguishes relational inferences from propositional inferences, is equally necessary for another sort of inference, namely, those which involve quantifiers. These are words such as *all* and *some* which allow the 'quantity' of items to be specified. The prototype of all quantified inference is the *syllogism*. A typical example is the following deduction:

Some criminals are extraverts.

All criminals are neurotic.

Therefore, some neurotics are extraverts.

The validity of this argument obviously depends upon the quantifiers, but it also depends upon the structure of the premises and the way they relate to one another. This is easily demonstrated by converting the second premise to, 'All neurotics are criminals'; it is now no longer possible to draw any valid conclusion about the relation between neurotics and extraverts. Much of the traditional 'scholastic' logic, largely based on Aristotle's work, consists in an analysis of these structural properties of the syllogism. The psychological problem, however, is to determine what mental processes are involved in the deduction.

Syllogistic inference has been studied by psychologists in great detail, yet the process is poorly understood. There is no real theory of deduction, but only a number of scattered hypotheses about the factors which lead to mistakes. One reason for this disappointing state of affairs is the sheer complexity of quantifiers. This is shown by a striking aspect of the logical calculus which deals with them. For the propositional calculus,

✓there is a simple 'mechanical' procedure for deciding whether or not an inference is valid. But for the calculus dealing with quantifiers, there is no such procedure and, in principle, there cannot be one (Church, 1936). An obvious reflection of this complexity is the number and variety of possible quantified inferences—even syllogisms, which are a minute part of the field, exist in a greater variety than can be encompassed in a single experiment. That they should have been studied by psychologists more often than any other sort of quantified inference is thus hardly surprising. Yet it is a pity; there are other sorts of inference and other sorts of quantifier, e.g.:

> Most of John's friends are psychoanalysts.
> All of Mary's friends are behaviourists.
> There are a few of her friends that a lot of John's friends like.
> Therefore, some psychoanalysts like some behaviourists[1].

In discussing propositional reasoning, we posed the question of the individual's rationality: was he able to make valid deductions and refrain from fallacious ones? The same question must be asked about quantificational reasoning; and the answer given by the experimental psychologist is rather less optimistic. A number of studies have purported to show that the individual is swayed by his emotions, attitudes, and prejudices (e.g. Janis and Frick, 1943; Lefford, 1946; Kaufmann and Goldstein, 1967). However, the most that can be safely claimed is that individuals tend to accept that a *given* conclusion, which they find congenial, has been validly derived. Whether there is an actual effect upon deduction is open to doubt.

Perhaps a more serious charge against the individual's rationality is that he is prey to 'atmosphere' effects. The atmosphere produced by the premises predisposes him to accept conclusions with a congruent atmosphere. For instance, the following premises:

---

[1] Whether or not this inference is valid is an interesting question. There is no logical calculus adequate to accommodate it (cf. Rescher, 1968, p. 133) —an admission of the paucity of logic for the analysis of everyday arguments. Its validity seems to hinge upon whether *a lot* is interpreted in an absolute or proportional sense. If it is taken proportionally, i.e. 'a good proportion', then the inference is presumably valid.

Some of the voters are illiterate.

None of the voters are peasants.

create an atmosphere favourable to particular (*some*) and negative statements such as the following (fallacious) conclusion:

Some of the peasants are not illiterate.

Much of the impetus to study syllogistic inference stems from the early investigations of the phenomenon by Woodworth and Sells (1935) and Sells (1936); and studies continue to be devoted to the topic (e.g. Chapman and Chapman, 1959; Simpson and Johnson, 1966; Begg and Denny, 1969). However, to describe the findings in more detail it is necessary to give an outline of the logic of the syllogism.

A syllogism consists of two premises and a conclusion, and, in its traditional conception, these are selected from four basic types of statement:

The universal affirmative statement: All x are y (symbolized by 'A').

The particular affirmative statement: Some x are y (symbolized by 'I').

The universal negative statement: No x are y (symbolized by 'E').

The particular negative statement: Some x are not y (symbolized by 'O').

The types of statement that occur in any particular syllogism specify its *mood*. Thus, our earlier example, 'Some of the voters are illiterate. None of the voters are peasants. Therefore, some of the peasants are not illiterate', is a syllogism in the IEO mood. Since each of the three statements in a syllogism can be A, E, I or O, there are 64 possible moods. But it is also necessary to specify the structural relations between the statements. Granted that the conclusion is analysed into subject and predicate, S–P, it is clear that, as in a series problem, these terms must be related by a middle term, M, which occurs in both of the premises. The traditional analysis recognizes that the order of the two premises is logically immaterial—it may not be, psychologically—and decrees that the subject of the conclusion should occur in the second premise. There are accordingly four possible *figures* for the structural relations of the syllogism:

Figure 1	Figure 2	Figure 3	Figure 4
M–P	P–M	M–P	P–M
S–M	S–M	M–S	M–S
S–P	S–P	S–P	S–P

Since each of the 64 moods could occur in any of these figures, there is a total of 256 syllogisms recognized by traditional logic. Only 24 of them are actually valid. (Since the order of the premises may matter to the psychologist, he should recognize that there are 512 possible syllogisms, of which 46 (*sic*) are valid.)

The atmosphere effect concerns only the mood of syllogisms. Woodworth and Sells (1935) asserted that affirmative premises create an atmosphere favourable for an affirmative conclusion while negative premises create an atmosphere favourable for a negative conclusion. The quantifiers in premises have a similar effect: universal premises suggest a universal conclusion while particular premises suggest a particular conclusion. Various sub-principles were subsequently proposed by Sells (1936) to explain what happens with heterogeneous syllogisms. But the essential theory can be succinctly summarized, following Begg and Denny (1969), in two principles:

(1) Whenever at least one premise is negative, the most frequently accepted conclusion will be negative; otherwise it will be affirmative.

(2) Whenever at least one premise is particular, the most frequently accepted conclusion will be particular; otherwise it will be universal.

These two principles can work in tandem, predicting for instance that the most frequently accepted conclusion from:

Some A are B

No B are C

will be either:

Some A are not C

or:

Some C are not A.

Only the first of these conclusions is, in fact, valid.

A variety of techniques have been used in the experimental studies. Subjects have been asked whether a given conclusion is 'true' or 'false', or whether it is 'absolutely true, probably true, indeterminate, probably false, or absolutely false'. They have been asked to pick out the correct conclusion from a set of alternatives. But, provided the material is symbolic (e.g. 'Some x's are y's', etc.), the results are almost invariably consistent with the atmosphere effect. There is, however, only one study where the subject genuinely has to *make* an inference, rather than to evaluate one that has been made for him (Sells and Koob, 1937). And this study investigated a very limited number of types of syllogism. Hence, there is no convincing evidence that 'atmosphere' does influence the process of inference.

What could be the mechanism of the atmosphere effect? Sells (1936) seems to have considered it a special kind of 'set'. The sort which leads to careless grammatical mistakes such as, 'The laboratory equipment in these situations were in many instances . . .', or which underlies such puzzles as:

> 'If an aeroplane carrying a party of English tourists crashed exactly on the border between Canada and the U.S.A., where would the survivors be buried?'

Of course, the answer is that they don't bury the survivors, but the 'set' induced by the stipulation of the nationality of the passengers, etc., will often mislead individuals into overlooking the absurdity of the question. In a similar fashion, according to Sells, the premises of a syllogism induce a predisposition to accept certain sorts of conclusion. This is a most damaging attack on the individual's rational ability. It suggests that the process of deduction is a purely superficial manipulation of verbal tags in a manner more akin to rhyming than to reasoning. It is no use arguing that the individual falls back on such procedures only in the case of fallacies, for how does he recognize them? Either he has recourse to other more basic strategies—in which case the atmosphere effect is a subsidiary and perhaps trivial phenomenon, or else he is prey to it for the whole universe of syllogisms, in which case his rationality *is* seriously impaired.

Woodworth and Sells seemed to have been aware that there

was more to syllogistic inference than atmosphere. This cannot be said with such certainty of their successors. Such is the sway of the phenomenon that many of them have often ignored the figure of the syllogism and merely pooled all the data in terms of mood. What is extraordinary about this preoccupation with atmosphere is that even at the time of the original enquiries there were good reasons for supposing that it was a phenomenon of limited applicability. Some years previously, Wilkins (1928) had investigated syllogistic reasoning, using a variety of problems and deliberately varying the nature of their content. She observed that fewer errors were made with familiar everyday materials (e.g. 'All students of literature make use of reference libraries', etc.) than with symbolic materials (e.g. 'All x's are y's', etc.) or unfamiliar materials (e.g. 'All foraminafera are rhyzopoda', etc.). But a more crucial finding, which has never received the prominence it deserves, concerns the pattern of errors that occurred with the different types of materials. Consider, for example, the problems with premises having the form:

> All B are C
>
> All A are B

With the symbolic material, the most seductive error in Wilkins' test was to evaluate the conclusion, 'All C are A', as valid. This is completely consistent with the atmosphere effect. Yet with the familiar everyday materials, this mistake hardly ever occurred. Indeed, the main mistake here was to accept the conclusion, 'Some C are not A', as valid. This error violates *both* the atmosphere principles. The percentages of subjects making these various errors are worth quoting:

	Familiar material	Symbolic material	Unfamiliar material
All B are C			
All A are B			
∴ All C are A	1·3%	38·0%	30·6%
∴ Some C are not A	32·4%	12·7%	15·0%

These findings are fairly typical of Wilkins' results, which suggest that atmosphere effects are much less general with familiar material. Indeed, it seems that different principles may govern reasoning with familiar as opposed to unfamiliar material.

Reasoning with familiar materials has, of course, its own particular dangers. The individual may be tempted to abandon logical considerations in favour of causal principles. Mary Henle (1962) has shown, in a unique qualitative study of syllogistic inference, that subjects may be capable of drawing valid inferences, yet fail to accept the task as a strictly logical enterprise. Her results are strongly reminiscent of those that we obtained when subjects were asked to make propositional inferences with an everyday content. For example, she presented graduate students with an argument which was essentially of the following form:

It's important to talk about things that are in our minds.

We spend so much of our time in the kitchen that household problems are in our minds.

Therefore, it's important to talk about household problems.

The conclusion runs counter to common sense; and, regardless of whether a subject evaluated the inference correctly, he often departed from the logical task in hand. Frequently, a subject would deny the truth of a premise (e.g. 'It's *not* important to talk about things that are in our minds unless they worry us') or, alternatively, he would seek to extend or justify it (e.g. 'by talking about a problem, it can be solved or worked through'). Other subjects ignored one or other of the premises, and correctly pointed out that the conclusion did not then follow validly (e.g. 'The fact that a woman spends much time in the kitchen has nothing to do with whether or not it is important to talk about the problems'). Similarly, an additional premise might be inserted into the argument, or the meaning of a given premise modified. In a number of cases, particular premises were even re-interpreted so as to be universal. The premises of the following syllogism:

Many youngsters don't get enough vitamins.

Some vitamin deficiencies are dangerous to health.

Therefore, the health of many youngsters is endangered.

were sometimes translated into the implicitly universal form:

Youngsters don't get enough vitamins.

Vitamin deficiencies are dangerous to health.

and the inference deemed valid, which it is after such a re-interpretation. A similar preference for universal statements has been demonstrated in a recent experimental study (Revlis, Lipkin, and Hayes, 1971). But it will be noted that in Henle's study the statements lack explicit quantifiers, and provide a vague and slippery way of passing almost imperceptibly from the particular to the universal. They are an ideal medium for the expression of prejudice, since they appear to have the force of a universal statement while being tolerant of exceptions (cf. Gilson and Abelson, 1965). In short, the difficulties with familiar material are more like those we described in the chapter on 'pure' and 'practical' reasoning than those associated with atmosphere effects.

Another strong argument in favour of the subsidiary role of atmosphere comes from Sells' (1936) own study. There is a marked contrast between the acceptance of valid and invalid conclusions where both conform to the principles of atmosphere. For example, given premises of the form:

All B are A

All C are B

the conclusion, 'All C are A', was accepted as valid by 94 per cent of Sells' subjects. But the conclusion, 'All A are C', was accepted as valid by only 45 per cent of his subjects. Both conclusions ought to be equally acceptable according to the theory; and it is an admission of the subsidiary role of atmosphere to point out that only the first conclusion is genuinely valid.

In order to investigate the atmosphere effect in more detail, we carried out an experiment[1] (Johnson-Laird, unpublished) which involved a number of departures from the usual investigations in this area. First, the subjects were given neither a conclusion to evaluate, nor a multiple-choice between alternative conclusions. They were simply presented with two premises and asked to write down the conclusion which followed from them in their own words. Second, they were given only premises from which a valid conclusion could be derived—a fact to which their attention was drawn in the instructions. This contrasts with previous studies which have concentrated their attention upon invalid inferences. Third, the problems involved familiar everyday material, e.g. 'All the nuns are nurses. None of the nurses are midwives.' This material was neither

[1] We are grateful to Diana Shapiro and Paul Byerley for assistance in preparing the materials and conducting the experiment.

contentious, nor likely to arouse questions of truth or falsity.

It may be useful in describing the material to give an alternative account of the syllogism, which is more pertinent to the psychologist. Although, logically, there are four basic statements, each premise in a syllogism can be one of eight different types of sentence. This is because the middle term, which must occur in both premises, can either be the subject or the object of the sentence. Hence, there is a total of 64 possible types of premise combination. Only 27 of these pairs of premises yield valid conclusions. These are presented, together with the strongest conclusion they yield, in Table 6. Obviously, if 'All A are C' is a valid conclusion, then so, too, is the weaker conclusion, 'Some C are A.'

In the experiment, each of the 20 subjects received a booklet made up, in a different random order, of the 27 problems couched in a familiar content.

The main point of the experiment, of course, was to see to what extent the subjects' errors were compatible, or incompatible, with the atmosphere effect. Allowing for the fact that the order of the premises is logically immaterial, and that 'Some A are B' is logically equivalent to 'Some B are A', and 'No A are B' is equivalent to 'No B are A', the inferences fall into seven basic sorts: AAA (2 problems), AAI (1 problem), AII (4 problems), AEE (4 problems), AEO (4 problems), IEO (8 problems), and AOO (4 problems). With problems of the AII and AEE sorts, no *error* can be compatible with the atmosphere of the premises since any response which is compatible with their atmosphere is also correct. But errors on the remaining five sorts of problem can be compatible, or incompatible, with the atmosphere. The average numbers of such errors *per* problem are given in Table 7.

There were reliably more errors which were incompatible with atmosphere (an overall average of 3·9 per problem) than which were compatible with atmosphere (an overall average of 1·8 per problem). But what the results in Table 7 show, and analysis confirms, is that the tendency to conform to atmosphere varies a great deal from one sort of problem to another. The AII and AEO problems tend to elicit 'atmosphere' errors, but the IEO and AOO problems do not tend to do so.

K

TABLE 6 *The 64 possible pairs of syllogistic premises, together with the valid conclusions which may be drawn from 27 of them. (The 8 columns represent the first premise in a problem the 8 rows represent the second premise)*

First premise (columns) / Second premise (rows):

Second premise \ First premise	All A are B	All B are A	Some A are B	Some B are A	No A are B	No B are A	Some A are not B	Some B are not A
All c are B		∴ All c are A			∴ No A are c	∴ No A are c	∴ Some A are not c	
All B are c	∴ All A are c	∴ Some A are c	∴ Some A are c	∴ Some A are c	∴ Some c are not A	∴ Some c are not A		∴ Some c are not A
Some c are B		∴ Some A are c			∴ Some c are not A	∴ Some c are not A		
Some B are c		∴ Some A are c			∴ Some c are not A	∴ Some c are not A		
No c are B	∴ No A are c	∴ Some A are not c	∴ Some A are not c	∴ Some A are not c				
No B are c	∴ No A are c	∴ Some A are not c	∴ Some A are not c	∴ Some A are not c				
Some c are not B	∴ Some c are not A							
Some B are not c		∴ Some A are not c						

TABLE 7 *The average number of errors (per problem) compatible with, and incompatible with, the atmosphere effect*

The sort of syllogism	Number of problems	Errors compatible with atmosphere	Errors incompatible with atmosphere
AAI	I	3·0	0
AEO	4	5·7	2·2
AAA	2	2·5	3·0
IEO	8	0·2	4·9
AOO	4	0·7	5·2

These findings suggest that, at the very least, the notion of an atmosphere effect needs to be supplemented by further principles to account for its variability from one problem to another, and to account for other sorts of error. However, taken in conjunction with Wilkins' differences between familiar and symbolic material and with Sells' differences between valid and invalid inferences, they suggest a more radical alternative. Perhaps, there is no atmosphere effect in syllogistic reasoning at all, but merely an amassed set of data which, when casually viewed, gives rise to the illusion of such a phenomenon.

The process of syllogistic inference seems to demand, first, the interpretation of the premises, and, second, their combination into some sort of representation from which the conclusion can be directly derived. An interesting illustration of this point is provided by Chapman and Chapman (1959). They were among the first to propose an alternative to the atmosphere effect, and their theory postulates that invalid inferences arise from mistakes in both processes. The mistakes in interpretation consist in illicitly converting A and O premises; and the mistakes in combination consist in what the Chapmans call 'probabilistic' inference—a phenomenon which will be described subsequently.

Both processes were, of course, invoked in the discussion of three-term series problems, and it is natural to try to extend that analysis to deal with syllogisms. However, there are some striking differences between the two sorts of problem. With syllogisms, for instance, the process of combination is likely to be very much more demanding than it is with series problems. This is confirmed by the impracticability of the procedure in which terms are separately stored with their appropriate 'weights' (the 'weighing machine' approach of Chapter 9). It would be ridiculous to interpret 'All A are B' by separately storing 'All A' and 'B'. Such an approach is likely to produce the 'eristic' arguments of the Sophists, e.g. 'That dog is a father; that dog is his; therefore that dog is his father', which were deliberately nonsensical (cf. Kneale and Kneale, 1962, p. 12). Yet despite the shift in relative importance, it is clear that *both* processes are necessary for syllogisms. The present chapter accordingly falls into two sections: in the first we consider the interpretation of premises, and in the second their combination.

In order to convey the issues involved in the interpretation of syllogistic premises, it is necessary first to say something about the linguistics of quantifiers. The reader who has no patience with the apparatus of grammatical transformations, which we owe to Chomsky (1957, 1965) and, in this particular case, to Klima's (1964) penetrating study of negation, is advised to skip the following argument.

Our analysis, presented in full (Johnson-Laird, 1970a), aims to delineate the essentials of English quantifiers. Let us consider initially the number of different ways of expressing the negation of a simple sentence containing a single quantifier, e.g. the negation of 'all the girls like John'. This can, of course, be expressed by, 'It isn't the case that all the girls like John.' But there are more economical ways, in both active sentences:

Not all the girls like John.

Some of the girls don't like John.

All the girls don't like John. (In one meaning of this sentence.)

and in passive sentences:

John isn't liked by some of the girls.

John isn't liked by all the girls. (In one meaning of this sentence.)

The central tenet of transformational theory is that the best way of giving a formal specification of sentences is to derive them from some underlying structure, closely related to their meaning[1]. Such derivations involve a series of grammatical transformations, which permute or delete elements of the underlying structure to yield, ultimately, the structure corresponding to the actual sentence. Our problem is accordingly to derive the above set of synonymous sentences from an underlying structure common to them all. The essence of this structure is that it contains an element representing negation which is placed prior to the sentence it negates. It is a structure which, ignoring unnecessary complications, has the following form:

neg (all the girls like John)

[1] Just how close is a matter of very considerable controversy in current linguistic circles.

Since the negative element is ultimately realized by *not*, we need transformations which move it into the position at the auxiliary verb and, if necessary, move it out again to incorporate it into the quantifier, yielding *not all*. But we also need a transformation which converts *all* into *some* and which, at the same time, removes the quantifier from within the scope of the negative. We can tell that the quantifier is no longer within the scope of the negative because the resulting sentence, 'Some of the girls don't like John', is synonymous with, 'There are some of the girls who don't like John'; and the negative clearly does not include 'There are some of the girls'.

The other main negative sentence is one which denies that any of the girls like John. This has an underlying structure of the form:

neg (some of the girls like John)

It will be noted that the existential quantifier *some* is used because the underlying meaning corresponds to, 'It is not the case that some girls like John.' This can be expressed in active sentences by:

> None of the girls like John.
> All the girls don't like John. (In the other meaning of this sentence.)

and in passive sentences by:

> John is liked by none of the girls.
> John isn't liked by any of the girls.
> John isn't liked by all the girls. (In the other meaning of this sentence.)

These sentences reveal that the existential quantifier is represented by *any* when it occurs within the scope of the negative, and that this becomes *none* when the negative is incorporated into it. Otherwise the transformations operate as before, and it is possible to convert *some* (*any*) into *all*—once again, this transformation removes the quantifier from within the scope of negation. It is important to bear in mind that unless a quantifier is within the scope of negation it cannot incorporate the negative.

This linguistic analysis makes transparent a fact which the traditional terminology may have obscured. There is a close relation between the A and the O statements, and between the

I and the E statements. O corresponds to the negation of A, and E corresponds to the negation of I:

Some A are not B is derived from neg (All A are B).

No A are B is derived from neg (Some A are B).

The analysis also reveals that one essential difference between the two ways of expressing O statements is in the scope of their negatives. The negative in 'Not all A are B' has a wider scope than in 'Some A are not B'. Such sentences, incidentally, provide an obvious way of testing Clark's (1972) hypothesis that the smaller the scope of the negative, the easier the sentence is to understand.

We devised an experiment, conducted by Jean Waddington, to investigate how syllogistic premises are interpreted. Twenty-four subjects were asked to classify a set of diagrams according to whether they were truthfully or falsely described by a statement. Each subject performed the task for the four types of statement used in the syllogism, and for a further set of statements synonymous with them but differing in structure:

(A)	All x are y.	(A')	No x are not y.
(I)	Some x are y.	(I')	Not all x are not y.
(E)	No x are y.	(E')	All x are not y.
(O)	Some x are not y.	(O')	Not all x are y.

The seven diagrams are shown in Figure 14, where the continuous line indicates that a circle was drawn in red (representing x), and the broken line indicates that it was drawn in green (representing y). These sorts of diagram were used by the Swiss mathematician, Euler, for pedagogical purposes, and their principle is simple. Each circle represents a different class, so two overlapping circles indicate that the two classes have some members in common, and one circle lying within the other indicates that all the members of the first class are included in the other class.

Each sentence had a different lexical content which was intended to make a generic assertion rather than to describe specific events. This was in order to investigate a further aspect of the interpretation of the existential quantifier. In everyday life the statement, 'Some grass is green' carries a strong presumption that some grass is *not* green, otherwise the stronger statement, 'All grass is green', would have been made. But this sort of presumption has to be abandoned in logic, because the existential quantifier means *at least some*—it does not rule out the possibility of *all*. Hence subjects in experiments on syllogistic reasoning are invariably taught to interpret *some* in its 'logical' fashion. The psychologist's preoccupation with syllogisms has perhaps obscured an interesting point about ordinary language. Sometimes the 'logical' interpretation occurs spontaneously and, of course, sometimes it does not. Although our subjects were told to forget about the truth or falsity of the sentences as descriptions of the real world, we tried to influence their interpretations of the I statement by varying the lexical material. Half the subjects received 'universal,

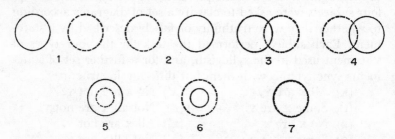

Figure 14. The set of Euler diagrams used in the experiment

material which could be plausibly extended to include *All* x *are* y, e.g. 'Some beasts are animals.' The other half of the subjects received 'non-universal' material which could not be extended in this way, e.g. 'Some books are novels.' If the extension is made, then obviously diagram (6), where all x lies within y, will be classified as truthfully described; otherwise it will be classified as falsely described.

The frequencies with which the diagrams were classified as truthfully described by each of the four main types of statement are given in Table 8, together with the average times taken to make the classifications. Summarizing the results of the experiment, it is clear that subjects had little difficulty in appreciating that *All* x *are* y refers to a situation where x is either included in y or is co-extensive with it, and that *No* x *are* y refers to the situation where the two classes are quite distinct and separate from one another. With the other two main types of statement, however, difficulties did emerge. The lexical content certainly seems to influence whether *some* is treated as consistent with *all*, at least in the case of the affirmative I statement. Table 9 presents the frequencies of the two classifications of diagram (6) as a function of the lexical material. The frequencies show that

TABLE 8 *The overall frequencies (max = 24) of 'true' classifications of the Euler diagrams for the main types of statement*

Statements	Diagrams					Average classification time (sec.)
	(1)	(3)	(5)	(6)	(7)	
(A) All x are Y	0	2	3	24	22	25·0
(I) Some x are Y	1	23	16	12	7	24·1
(E) No x are Y	24	1	2	0	1	24·9
(O) Some x are not Y	8	24	18	2	2	27·5

the nature of this material reliably overrode the instructions to ignore its relevance to the real world: where it suggests a 'universal' interpretation of the form *at least some and possibly all*, it tends to be given one. With the negative statement, *some* x *are not* Y, there was a general tendency to assume that *some* is inconsistent with *all*, i.e. the statement is taken to imply *some* x *are* Y. This bias, apparently unaffected by the content of the statement, might have been expected from our earlier analysis of the preconceptions involved in the normal use of negatives.

TABLE 9 *The frequencies of the two classifications of diagram (6) as a function of whether the lexical material of (1) Some x are Y was 'universal' or 'non-universal'*

	Diagram (6) classified as:	
	True	False
'Universal' lexical material	9	3
'Non-universal' lexical material	3	9

Turning to the other four sorts of statement, the classification of *not all* x *are* y was very similar to that of *some* x *are not* y, but it took reliably longer to classify (an average of 34·0 sec. in comparison to an average of 27·5 sec.). This finding is, of course, precisely what is to be expected from Clark's (1972) hypothesis about the scope of negation. The classification of *all* x *are not* y confirmed the ambiguity of this sentence which was established in our linguistic analysis; and the two interpretations occurred with about equal frequency. The two double negatives, *no* x *are not* y and *not all* x *are not* y, took a considerable time to decipher—approximately twice as long as their equivalent affirmatives (A) and (I)—but their classifications were very nearly as consistent as those of the affirmatives.

The fact that very nearly half the subjects interpreted *some* x *are not* y in an identical way to *some* x *are* y suggests one potent reason why O statements are illicitly converted. They tend to be taken as logically equivalent to I statements, which of course may be validly converted. The two sorts of statement merely emphasize, according to this argument, different aspects of the same underlying situation. But the results offer no enlightenment on the question of the illicit conversion of *All* x *are* y. How is this phenomenon to be explained?

Once again, it could be argued that it is merely due to the operation of an atmosphere effect. Such a suggestion was indeed made by Sells (1936), but it was rejected by the Chapmans. They argue that such conversions are often plausible, especially in mathematics where the copula *are* is often treated as equivalent to *are equal to*. This sort of interpretation, they suggest, may transfer to the laboratory, particularly if the material is symbolic. Of course, the individual's implicit knowledge of his language (or the world) will inhibit him from arguing: 'All dogs are animals', therefore 'all animals are dogs'. It is easy enough to devise concrete material which contains no definite cues of this sort, and, interestingly enough, the mere fact that it is concrete seems to exert a useful corrective influence. For example, Wilkins (1928) found that given the premise, 'all freshmen take History 1', only eight per cent of her subjects accepted the converse conclusion: 'all students taking History 1 are freshmen'. But 20 per cent of them accepted the equally invalid conclusion, 'some students taking History 1 are not freshmen'. With purely symbolic material (all A are B), the corresponding percentages for the two inferences were 25 per cent (all B are A) and 14 per cent (some B are not A). A still more marked interaction between structure and content occurred with inferences from 'all the men belonging to the Athletic Club belong to this Club' (All A are B). The percentages of subjects accepting the conclusions with the symbolic and familiar material were:

	Familiar material	Symbolic material
All B are A	3·7%	25·0%
Some B are not A	21·0%	14·0%

A similar difference in the tendency to accept illicit conversion seems to occur as a function of whether the material is verbal or pictorial. Susan Argent (personal communication) found that given a statement of the form, 'If it's a diamond, then it's green', 20 out of her 24 subjects considered that it therefore followed that, 'All green shapes are diamonds.' Yet only six of the subjects made the same mistake when given drawings, or descriptions of them, to evaluate with respect to the given statement. Argent's use of the conditional reminds us of the close connection between conditional and universal statements. Similar factors may underlie their illicit conversion. However, the conditional is ambiguous since it can be legitimately used to imply its converse in a way which is not possible for the universal.

A quite independent line of thought on the problem of conversion comes from Piaget's investigations of the child's grasp of quantifiers (Inhelder and Piaget, 1964). Children between the ages of about 5–7 years, in the upper end of what Piaget calls the stage of 'pre-operational' thought, show a characteristic inability to handle class inclusion. This is very simple to demonstrate. The child is presented with a collection of blue circles together with some red and blue squares. He is then asked, 'Are all the circles blue?' The characteristic error is to reply, 'No', because 'there are blue squares', or because 'there are red and blue squares'. Inhelder and Piaget found that this sort of mistake is more frequent when the quantified term concerns colour rather than shape (e.g. 'Are all the blue things circles?'); and it is still further enhanced when the quantified term refers to weight (cf. Lovell, Mitchell, and Everett, 1962). It seems that the task is easier when the quantified term denotes a more concrete dimension or, as Inhelder and Piaget put it, when it denotes a better graphic collection.

The attempts of Inhelder and Piaget to explain the child's mistakes smack a little of circularity. They argue that 'All A are B' is taken as equivalent to 'All B are A' because the child assumes that all A are *all* B rather than all A are *some* B[1]. This is because he cannot see that A is included in B. Thus, failure to grasp the relation of inclusion leads to errors with *all* and *some* (Inhelder and Piaget, 1964, p. 73). Later on, however, the authors (p. 97) argue that error in handling *all* and *some* lead to errors with inclusion. It really seems that the two factors are indissolubly linked: the verbal mastery of class inclusion necessitates a firm grasp of the distinction between *all* and *some*.

Inhelder and Piaget do, however, make one most illuminating point about illicit conversion. They claim that the child has no difficulty in appreciating that, say, the class of circles consists of two subclasses, the red ones and the blue ones. But once he separates the subclass of blue circles from the remainder, whether in reality or in his mind, the class of circles ceases to exist for him. This is because: 'when the word "all" is applied to a collection, it introduces a property which the collection possesses as an entity. . . . Thus "all the circles are blue" means that the collection as a whole is *exclusively* and *entirely* blue and made up of circles. . . .' Without in any way wishing to imply a regression to a more childish way of interpreting statements, this remark suggests the following explanation of the adult's interpretation of universal statements. He tends to interpret the statement, 'All x are y', by setting up a representation of the class of instances corresponding to x, and

---

[1] This rather odd device of quantifying the predicate is due originally to Sir William Hamilton, the nineteenth-century Scottish logician. Although relatively harmless in the expository use made of it by Inhelder and Piaget, the scheme as a whole is unworkable (cf. Kneale and Kneale, 1962, p. 353). To raise just one difficulty: is the *some* in 'all A are some B' to be taken as *at least some* (in which case A and B could be co-extensive) or as *some but not all*?

tagging each instance with the attribute y. When the statement is abstract or symbolic, the class x is treated as an entity, and the individual is likely to focus his attention solely upon it, even when considering the converse statement, 'all y are x'. It becomes the universe of discourse, and, of course, within such a restricted universe, the converse follows quite validly. To illustrate this notion, let us represent the class x by triangles and the property y by cross-hatching. The statement, 'All x are y', with an abstract content, is thus interpreted by a representation isomorphic to the part of Figure 15 lying within the dotted line. This might be a visual image, or a more abstract

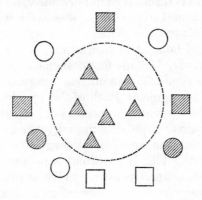

Figure 15. The interpretation of 'All x (triangles) are y (cross-hatched)

representation. It might even consist of the representation of a single triangle tagged with the information that 'any' triangle possesses the attribute y. In the case of meaningful and familiar material, however, knowledge of the world will prevent the individual focussing solely upon the quantified term. The representation will thus in effect include the items lying outside the dotted line in Figure 15—items which are not x's but which sometimes possess the attribute y. This sort of representation is, in turn, likely to give rise to the invalid conclusion (reported by Wilkins, 1928) that 'Some y are not x.'

One factor which encouraged the illicit conversion of conditionals was the cognitive load of the problem: we saw in

Chapter 6 that subjects would convert a conditional if it enabled them to solve a problem. Since illicit conversion often turns a syllogism from being invalid into being valid, one would expect it to occur more often in such syllogisms than in the statement judged in isolation. Of course, this prediction provides only indirect evidence for the Chapmans' idea that illicit conversion occurs in evaluating syllogisms. However, results contrary to the prediction would place the theory in jeopardy. In fact, all available data support the prediction. Sells (1936) found that A statements were judged to have valid converses by 33 per cent of his subjects. He tested 18 types of syllogism where an invalid conclusion would become valid if an A premise were converted, and, on average, they were judged valid by 66 per cent of his subjects. The percentages ranged from 45 to 80 per cent, and none of them was lower than the critical 33 per cent. Similarly, Wilkins found that the converse of an A premise with a symbolic content was accepted on average by 21 per cent of her subjects. Each of the 17 relevant syllogisms was accepted by a greater proportion of her subjects, with an average of 41 per cent judging the inference as valid.

The same enhancement of illicit conversion does not occur with O statements. This is consistent with our view that conversion of O statements rests upon a different principle, namely, the fact that they are often construed as equivalent to I statements. The fallacy, here, is also much more potent—indeed, one might argue that it is so prevalent that there is little room for any enhancement of the effect by embedding the statement in a syllogism.

After this detailed examination of the interpretation of premises, we can turn to the process of their combination in syllogistic inference. We mentioned that Chapman and Chapman (1959) suggested that one source of error was the use of 'probabilistic' inferences. This means that the reasoner tends to assume that items which have something in common are (likely to be) the same, and that things that lack common qualities are not (likely to be) the same. For example, given the premises:

    Some A are B.
    Some C are B.

the reasoner is likely to conclude that: Some A are C, because they both have the attribute B in common. And, given the premises:

No A are B.

No C are B.

he is likely to deduce that: No A are C, because they both lack the attribute B.

Unfortunately, the theory is inherently vague. It is difficult to determine exactly what prediction it makes for the premises:

No A are B.

Some C are not B.

Should the individual be predisposed to conclude that 'No C are A', or that 'Some C are not A'? The Chapmans point out that their subjects' preferences were, indeed, more or less equally split between these two alternatives. Alas, this ingenious exploitation of an inherent vagueness in the theory does not always work. Given the premises:

All A are B.

Some B are C.

there should be an equal preference for the conclusions, 'All C are A', and, 'Some C are A.' But the subjects opted overwhelmingly for the latter alternative.

It seems that we need an entirely fresh approach to the problem of combination in syllogistic inference; and there are two pertinent facts which need to be taken into account in its development. First, syllogisms differ widely in their difficulty. There are some which are straightforward and which most intelligent adults can solve in a few seconds. There are others, however, which are extremely difficult. This is soon appreciated by the reasoner, yet even after several minutes of thought he may still produce a fallacious answer. Second, even the easiest of syllogisms tends to take a considerable time to solve in comparison to a three-term series problem.

These two facts imply that the process of combination is essentially a *series* of processes rather than a single act, and hence different individuals are likely to proceed in different ways. If we look for some single unified process, we are likely to look in vain. We propose accordingly to present a speculative outline of some aspects of these processes. Our remarks are in no way comprehensive, and even the fragmentary picture that they convey contains a number of details which have yet to be tested.

If a difficult syllogism is given to an intelligent individual, in a relaxed and informal situation, one can often observe traces of a series of processes. On presenting the premises, say:

None of the musicians are inventors.

All the inventors are professors.

an articulate individual is likely to announce an obviously tentative answer after a relatively short time:

None of the musicians are professors.

If one then asks, 'are you sure?', or merely refrains from comment, a considerable amount of time will probably elapse during which it is clear that intense cogitation is going on. A series of successive approximations, culminating in the correct conclusion will probably be forthcoming, e.g.:

None of the professors are musicians.

None of the professors who are inventors are musicians.

Some of the professors are not musicians.

The second of these answers is of great interest: it is a logically impeccable conclusion in which the middle term of the premises has been only partially digested. Not until the final answer is the process completely carried out. In the experiment which we conducted on syllogistic reasoning (cf. pp. 136–9), we observed that some subjects seemed to be incapable of passing beyond certain stages in the series. Some held fast to their initial answer, others produced a variety of intermediate answers, e.g. 'The professors who are inventors are not musicians', 'All the inventive professors are not musicians.' Only a few subjects (three out of 20 in the case of this particular inference) produced the most economical answer.

It seems that the reasoner initially constructs his first approximation to the answer, working in an intuitive fashion, and then submits it to a series of logical checks. Such checks probably involve trying out various ways of combining the information in the premises. They will sometimes lead to a revision in the answer, and even perhaps to the decision that no definite conclusion can be derived from the premises. Of course, the thoroughness with which the checks are carried out will vary from individual to individual, depending upon both his logical acumen and his enthusiasm for the task. But it also seems to depend upon the syllogism itself. The processes of combination are naturally easier for some problems than for others; and they are also facilitated when the content of the problem involves familiar everyday matters.

What principles determine the initial rapid construction of a conclusion? It is plausible that the individual, untrained in formal logic, appreciates that if there is a 'restricted' premise, concerning only *some* members of a class, then the conclusion must be similarly restricted. Likewise, he appreciates that if there is a negative premise, the conclusion must also be negative. (This second principle does admit exceptions, however, since 'some A are not B' is often taken to imply 'some A are B'.) These two principles, of course, correspond exactly with the rules for the atmosphere effect. But in this case they are reflections of an underlying logical knowledge of what properties of premises are transmitted to conclusions, rather than recipes for the purely superficial matching of verbal elements. Unfortunately, the principles fail to specify which term should occur in the subject and which term should occur in the predicate. For example, given premises of the form: Some B are A; All B are C, they merely stipulate that the conclusion will be an I statement. It could be, 'Some A are C', or it could be, 'Some C are A.' It is vital to rectify this deficiency because our subjects showed a very distinct bias in framing their conclusions—a bias which probably had its origin in the initial stages of the inference. The equivalent deficiency in framing the rules of the atmosphere effect has presumably been overlooked because the empirical studies almost invariably require the subjects to evaluate given conclusions.

In thinking about the missing principle governing the initial stage of inference, we were originally attracted by the analogy with three-term series problems. It seemed that some individuals might proceed by trying to arrange the terms of the syllogism into a 'natural' order: an order which, following Hunter's (1957) model for series problems, would have the terms arranged in a sequence allowing the middle term to be expunged, e.g.

L

Some A are B.
All B are C.
Therefore: Some A are C.

If the terms were not naturally laid out in this order, then it would be necessary to re-arrange them. Depending upon the mood and the figure of the syllogism, the two premises might have to be re-ordered, or an individual premise might have to be converted, as the Chapmans had already suggested. For example, premises of the form:

Some B are A.
All B are C.

can be brought into the appropriate order by converting the first premise to 'Some A are B.'

It may be true that some subjects proceed in this way, but the results of our experiment suggest that the majority do not do so. The crucial evidence concerned problems which become identical after the valid conversion of a premise. These problems, according to the hypothesis, ought to yield identical conclusions. Yet, to our surprise, we found systematic differences between them. Table 10 gives the frequencies with which two different conclusions were drawn for the two IA problems illustrated above.

TABLE 10 *The frequencies of two alternative valid conclusions from IA premises*

Form of conclusion	Premises	
	Some A are B All B are C	Some B are A All B are C
Therefore: Some A are C	13	3
Therefore: Some C are A	2	9

If the subjects were simply converting the first premise of the second problem, then they should tend to draw the same initial conclusions for both inferences. There should be no reason subsequently to modify these conclusions since both problems are simple, and the observed differences should not occur. The difference was also reliable where the premises were stated in the opposite order; and an analogous difference is shown in Table 11 for AE premises. This difference was again maintained when the premises were stated in the opposite order.

TABLE 11 *The frequencies of two alternative valid conclusions from* AE *premises*

| | Premises | |
Form of conclusion	All A are B No B are C	All A are B No C are B
Therefore: No A are C	12	5
Therefore: No C are A	1	9

Obviously, the two principles governing the formulation of the initial conclusion need to be supplemented by a principle which accounts for this bias. In purely descriptive terms, it seems that the individual examines first the 'restrictive', or negative premise. If the quantified term is an end-anchor, i.e. *not* the middle term, it forms the subject of the conclusion, and it is only necessary to determine the end-anchor of the other premise in order to complete the conclusion. If, on the other hand, the quantified term is not an end-anchor, the subjects then examine the other premise. Its end-anchor becomes the subject of the conclusion, suitably restricted or negated, and the predicate consists of the end-anchor of the first premise. It is difficult to formulate a more general underlying psychological principle until we have more information about what happens with those invalid inferences where both premises are negative, or restricted. Indeed, a study in which subjects were encouraged to give spontaneous and immediate answers, perhaps within a few seconds, might be most revealing.

After the initial stage, there is likely to be a series of logical checks which seem to demand an essentially representational approach. We can best illustrate the sort of process that seems to occur by considering a deduction which we have only observed informally.

If a subject is presented with premises of the form:

All A are B.

All C are B.

his initial conclusion is likely to be:

Therefore: All A are C.

This is presumably derived by the operation of the principles governing the initial stage of inference. But suppose the subject holds fast to his conclusion, even after some thought, as indeed did many of Wilkins' (1928) and Sells' (1936) subjects. There are two alternative explanations of his behaviour. First, he may have gone on to set up a representation of the first premise isomorphic with the following diagram:

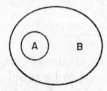

and then superimposed upon it an identical representation of the second premise, to yield:

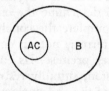

Second, the subject may have illicitly converted one of the premises before combining their representations. This is only likely, however, when the premises have a symbolic content.

After some thought the subject is likely to realize his error, and to conclude instead that:

Therefore: Some A are C.

Such an error, unlike the first one, is difficult to explain in terms of illicit conversion, but it is readily explained representationally. In combining the representation of the second premise with that of the first premise, the subject has discovered that it is not necessary to make an exact superimposition:

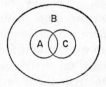

Finally, a subject who continues to experiment with the combination of the premises is likely to realize that it is not even necessary for A and C to have members in common:

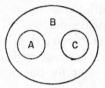

Hence, no valid conclusion can be drawn from the premises.

Our conception of a series of logical checks should now be clear: with syllogisms, the information contained in the premises can be combined in different ways, and it is necessary to carry out a series of 'experiments' to check the validity of the initial conclusion. The common errors which subjects make suggest that there is a general factor governing the order in which such checks are carried out. Subjects seem to be biased towards attempting to *verify* a conclusion, whether it is their own initial answer, or one given to them by the experimenter to evaluate. They seek to determine whether the premises could be combined in such a way as to render the conclusion true. Of course, this merely shows that conclusion and premises are consistent, not that the conclusion follows from the premises. The crucial test in combining premises involves falsification. The reasoner must try to discover whether there is a combination which would render the conclusion false. If there is, then the inference is invalid; if there is not, then the inference is valid. This bias towards verification is a theme which will crop up again and again in our subsequent analysis of reasoning tasks.

We have established in this chapter a number of aspects of the processes of interpretation and combination. The illicit conversion of premises, especially notable when they are symbolic, depends upon two quite distinct phenomena. In the case of A statements, there is a tendency to treat the quantified term as an entity and to substitute it for the complete universe of discourse. In the case of O statements, there is a more entrenched tendency to treat them as logically equivalent to I statements. However, the role of illicit conversion in syllogistic inference is more problematic. While it may be an important factor in the evaluation of abstract syllogisms, our results suggest that it is less prevalent in making inferences from concrete premises. The initial conclusion seems to be determined by three underlying principles which take into account the presence of negative, or restricted premises, and the location of end-anchors. The subsequent logical checks appear to be determined to some extent by the desire to *verify* the initial conclusion.

12

Immediate Inferences
with Quantifiers

One obvious extension of quantified inference is into problems involving more than two premises, but the psychological investigation of such problems is likely to await a better understanding of syllogistic inference. However, a new departure that is more amenable for empirical study concerns immediate inference with sentences containing more than one quantifier. The A, E, I and O statements of the syllogism each contain just a single quantifier; but there seem to be few obvious restrictions on the number of quantifiers an English sentence may contain. Sentences with two quantifiers yield fairly straightforward immediate inferences, e.g.:

Not all species are found in all continents.

Therefore, some species are not found in some continents. This simple inference and its converse, which is equally valid, clearly depend solely upon the meanings of the statements involved. There is no question of combining semantic representations as in syllogistic inference, and it may be safely assumed that such inferences depend upon linguistic principles. It is clear, however, that the linguistic properties of such sentences are considerably more complicated than those with a single quantifier. The potential ambiguity of sentences containing quantifiers has already been touched upon, but when we consider sentences with more than one quantifier ambiguity becomes almost inevitable. Thus, a sentence such as:

All the doctors interview some patients
could mean that certain patients *in particular* are interviewed by all the doctors, or merely that every doctor interviews patients. The ambiguity turns upon which quantifier is taken as the more important. (In logical terms, it depends upon which

quantifier is within the scope of the other.) The distinction can be represented in the underlying structure by some sort of tag: we shall use simple indices with the convention that an index of 1 is used for the most important quantifier. Hence:

All$_1$ the doctors interview some$_2$ patients.

represents the statement that for any doctor there are some or other patients that he interviews. Whereas:

All$_2$ the doctors interview some$_1$ patients.

represents the statement that there are some patients, in particular, whom all the doctors interview.

These ambiguities are, of course, subtle. They usually pass unnoticed in ordinary discourse, either because they are not critical to the argument, or because the context of the sentence renders them unambiguous. However, they do raise an interesting psychological question. Although the passive sentence, 'Some patients are interviewed by all the doctors', should be equivalent to the active sentence, 'All the doctors interview some patients', it does not seem intuitively to be quite so ambiguous. More precisely, the passive suggests one interpretation (certain patients, in particular, are interviewed by all the doctors), while the active suggests the other (all the doctors interview patients). This difference could be a function of the voice of the sentences, or, as seems more likely, it could be due to the order of mention of the quantifiers. This factor can be described in terms of the distinction between 'topic' and 'comment' (cf. Lyons, 1968, p. 334). The 'topic' of a sentence is the person or thing about which something is said, and it is usually denoted by the first nounphrase in the sentence. The actual statement that is made—by the remainder of the sentence—is the 'comment'. Hence, when the topic corresponds to the underlying object of the sentence, the passive voice is likely to be selected in order that it may be mentioned first. This hypothesis has received abundant support from psychological experiments. It has been shown that increasing the importance of the object makes a passive description more likely (Carroll, 1958; Johnson-Laird, 1968a). The passive is also interpreted so as to lend an increased importance to the object (Johnson-Laird, 1968b). One consequence of this 'topicalization hypothesis' is that when *some* occurs in the topic, it is likely to be treated as the predominant quantifier—it is most unlikely that the topic will concern 'some or other persons or things'. By parity of reasoning, when *some* occurs in the comment, it is likely to be treated as the subsidiary quantifier. In short, a sentence such as, 'Some patients are interviewep by all the doctors', should tend to be interpreted to mean that there are some particular patients who are interviewed by all the doctors; and a sentence such as, 'All the doctors interview some patients', should tend to be interpreted to mean that all the doctors interview patients. How can such predictions be tested?

One way which we tried was to ask subjects to give their own paraphrases of the sentences. A large variety of sentences containing two quantifiers was given to 36 subjects. The sentences differed in their fundamental logical form and in their lexical content. The results were disappointing. For example, a sentence of the form:

All men know some women.

was paraphrased as:

Some women are known by all men (or every man).

by all 18 subjects who received it. The corresponding passive sentence of the form:

Some women are known by all men.

was not paraphrased in quite so uniform a fashion. But 12 of the 18 subjects produced the paraphrase:

All men know some women.

It is perhaps hardly surprising that subjects, asked to paraphrase ambiguous sentences, should have responded in the main with ambiguous paraphrases.

It was plainly necessary to evolve a more revealing technique, but unfortunately the simple Euler circles cannot be used to discriminate between sentences with two quantifiers. The solution was provided by using a series of matrix diagrams, which the subjects had to classify with respect to the sentences. A typical diagram is shown below (based on Johnson-Laird, 1969a).

To appreciate how such a matrix has to be interpreted, imagine that it is paired with the sentence, 'Every man knows some woman.' Each row in the matrix then represents a man, and

I	I	O
I	I	O
I	I	O

each column represents a woman. A '1' indicates that the man in whose row it occurs *knows* the woman in whose column it occurs; and a 'o' indicates that the man does *not* know the woman. Hence the above matrix is likely to be considered to represent a situation which is truthfully described by the sentence.

In the experiment that was performed utilizing this technique, we used ten such matrices (Johnson-Laird, 1969a). They constitute a representative sample from the complete set of such matrices, and were selected to enable the likely interpretations of sentences to be reflected in the pattern of their classifications. The rows of the matrices always represented the underlying subject of the sentence and the columns represented the underlying object. The 10 diagrams are shown in Table 12, together with the predicted classifications for

TABLE 12 *The predicted classifications for four affirmative sentences (Johnson-Laird, 1969a). A '1' indicates that the matrix is classified as truthfully described by the sentence and a 'o' that it is classified as falsely described*

	1	2	3	4	5	6	7	8	9	10
	000	100	100	100	111	111	110	110	111	111
	000	000	100	010	000	100	101	110	111	111
	000	000	100	001	000	100	011	110	000	111
(1) Every man knows some woman	0	0	1	1	0	1	1	1	0	1
(2) Some woman is known by every man	0	0	1	0	0	1	0	1	0	1
(3) Every woman is known by some man	0	0	0	1	1	1	1	0	1	1
(4) Some man knows every woman	0	0	0	0	1	1	0	0	1	1

examplars of the four affirmative sentences used in the experiment. These predictions are based upon our assumption that *some* would be treated as meaning *some in particular* when it occurred in the first nounphrase, or topic of the sentence, otherwise it would be treated as *some or other*.

In addition to the affirmative sentences, each of the 24 subjects classified the diagrams for four negative sentences. The sentences were presented in a counterbalanced order, and each of them had a different lexical content.

Since we were fundamentally concerned with whether the subject made the predicted classification, or its correlate based on the opposite interpretation of the quantifiers, each subject's classifications were scored with respect to both of these interpretations. The higher score was taken as an index of which interpretation had been made. This procedure made it possible to take into account all the data including those trials where a subject might have made a predicted interpretation, or its correlate, but for a trivial mistake. The score assigned to a subject could range from +8 to −8, in terms of the number of predicted classifications he made, minus the number of correlated converse classifications. The overall average score was +5·2; and all 24 subjects had positive scores. There were just seven occasions (out of a possible 96) when a subject classified an active and its correlative passive in an identical fashion.

The results with the negative sentences were consistent with the general nature of the predictions, but in one respect they were rather shocking. The negatives, as was expected, took reliably longer to classify, and yielded a reliably larger number of discrepancies from the predicted classifications. However, as the result of a close examination of the subjects' classifications it emerged that the negatives were more ambiguous than had been appreciated before the experiment. It was evidently necessary to scrutinize the linguistics of negative sentences containing two quantifiers.

The first point to emerge concerned the transformation which exchanges one quantifier for the other, while at the same time removing the quantifier from within the scope of negation (cf. pp. 141–2). It will be recalled that this was required in order to derive sentences such as, 'Some of the girls don't like John', from an underlying structure common to, 'Not all the girls like John.' Where there is more than one quantifier in a sentence, this transformation must be applied to the quantifiers in the order of their importance, starting with the item with index 1. Hence, for example, an underlying structure of the form:

neg (some$_1$ doctors interview all$_2$ the patients)

can be expressed in several different ways. First, there is a straightforward realization of the sentence, with both quantifiers within the scope of the negative:

No doctors interview all the patients.

Second, the predominant quantifier can be transformed and removed from within the scope of the negative:

All doctors do not interview all the patients.

This sentence is, of course, highly ambiguous and can be derived from other underlying structures; however, it is capable of receiving the required interpretation. Once the quantifier with index 1 is removed from within the scope of negation, the way is clear to transform the other quantifier. This yields a third version where neither quantifier is within the scope of the negative:

All doctors do not interview some of the patients.

There are other ways of expressing the underlying meaning, e.g. using passive sentences (cf. Johnson-Laird, 1970a), but enough has been said to show how the transformation works.

The analysis of this transformation suggests a way to put Clark's (1972) hypothesis about the scope of negatives to a further test. The reader will recall that according to this hypothesis the smaller the scope of the negative, the easier the sentence will be to understand. Unfortunately, there is often a tendency, as the above examples show, for ambiguity to increase as quantifiers are removed from the scope of negation by the operations of the transformation. However, there are some sentences which are not confounded by this additional source of difficulty. For instance, sentences of the form, 'some doctors do not interview some of the patients' ought to be easier to understand than those of the form, 'not all doctors interview all the patients'. Although the two sentences are synonymous, the former has both its quantifiers outside the scope of the negative, whereas the latter has both its quantifiers within the scope of the negative.

It should now be abundantly clear that the study of inference with 'multiply-quantified' sentences is going to involve ambiguity. The whole topic of reasoning with ambiguous sentences has been relatively ignored by psychologists, yet ambiguity may be the source of many deductive errors, especially as it is likely to pass unnoticed in daily life. The following inference does not seem to involve ambiguous material:

Italians like opera more than Germans.
Germans like opera more than the English.
Therefore, Italians like opera more than the English.

Yet each statement is ambiguous as the following inference should make clear:

Italians like opera more than Germans.
Italians like Germans more than ballet.
Therefore, Italians like opera more than ballet.

The fact that the first premise in both inferences does double duty is probably not detected until the inferences are examined in detail.

What is more problematic is how subjects would evaluate the following sort of inference:

Every toy is liked by some child.
Therefore: some child likes every toy.

If these two ambiguous sentences are interpreted according to the principles which seemed to govern the findings of our interpretative experiment, then this inference should be judged as invalid. Such interpretations would also cause the converse inference:

Some child likes every toy.
Therefore: every toy is liked by some child.

to be judged as valid. However, both the premise and the conclusion are, in principle, ambiguous. Hence, should a subject construe them so that the second quantifier in each sentence is predominant, then exactly the opposite evaluations would be made.

An experiment was carried out (Johnson-Laird, 1969b) to determine whether the evaluation of these inferences could be related to the way the sentences were interpreted in the previous experiment. Pairs of inferences were made up from the actual sentences used previously, with each pair consisting of an active and its correlated passive. In this way, it was possible to compare the inferences from active to passive with those from passive to active. The inferences made up from the affirmative sentences consisted of:

(1) (a) Every man knows some woman.
        Therefore: Some woman is known by every man.
    (b) Some woman is known by every man.
        Therefore: Every man knows some woman.
(2) (a) Every woman is known by some man.
        Therefore: Some man knows every woman.
    (b) Some man knows every woman.
        Therefore: Every woman is known by some man.

Each of 24 subjects judged the validity of these inferences together with four pairs of inferences with negative sentences. They were presented in a counterbalanced order, and each inference involved a different lexical content. The main feature of the procedure was that premise and conclusion were always presented separately in order to minimize approaches to the task in which the individual attempted to match purely super-ficial characteristics of the sentences.

The results were evaluated with respect to both the theoretical and the practical ambiguity of the sentences. It is a simple matter to predict how the inferences should be evaluated according to our hypothesis that when *some* occurs in the topic it is interpreted as *some in particular*, and when it occurs in the comment it is interpreted as *some or other*. The average number of judgements in accordance with these predictions was 5·2 (out of a maximum of 8), and this bias in favour of our hypo-thesis was very reliable.

In order to test whether the evaluations could be accounted for by the actual practical ambiguity of the sentences, the results were compared with those from the earlier inter-pretative study. The evaluations of the pairs of related in-ferences were classified into four categories:

(1) Both inferences were judged as valid, i.e. the sentences are judged to imply one another (symbolized by ←→).
(2) The sentence with *some* in the topic (the first nounphrase)

is judged to imply the sentence with *some* in the comment (the second nounphrase), but the converse inference is judged as invalid. This category corresponds to our theoretical prediction, and is symbolized by ⟶.

(3) The sentence with *some* in the comment is judged to imply the sentence with *some* in the topic, but the converse inference is judged as invalid. This is contrary to our theoretical prediction, and is symbolized by ⟵.

(4) Both inferences are judged as invalid, i.e. neither sentence is judged to imply the other (symbolized by ⟵/⟶).

It is a simple matter to work out the frequency with which each category ought to occur on the basis of the interpretations given in the previous experiment. These frequencies, together with those actually obtained in the present experiment, are shown in Table 13.

TABLE 13 *The number of subjects making each category of response for the affirmative inference, together with the comparable results from the interpretative study*

	Inference 1 (a and b)				Inference 2 (a and b)			
	⟷	⟶	⟵	⟵/⟶	⟷	⟶	⟵	⟵/⟶
Interpretation	2	16	2	4	1	12	2	9
Inference	5	12	3	4	5	14	2	3

It is evident that the results of the two experiments are consistent, given that two entirely different sets of subjects were tested. This homogeneity was maintained, although to a lesser degree, with the negative sentences.

There was a reliable tendency, evident in all pairs of inferences, for both inferences to be judged as valid more often than would be expected from the interpretative results (cf. the category ⟷ in the Table). This suggested that the two sentences were more often considered to be synonymous in the inference task, perhaps because there was a bias towards interpreting the conclusion in the same way as the premise. In other words, there might be a *semantic* atmosphere effect, with the meaning of the premise influencing the interpretation of the conclusion. However, there was a possible alternative explanation: having judged one inference as valid, a subject might be biased towards judging the other related inference, occurring later in the series, as also valid. If this were so, a similar affect should occur when the first inference was judged invalid. Hence, there should also be a greater tendency for *neither* inference to be judged as valid than would be expected from the interpretative data. But it is clear from the category ←/→ in Table 13 that there was no such tendency, and this suggests that the effect is primarily due to processes occurring within the inference.

It seemed that there was a semantic atmosphere effect in evaluating inferences with doubly-quantified sentences. Yet one further finding proved to be important in the light of subsequent events. This was that more subjects noticed the ambiguity of the sentences in the inferential task than in the interpretative task. This was an unexpected result because it seemed much more likely that an individual would detect ambiguity in an experiment explicitly concerned with the interpretation of sentences. Perhaps the critical factor was the context provided by the other related sentence in the inferential task.

The possibility of an atmosphere effect created by the *meaning* of a premise suggests that ambiguity may become critical when an ambiguous sentence provides the 'pivot' of an argument, being deduced in one meaning, and then being used in another meaning as the basis of a further deduction. One example is suggested by the work of Abelson and his associates. Gilson and Abelson (1965) have shown that subjects will accept generalizations of the form, 'Families buy magazines', even though there is evidence of clear counter-examples. The acceptability of the generalization is generally greater when one knows that all families buy some magazines than when one knows merely that some families buy all magazines; however, this phenomenon varies greatly from one verb to another in a way which is mysterious (Abelson and Kanouse, 1966). The crucial point, however, is that once a generalization like, 'Communists are treacherous', has been established on the basis of evidence which contains counter-examples, it is easy to forget them, or to suppress them, and to go on using the generic assertion without any qualifications as the basis of further arguments.

It is debatable whether assertions like, 'Families buy magazines', are truly ambiguous as opposed to intrinsically vague. The 'pivot' is truly ambiguous, however, in the following example:

Not all the candidates are illiterate.

Therefore: all the candidates are not illiterate.

Therefore: no candidates are illiterate.

The pivot sentence, 'all the candidates are not illiterate', as our earlier linguistic analysis showed (cf. pp. 141–2), has two alternative meanings: one is synonymous with the initial premise, and the other is synonymous with the final conclusion. The possibility that an individual might be seduced into thinking that such inferences were valid was very attractive. But we have carried out a number of studies with both Diana Shapiro and Roger Goodwin which have all been fruitless. The rationality of our subjects has triumphed in every case. Whenever an ambiguous 'pivot' has been used—and we have tried a variety of different sorts of ambiguity—the majority of subjects have always considered one or other of the two inferences as invalid. They have refused to countenance both interpretations of the 'pivot' within the same inference. We have therefore come reluctantly to the conclusion that perhaps the semantic atmosphere effect is a spurious by-product of the results of two experiments which utilized very different techniques. We have quite failed to detect it in the subsequent studies of ambiguous 'pivots'.

There are whole domains of quantified inference which still await psychological investigation, and which are likely to continue to await it until we have a better understanding of the more fundamental patterns of inference. There is, however, a strange kind of reconciliation between formal logic and ordinary inference which occurs at a slightly higher level of complexity, i.e. with statements involving three quantifiers such as, 'all the doctors diagnosed some of the vitamin deficiencies in all their patients'. It has been proved that for inferences with materials of this sort, there is no automatic

M

procedure for determining whether an inference is valid (Wang, 1963). The skilled logician may be fortunate enough to discover a proof, but he can resort to no mechanical procedure which will guarantee one. This is in marked contrast to the propositional calculus where such procedures do exist. It follows, of course, that the individual's logical ability is similarly restricted; like the logician, he must operate with heuristic, or 'hit-or-miss', procedures which do not guarantee solution.

It is appropriate that at this point our investigations into deductive reasoning, in its narrowest sense, come to an end. We have examined all the main ways in which a conclusion may be drawn from a set of premises. But this does not mean that the full range of psychological problems of deduction has been exhausted. There are higher-order problems of inference, e.g. those connected with scientific thought, to which we now turn.

13

Testing a Hypothesis:
Error and its Correction

In previous chapters we have been mainly concerned with the psychology of inference. Some of these inferences which we have examined are obviously intrinsic to scientific thought, but such thought demands an important further step which we have not considered: the formulation and testing of general hypotheses. The principles by which hypotheses are discovered, or invented, are little understood, but the testing of hypotheses is a more tractable matter. It involves both inference and observation, but we shall naturally concentrate on its deductive aspect. Deduction enters into this process in several quite distinct ways. It may be necessary to deduce an empirical prediction from some theoretical hypothesis. Alternatively, it may be necessary to make inferences from the observations about the status of the hypothesis itself. By themselves these tests are plainly forms of inference which have been discussed in previous chapters: they involve drawing conclusions from premises. But put the two together, and an interesting hypothetico-deductive task emerges. It is necessary to determine which particular observations from a large number of possibilities would constitute a crucial test of the hypothesis in question. A concrete example may be helpful.

Suppose a scientist postulates the modest hypothesis that a substance, x, is associated with obesity. A direct way to test it would be to inject x into a group of rats in order to determine whether it in fact results in obesity. However, suppose for the sake of argument, that x cannot be isolated for experimental manipulation, but can only be detected in the blood stream. Then the critical question arises whether the blood of fat rats or thin rats should be examined in order to test the hypothesis.

There is a natural tendency to say that fat rats should be examined. But this is a mistake. The hypothesis does not assert that obesity is necessarily due to x, but merely its converse: that x is sufficient to produce obesity. Hence, in order to test the hypothesis under these conditions, it is crucial to examine the blood of the thin rats. If it is found to contain x, then the hypothesis clearly stands in need of modification. Of course, if the hypothesis is assumed to imply its converse, i.e. if a relation of equivalence is postulated between x and obesity, then it would be necessary to examine both fat and thin rats. But in our example, the hypothesis is in the weaker logical form of the conditional statement: 'If x is present then obesity is present.'

Men are particularly prone to making general assumptions. If one asks how, psychologically, science is possible, one contributory cause must be a pre-eminent ability to generalize and to test generalizations. Indeed, prejudice is perhaps no more than the pathology of this tendency: an inability to submit certain generalizations to a proper test. Hence it is hardly surprising that the testing of generalizations is not peculiar to science. However, a mirror image of such a task is perhaps more common in everyday life: the test of whether certain objects or events conform to a given rule. In these cases it is not so much the rule which is tested, but the objects or events which may infringe it. The most familiar examples are to be found in the law and in standards of control in industry. Whenever there is some pre-established criterion, or rule, governing acceptance and rejection, the same hypothetico-deductive question arises with respect to the observations which constitute a crucial test of whether the cases in question infringe the criterion. This is obviously analogous to the scientist's question about those individual observations which would be a crucial test of his hypothesis. The fundamental psychological issue is to discover how the individual is prone to tackle such tasks, and the practical problem is to devise a laboratory study which mirrors the logic of the situation. This was solved in a pilot study (Wason, 1966), and examined in more detail in a full-scale experiment (Wason, 1968a). If you had been a subject in the pilot study, then four cards would have been placed in front of you, showing the following symbols:

E   K   4   7

You know that each of these cards has a letter on one of its sides and a number on its other side, and you are then presented with the following rule which refers only to the four cards:

> *If a card has a vowel on one side, then it has an even number on the other side.*

Your task is to name those cards, and only those cards, which need to be turned over in order to determine whether the rule is true or false.

The vast majority of subjects say either 'E and 4', or 'only E'. Both answers are wrong. The correct answer is 'E and 7'. Any odd number on the other side of E falsifies the rule in exactly the same way as would any vowel on the other side of the 7. The task is analogous to determining how best to test the hypothesis, 'if x is present then obesity is present'. The subjects' mistakes are similar to (a) investigating the blood of the fat rats, and (b) failing to investigate the blood of the thin rats. The solution to our abstract problem may now seem fairly obvious. Yet some of the highly intelligent subjects tested in both experiments took a considerable time before they saw it was correct, and a few even continued to dispute its correctness. And yet a computer could readily be programmed to solve the problem, as some subjects have been quick to point out after they had failed to solve it. It may be hard for the reader, guided by our concrete example, to appreciate the extreme difficulty of the task. (If he wants a proof of it, let him try it out on his friends.) Time after time our subjects fall into error. Even some professional logicians have been known to err in an embarrassing fashion, and only the rare individual takes us by surprise and gets it right. It is impossible to predict who he will be. This was all very puzzling and, if anything, made it harder to understand the origins of scientific enterprise. But we wondered whether our subjects' difficulties were due to the very simplicity of the problem. It is really simple. This was demonstrated in a small experiment (Wason, 1969a) in which the procedure was reversed. The subjects were first given the solution, then given the problem, and finally asked to justify the solution in their own words. We were quite astonished to find that, after some hesitation, all the 20 subjects tested gave the correct reasons for the solution. Thus the problem is evidently not obscure when it is regarded with unprejudiced eyes: clearly it is the attempt to solve it which makes it difficult. In this way it contrasts sharply with a problem which does have a very complex logical structure. When the solution is shown to you, it probably means very little; it seems neither right nor wrong. This is worth demonstrating.

Suppose you are introduced to three men, and all that you know is that one invariably tells the truth, one invariably lies, and one tells the truth at random. Each man knows the identity of the others, but of course you don't know the identity of any of them. You are allowed to address three questions to the men, the answers to which must be 'yes' or 'no', in order to determine their identity. What questions do you ask?

This is the solution. Label the men arbitrarily as A, B and C. The first question to A is: 'Does B tell the truth more often than C?' If the answer is 'yes', address the next question to C; if it is 'no', address it to B. The second question is 'Does $2 + 2 = 4$?' And the third question (addressed to the same man) is: 'Is A the man who tells the truth at random?'[1]

Our problem is not like that at all. It is deceptive rather than complex, and to see why it is deceptive we must examine its logic. The rule is in the form of a conditional statement, 'if p then q', where p corresponds to the card showing E, not-p corresponds to K, q corresponds to 4, and not-q to 7. It is necessary to select p to ensure that no value, other than q, occurs with it, but there is a natural tendency to select it in order to see whether q does occur with it. This is making the right response for the wrong reason, attempting to verify the rule rather than to falsify it. It is unnecessary to select not-p because no value occurring with it would falsify the rule; and

---

[1] The essential point to realize is that if the answer to the first question is 'yes', then C cannot be the 'random' man; and if it is 'no', then B cannot be the 'random' man. Hence the second question determines the precise status of C (or B), and the third question exploits his identity to determine that of the others.

since no value would verify it, subjects seldom do select not-p. The distinction between verifying and falsifying becomes more crucial with the consequent of the conditional. A subject attempting to verify the rule will be tempted to select q (because p occurring with it would verify), and to refrain from selecting not-q (because nothing occurring with it would verify). The correct course of action, however, is to attempt to falsify the rule. This requires the subject to select not-q (because p occurring with it would falsify), and to refrain from selecting q (because nothing occurring with it would falsify). In short, the goals of verification and falsification coincide for the antecedent of the conditional and the correct selection is deceptively easy, but they diverge for the consequent and the correct selection is deceptively difficult.

Let us now concentrate on these two main errors of omisson and commission. The failure to select not-q is more fundamental because its selection would be correct even if the converse of the sentence were assumed to hold, i.e. if it were interpreted as a statement of material equivalence. But the error of selecting q would be no error at all under this interpretation. In fact, the solution under the equivalence interpretation is to select all four cards. This will be appreciated from a consideration of the truth table for equivalence described on p. 89. But what is most remarkable about this problem is that *the performance of a subject can seldom be predicted from a knowledge of the truth table which underlies his interpretation of the rule.* As we have seen, individuals tend to interpret the conditional according to a 'defective' truth table (see the experiment by Johnson-Laird and Tagart, 1969, described on p. 91). Thus, the not-p card would be deemed as irrelevant to the truth or falsity of the rule. This is consistent with the tendency to omit not-p. But a card combining p and not-q would be deemed as falsifying the rule, and this is inconsistent with the failure to select not-q.

We were initially very puzzled by the difficulty of the task, and set out to isolate aspects of it which might be responsible for leading the subjects into error. Surely, as a psychologist put it to us recently, it must have something to do with the procedure used in the experiment. Hence, our first line of attack was to manipulate procedural variables in order to see whether the logic of the problem would become more transparent.

In the example of the problem which we have discussed, any even number on the other side of the vowel would verify, and any odd number would falsify. Similarly, any vowel on the other side of the odd number would falsify. It might be better to restrict the task to a small finite number of symbols, and explain this to the subjects first of all. Hence, in a further experiment (Wason, 1969b), the task was made strictly binary. The subjects were trained to appreciate that only one of two possible stimuli could occur on each side of the cards before they attempted to solve the problem. There was no improvement in their performance.

When we discussed the use of conditionals in everyday discourse, we argued that they are normally used to suggest a temporal, or causal, relation between antecedent and consequent. Hence, the simultaneous presentation of values of them could have induced considerable perplexity. Accordingly a different version of the rule was substituted: 'Every card which has a red triangle on one side has a blue circle on the other side' (Wason, 1969b). This definitely removes any possible temporal connotation, and probably diminishes any possible causal connection. The latter, however, may not be entirely removed, and may have induced the subjects to concentrate more upon a supposed causal antecedent. In fact, in this experiment the majority of subjects selected just p. The error of selecting q was appreciably reduced without in any way affecting the more critical error of failing to select not-q.

It is also possible that the subjects in the original experiment confused the two sides of the cards, and, in particular, construed 'the other side of the card' (mentioned in the rule) as referring to the side which was face *downwards*. So in a further experiment (Wason and Johnson-Laird, 1970) we presented all the information on one side of the card, with masks concealing those values which in previous experiments had been on the other side (see Figure 16). The rule referring to the cards was: 'Every card which has a circle on it has two borders round it.' Inspection of the cards shows that the subjects can

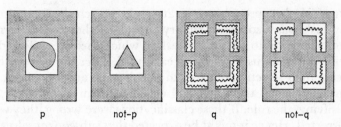

p   not-p   q   not-q

Figure 16. 'Selection task' material when all the information is potentially present on the same side of a card. The rule is: 'Every card which has a circle on it has two borders round it.' (Wason and Johnson-Laird, 1970)

see only whether (a) a circle is present (*p* and not-*p*), and (b) two borders are present (*q* and not-*q*). Once again performance was not improved. The experiment also demonstrated that the difficulty was not due to the failure to perceive the not-*q* card as designating the absence of *q*. There was no difference between performance when not-*p* and not-*q* were represented by stimuli other than *p* and *q* (a triangle and one border as in Figure 16), and when these values were represented by complete blanks.

An even greater concession to the subjects' possible confusions failed to make the task appreciably easier. The subjects had available a duplicate set of fully revealed cards which they could examine while they were performing the task with equivalent partially masked cards (Goodwin and Wason, 1972). The fully revealed cards function as visual aids to rectify any possible limitations imposed on memory, or imagery, by the partially masked cards in solving the problem. No significant differences were observed between a group who were given these reminders and a group without them.

Perhaps the difficulty was that the subjects were not sufficiently familiar with the rule? Wason and Shapiro (1971) overcame this by allowing their subjects to evaluate, or construct, examples of the four types of card for 24 trials in relation to a given conditional rule. They then carried out the selection task with four more partially concealed cards in relation to the same rule. Little facilitation was evident. This was not too surprising because a previous attempt to teach the structure of the task was also unsatisfactory. Athol Hughes (1966) turned the problem into a learning task in which the rules referred to different stimulus material at each trial. After the subjects had made their selection of cards to test the rule at each trial, they turned over all the cards and classified them as verifying, or falsifying, the rule. If these classifications were wrong, they were corrected. Hence it might be expected that subsequent selection errors would diminish. A contradiction, or inconsistency, between a correct classification of the cards and a previous incorrect selection of them might lead to insight, just as it did in the experiment discussed previously in Chapter 6 (Wason, 1964), when valid inferences explicitly contradicted previously made fallacious inferences. The technique proved to be singularly unilluminating in Hughes' experiment, apparently because the subjects tended to detach the selection and classification parts of the task. About a third of the subjects failed to meet the criterion of success over a period of 15 trials. In our experience a learning task is unsatisfactory as an index of inferential processes because it provides little information about either the cause, or the nature, of error.

Paolo Legrenzi (1971), however, in two elegant experiments turned the task round. The subjects did not have to check the four types of card in relation to a given rule. On the contrary, they knew from the start how the four cards stood in relation to the rule; what they did not know was the nature of the rule itself. Their task was to attempt to discover the rule which governed the cards and, in the first experiment, to express it in their own words. They then carried out the 'selection task' with four more partially concealed cards. In the second experiment the procedure was the same but the subjects were obliged to express the rule as a conditional statement. In both experiments the subjects, who had derived the rule for themselves, performed better on the selection task than a control group who were presented with the rule directly.

It is not altogether clear why this technique should be better than that used by Wason and Shapiro, and by Hughes. Perhaps the synthetic activity of deriving the rule from given instances allows the subjects to appreciate all its consequences to a greater extent than does the more analytic activity of seeing how the instances stand in relation to a given rule. In addition, Legrenzi's technique probably requires considerably more mental effort which would further enhance its productiveness.

Finally, a variety of different instructions were tried out. An instruction to pick out cards which 'could break the rule' (Wason, 1968a) was intended to emphasize falsification. It merely induced several subjects to select just not-p and not-q, apparently on the grounds that they 'already broke the rule', i.e. were unmentioned in it. Similarly, an instruction to select cards to determine 'Whether the statement is a lie' (Hughes, 1966) had only a slightly favourable effect on performance.

Most of these experimental modifications could be regarded as 'failures' because they did not improve the subjects' performance. However, these 'failures' were clarifying the difficulty of the problem for us. In eliminating potentially artefactual variables, they revealed the obdurate nature of the 'selection task': after each successive variable proved innocuous, the occurrence rather than the non-occurrence of errors proved valuable. It was these errors which enabled us to discover ways in which the subjects might be induced to gain at least some insight. The first step in discovering such a method was the realization, gradually borne in upon us by each fresh negative result, that the cause of error was no brief momentary lapse of attention but some much deeper fixation.

The first really revealing technique was related to the self-contradiction device used in a previous experiment (Wason, 1964). But in many ways it was an improvement because it did not involve an explicit self-contradiction. Instead it engaged the subject in a dialogue with the experimenter about the effects of a conceptual conflict, induced either by the subject's inferences, or by the experimenter's actions. Basically, this method exposed the subjects to inconsistencies between their initial selection of cards and their subsequent independent evaluations of specific cards as falsifying, or verifying, the rule. It aimed to create a sense of discrepancy, an intimation that something was wrong. And from this awareness it was hoped that thought would be aroused which would correct the error.

These contradictions, which aimed primarily to induce

insight into the relevance of not-q, rather than the irrelevance of q, were of two kinds: (a) hypothetical and (b) concrete. Hypothetical contradiction occurs when a subject says that a value of not-q on the other side of a card showing a value of p (or a value of p on the other side of a card showing a value of not-q) would falsify the rule, and yet still refrains from selecting the not-q card as relevant to the solution. There is an incongruity between his evaluation and his initial selection, but it is only hypothetical. The inference is about a consequence which would follow only if there were a value of p and not-q on the same card. In contrast, concrete contradiction occurs when the card showing a value of p is *actually* turned over to reveal a value of q on the other side, verifying the rule; and then the card showing a value of not-q is *actually* turned over to reveal also a value of p on the other side, falsifying the rule. In other words, a card (p), which is almost inevitably selected initially, fulfils the subject's intention, and is found to make the rule true in reality; but a card (not-q), which is usually ignored initially, is then found to make the rule false in reality. What seemed incorrigibly true a moment ago suddenly turns out to be false. The clash is obvious and explicit, and not merely an inconsistency in thought between an intention and an inference.

In the first experiment to use these techniques (Wason, 1969b), the contradictions were seriated over the task, starting with the two less powerful hypothetical contradictions, and culminating with the traumatic concrete contradiction. At the initial selection of the cards only two out of the 36 subjects had selected not-q. At the end of the experiment 26 more subjects had incorporated not-q in their selections, and 15 of them achieved the correct solution: p and not-q. In the next experiment to use them (Wason and Johnson-Laird, 1970) the subjects were immediately confronted with the concrete contradiction after their selection, the hypothetical contradictions being induced subsequently in an unstructured interview about the roles of the q and not-p cards. The immediate concrete contradiction may, in fact, have been too traumatic because only 26·5 per cent of the subjects (nine out of 34) changed to the correct solution immediately after agreeing that the 'p and q' card verified and the 'not-q and p' card falsified.

Moreover, at the conclusion of the interview, which was designed to help the subjects, 38·2 per cent had still failed to reach the correct solution.

However, it is evident that in both experiments the creation of conceptual inconsistencies in this problem does allow a significant number of subjects to gain insight and overcome an apparently deep-seated error. The next chapter postulates a formal explanation of error and insight.

It is important to stress, yet again, that the subjects do not initially choose the cards at random (see Table 14). They tend to make, to an overwhelming extent, just two errors: they fail to select the not-q card, which could falsify the rule, and they do select the q card, which could not falsify it. This regularity in their behaviour makes it feasible to suggest an explanation in terms of an 'information-processing model'.

TABLE 14 *Frequency of Initial Selection of cards in four experiments*

p and q	59
p	42
p, q and not-q	9
p and not-q	5
others	13

$$N = 128$$

Let us begin by considering how a computer might be programmed in order to solve the problem. This will serve as a base-line against which to compare human performance. The computer would first retrieve the truth table appropriate to the rule, 'if p then q', and then scan each of the four ways in which the values of p and q can be combined in relation to truth and falsity. In doing this it would make no difference whether the truth table was that of material implication, which counts every combination as true except 'p and not-q', or the 'defective truth table' which assumes that any combination associated with not-p is irrelevant to truth and falsity. As we pointed out previously, it is this latter truth table which human subjects evidently use (Johnson-Laird and Tagart, 1969). Having retrieved either truth table, the computer would scan each card in turn with reference to its combinations of values. Its algorithm, or decision procedure, is then governed by the following simple principle: a card is selected if, and only if, a value on it could make the rule false. A moment's reflection shows that this leads to the selection of p and not-q since neither not-p, nor q, could falsify the rule.

It is quite evident from all the results, so far discussed, that subjects seldom do this, and that moreover their responses are even inconsistent with their own truth table for the rule. We have proposed two information-processing models which endeavour to describe their performance (Johnson-Laird and Wason, 1970a). The preliminary model incorporates two kinds of insight, corresponding to the avoidance of each of the two errors. It is concise, economical and rational: a model to please the logician. Its flow diagram is shown in Figure 17 and only its salient features will be described verbally.

If a subject lacks both kinds of insight he is assumed to examine each card in turn to see whether there could be a value on the other side which would verify the rule. Hence he will select the p and q cards. If he possesses insight (a), he will test those cards which could verify to see whether they could falsify the rule. If they fail to meet this criterion, they are rejected. Hence just the p card will be selected. If he possesses insight (b), he will select cards that could verify, and also test those cards which could not verify, to see whether they could falsify. The not-q card could falsify the rule. Hence the p, q, and not-q cards will be selected. The two insights are assumed to be additive, and it follows, if both are possessed, the correct selection will be achieved, i.e. p and not-q.

This preliminary model nicely takes account of the two errors which stand in the way of enlightenment, but it is almost certainly grossly wrong. Reference to Table 14 shows that the failure to select the not-q card, which corresponds to the lack of insight (b), is far more frequent than the error of selecting the q card, which corresponds to the lack of insight (a).

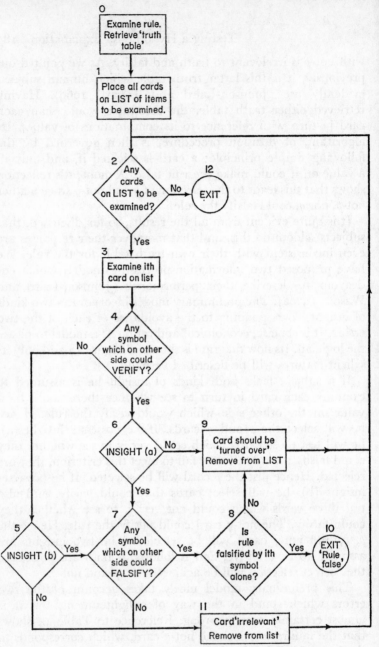

Figure 17. The preliminary model postulated to explain the abstract 'selection task' (Johnson-Laird and Wason, 1970a)

There is a large difference in frequency between 'just *p*' and
'*p*, *q* and not-*q*'. But it seems *a priori* most implausible to
suppose that one insight, (a), occurs about three times as often
as the other insight, (b). It is more plausible to suppose that the
two errors, which have the same logical status, have different
psychological sources. Indeed, the suspicion arises that the
selection of just *p* may not be the result of the (non-trivial)
insight that verifying cards should be rejected if they could not
falsify, but merely signifies that the subject does not assume that
the converse of the rule holds. In fact, this supposition was
frequently corroborated by the verbal testimony of the subjects.

Important further evidence for this suggestion is shown by the
fact that the rejection of the *q* card is evidently labile. When the
subjects were confronted with conceptual inconsistencies, a
rather disconcerting event frequently occurred. The mere
hypothetical consideration of possible values on the other side
of the *p* card induced a change in selection from just *p* to *p*,
q and not-*q*. Thus the subject appears to think that he has made
two mistakes rather than one; and in terms of the preliminary
model this corresponds to the simultaneous loss of insight (a)
and gain of insight (b). Such an event, in terms of two independent insights, is psychologically improbable and bizarre.
Moreover, the gain of insight (a) alone, i.e. the transition
from '*p* and *q*' to 'just *p*' was very rare.

A revised model was constructed to allow for these facts.
Its flow diagram is shown in Figure 18. It assumes that the
subject will initially focus only on items mentioned in the rule.
From this hypothetical 'list', only cards which could verify the
rule will be selected, as a function of whether he assumes that
the converse holds (selection of *p* and *q*), or does not hold
(selection of just *p*). Two levels of insight have been retained,
but unlike those in the preliminary model, they are no longer
independent. *Partial insight* consists in realizing that all cards
should be tested, and that those which could verify, and those
which could falsify, should be selected, i.e. *p*, *q* and not-*q*.
Even if *q* had not been selected initially, it will now be selected
because it could verify the rule. *Complete insight* consists in
realising that only cards which could falsify should be selected,
i.e. *p* and not-*q*. Thus the revised model is consistent with the

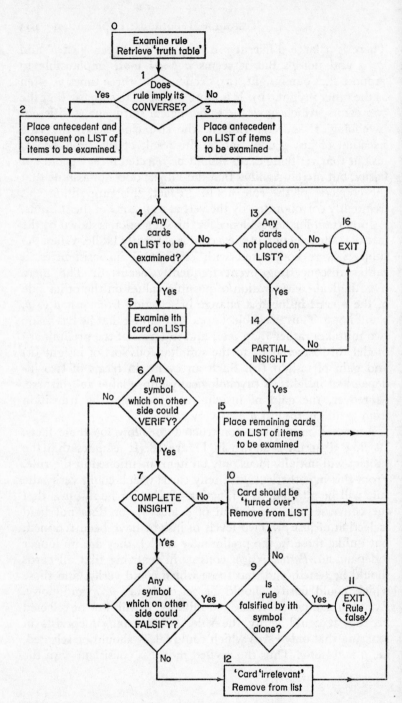

Figure 18. The revised model postulated to explain the abstract 'selection task' (Johnson-Laird and Wason, 1970a)

reasonable assumption that the q card is omitted as a function of two different psychological processes—one superficial, and the other more deep.

There is some empirical support for this model. We found in the pilot study (Wason, 1966) that, over a period of three trials, the error of failing to select the not-q card decreased, while the error of selecting the q card increased, as a function of turning over all the cards after each trial. In fact, between the first and second trials the number of subjects, who selected the q card for the first time, had doubled. This result was puzzling at the time: we can now say the subjects were moving from a state of *no insight* into a state of *partial insight*.

In general, the revised model shows how increase of insight is correlated with increase in awareness of the importance of falsification, as opposed to verification. With no insight only verification is considered relevant to the selection; with partial insight both verification and falsification are considered relevant; with complete insight only falsification is considered relevant. What has been lost in the logical elegance of the preliminary model has been compensated by a gain in psychological elegance in the revised model.

The experiment by Goodwin and Wason (1972), mentioned in the previous chapter, provided more detailed corroboration. The rule was expressed in the form, 'Every card which has p on one half has q on the other half', and half of each of the four cards was covered by a simple mask. The subjects were instructed to write down their reasons, both for selecting, or for rejecting, each card. Thus an additional virtue of this experiment was that the results were immune from any possible experimenter bias. The reasons tended to corroborate the psychological processes, postulated in the revised model to underly degrees of insight. Two protocols, associated with the extremes of *no insight* and *complete insight*, will be sufficient to illustrate this correlation.

No insight: selection of p *and* q

p: 'Only interested if it has q on it.'

not-p: 'It is irrelevant if it has q or not-q on it.'

q: 'Want to know if it has p on it.'

not-q: 'It is irrelevant if it has p on it.'

Episodic but graphic, these remarks clearly reveal that the subject is only content to try to verify the rule. They also, incidentally, provide a striking instance of 'irreversibility', which will be discussed more fully in the next chapter: the failure to appreciate that the significance of a card is the same regardless of which symbol is exposed on it.

Four out of the six subjects, who gave the correct solution, mentioned only falsification as governing their choices. The following is an example.

Complete insight: selection of p *and not-*q

p: 'I chose this because if it has not-q on it, it will disprove the rule.'

not-p: 'I ignored this because it has nothing to do with the rule.'

q: 'I ignored this because it may have p or not-p on it.'

not-q: 'I chose this because if it has p on it, then it will disprove the rule.'

One of the other two subjects, who did not simply mention falsification, stated that he selected p because it could either verify or falsify. However, he then changed his mind, and apparently regressed to *partial insight*, altering his selection to p, q and not-q. He then spontaneously regressed further to *no insight*, altering his selection again to p and q. It is plausible to suggest that his initial hold on *complete insight* was tenuous because he justified his selection in terms of both verification and falsification. During his reflection, the verification tendency increased, driving him first into *partial insight*, and then into *no insight*, in which the need to falsify had been completely vanquished by the need to verify. Thus, if this subject is discounted, only one out of the six, who were initially correct, justified their selections in terms inconsistent with those postulated by the revised model to underly *complete insight*.

One obvious implication of the results obtained from these investigations concerns Piaget's theory of thought. The main result, which is indisputable, in that highly intelligent adults fail to treat a rule as a rule, in the sense that they do not readily grasp all the consequences which could follow from it. Indeed, those subjects who fail to gain any insight justify the reasons for their selections in terms which, by any standard, are of a primitive kind. A typical example occurred in one pilot study. The subject was taken right through all the conceptual inconsistencies discussed in the previous chapter. When the concrete contradiction had been reached, i.e. when the relevant cards had actually been turned over, she said that the selection was to turn over all four cards. On being told this was wrong, she immediately replied, 'Presumably then only those I can see which have a red triangle and a blue circle on them. Those which have a red circle or a blue triangle don't comply with the sentence.' This kind of response, which was so characteristic, is somewhat disturbing. The subject seems tied to perceptual data—only those cards mentioned in the rule 'comply'. It is not that she tries to carry out the necessary combinatorial analysis, but fails to accomplish it. On the contrary, the necessity of such an analysis does not occur to her because her judgements are based only on what she can see—a kind of intellectual 'tunnel vision'. This supposition is strongly supported by the Goodwin and Wason (1972) experiment in which fully revealed duplicates of the test cards were available for inspection during the task. These potential aids to such an analysis failed to facilitate performance.

Our earlier analysis of propositional reasoning in Chapter 5 showed that Piaget's use of the propositional calculus as a model of deductive competence was open to serious criticism. The results on the present problem reinforce this criticism, but they also extend it by raising further difficulties for Piaget. The theory of 'formal operational thought' assumes that the adolescent is no longer tied to what he can see, or to 'concrete operations', but is capable of thinking in terms of propositions which take account of the possible and the hypothetical. He will be able to isolate the variables in a problem and subject them to a combinatorial analysis which nicely exhausts the possibilities (Inhelder and Piaget, 1958). But this, of course, is exactly what most of our subjects conspicuously fail to do. In his more recent publications Piaget is even more explicit about the processes which he assumes to occur in 'formal operations' (Beth and Piaget, 1966, p. 181). He claims that the adolescent, confronted by a complex causal situation, will ask himself

whether fact *x* implies fact *y*, and frequently do this by formulating a proposition in the form, 'if *p* then *q*'. In order to test
this proposition he will search for the counter-example, *x* and
non-*y*, i.e. *p* and not-*q*. Such a description reads like an account
of what our subjects do not do.

It is true that our problem is not causal, and (as we shall see
shortly), the failure to conform to the theory of operational
thought is most marked when the terms are abstract rather
than concrete. But in Piaget's theory these factors appear to be
minimized. He does, of course, admit (Tanner and Inhelder,
1960, p. 126) that the intelligent adult could only be expected
to engage in formal operational thought when confronted by a
challenging deductive problem. Our problem is not only
challenging, it is (to judge by our subjects' comments) also
instructive, surprising and amusing. And it arouses a high
degree of motivation. Still, the concept of *horizontal décalage*
could be invoked to show that our results are not critical. This
assumes that there is not a one-to-one relation between a task
and a developmental stage. As Flavell (1963, p. 23) puts it:
'Task contents do differ in the extent to which they resist
and inhibit the application of cognitive structures.' In our view
such a concept tends to make the theory untestable: it could
always be used to explain a discrepancy.

What may we conclude about the divergence between our
results and Piaget's theory? One answer would be that formal
operations are, in fact, only elicited by familiar tasks, and not
cognitive skills which can be applied to any problem whatsoever. In other words, they are really practical rules rather
than formal operations. Some evidence for this answer is provided by an experiment (Wason and Shapiro, 1971) in which
the problem was presented in a familiar guise. The conditional
rule was, 'Every time I go to Manchester I travel by train.'
The four cards showed respectively, 'Manchester' (*p*), 'Leeds'
(not-*p*), 'Train' (*q*) and 'Car' (not-*q*), and the subjects knew
they had been taken from a larger set in which each had a town
on one side and a mode of transport on the other side. The task
was to imagine that each test card represented a journey made
by the experimenter, and that the rule represented a claim
about them. The results showed that ten out of 16 subjects

made the correct selection of cards to determine whether the claim was true or false, as opposed to only two out of 16 in a control group in which abstract material was used. The precise causes of this facilitation are unclear. It could have been due to the concrete terms, the towns and modes of transport, mentioned in the claim; or it could have been due to the concrete nature of the relation (a journey) which connects these terms. But perhaps an even simpler hypothesis to explain the beneficial effects of the concrete material is that the 'story' provides a framework into which the subjects can project themselves by an act of imagination. And this framework, the experience of four journeys, allows the conditional nature of the rule to be grasped, in a way in which it is much less easily grasped when the terms and the connections between them are arbitrary.

Such an account is strongly supported by a subsequent experiment conducted in collaboration with Maria and Paolo Legrenzi (Johnson-Laird, Legrenzi and Legrenzi, 1972). Under the realistic, 'concrete', experimental condition the subjects were instructed to imagine that they were Post Office workers, engaged in sorting letters. Their task was to discover whether, or not, the following rule had been violated: 'If a letter is sealed, then it has a 5d stamp on it.' And instead of four cards, the material consisted of four *envelopes* arranged as follows: the back of a sealed envelope (p); the back of an unsealed envelope (not-p); the front of an envelope with an address and a 5d stamp on it (q); the front of an envelope with an address and a 4d stamp on it (not-q). The instructions were to 'select just those letters that you definitely need to turn over to find out whether or not they violate the rule'. Under the abstract, control, condition the rule was: 'If a letter has a D on one side, then it has a 5 on the other side', and the material consisted of the front of an envelope with a D on it (p); the front of an envelope with a C on it (not-p); the back of an envelope with a 5 on it (q); the back of an envelope with a 4 on it (not-q). (See Figure 19 for the material used in each condition.) In all other respects the procedure was the same as that used in the experimental condition.

There were 24 subjects in the experiment, and they were all

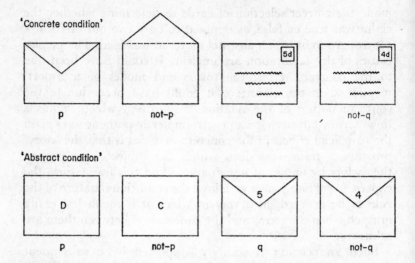

Figure 19. Material used in the 'envelope experiment' under both conditions

tested under both conditions in a counterbalanced order. Under the 'concrete' experimental condition 21 subjects were correct, i.e. selected *p* and not-*q*, and under the 'abstract' control condition only two subjects were correct. This truly astonishing result (which for once needs no statistics to interpret its significance) is all the more remarkable when one remembers the large number of previous experimental modifications designed to enhance the subjects' performance in the selection task. Equally remarkable, of course, is the fact that there was no transfer whatsoever between the concrete and abstract conditions: getting the solution correct with the concrete material led to no improvement when the task was presented in abstract form subsequently.

Unlike the Wason and Shapiro (1971) experiment, which we have just considered, the present experiment does more than provide a realistic framework into which the subjects can project themselves. It simulates exactly a real life activity. We are no longer concerned with a *card* which is assumed to 'represent' a journey—the card has become an envelope in the concrete condition which does not 'represent' anything but itself. And the results show that if, and only if, it is used in a way in which it might be used in a realistic context, then performance is dramatically improved. The conditional rule, which proved so recalcitrant, when its terms and connections were arbitrary, has become almost trivially easy when it is embodied in a real task.

Taken together, these two experiments force on us a radical reconsideration of the role of content in reasoning. The nature of the material would seem to be decisive in terms of whether the subjects exercise rational thought. With 'sensible material', in which there is no conflict between the logical and causal requirements, the task becomes much easier. The distinction drawn between pure and practical reasoning in Chapter 7 finds an echo with the present results on a much more difficult problem. Thus, one answer would be that formal operational thought is less general than Piaget supposes, and that it may, in fact, be specific to a wide variety of tasks in which a causal and a logical analysis coincide.

A rather different, and much more speculative, answer would be that the novelty of our problem, when presented in abstract terms, may induce a temporary regression to earlier modes of cognitive functioning. As we shall see in the next chapter, several startling cases were revealed of an apparent failure to appreciate the significance of a reversible operation—an operation which is of central importance in Piaget's theorizing, and a distinctive feature of 'preoperational thought'. It would imply that more recently acquired modes of functioning may be temporarily inhibited by rather unusual tasks, so that earlier modes begin to function. The evidence to back up this answer, however, is sketchy and we place no real credence upon it. The first answer is much more plausible.

Testing a Hypothesis: Prevention and Structure of Error

Our information-processing model constitutes a formal explanation of the psychological processes, connected with verification and falsification, which underly insight into the problem. But it does not attempt a more detailed explanation of the phenomena connected with these processes, nor with the way in which they interact during the attempt to solve the problem. Since there are wide individual differences with respect to the emergence of these phenomena it would be premature to incorporate them into the model. They are, however, of considerable intrinsic interest.

The present problem seems to create in many cases a deep-seated, ill-defined sense of perplexity. But just because more simple kinds of reasoning, discussed in earlier chapters, are relatively easy for our subjects, so the present problem possesses considerable advantages. It is not its difficulty which is primarily interesting. One can imagine that a metallurgist might investigate the strength of a new alloy by subjecting it to strains until it breaks. It is plausible to suppose that it may not just be the point at which it breaks, but the way in which it breaks which could provide information about its structural properties. In rather the same way, in our problem, it is not simply the occurrence of errors, nor even the processes which induced them, but their properties which may be illuminating. These properties are not manifested in the occurrence of an error, but they are revealed when the errors are confronted by contradictions and inconsistencies.

Our investigations suggest that there are at least two (and possibly three) components, or levels, within an error which are a consequence of the strategies employed by the subjects.

One component is trivial, and readily removed by reminding the subjects of their task. It is the preconception that the rule must be true, rather than under test for truth or falsity. The other two components are more fundamental, and in some cases more deep-seated. The first is the failure to appreciate that the cards are *reversible*, i.e. the significance of a card is the same regardless of which part of it is exposed. In the first experiment which systematically investigated the effects of contradiction (Wason, 1969b), the majority of subjects accepted the experimenter's correction, if they had denied that a red triangle (p), on the other side of the red circle (not-q) would falsify the rule. However, in one case, a subject confronted by this possibility, said: 'The sentence would be meaningless because it doesn't apply.' And when he was told it would make it false, he replied: 'It could do so but you are not doing it that way round.' When the relevant cards were actually turned over, this subject experienced the typical conflict, and acknowledged that the rule was, after all, false: 'Wait a minute. When it is put like that the sentence is not true. Either the sentence is true, or it is not true. You have proved one thing and then you have proved the other. You've proved a theorem and then its corollary (*sic*), so you don't know where you are ... there is only one card which needs to be turned over to prove the statement exactly: the red triangle (p).' It is evident that, when the cards are reversed again to their original position, it is as if they had never been turned over. The red circle (not-q) is still not selected: 'That is doing it the other way round.' Another subject behaved in a similar way: 'I am quite sure I am right. When it was the other way round it was all right.' Thus a card is apparently granted a different meaning according to which way up it is turned.

Irreversibility is more typically shown when the cards are not actually turned over, but discussed in hypothetical terms. The following dialogues between subject and experimenter (Wason and Johnson-Laird, 1970) are presented in symbolic terms in order to show their inconsistency with maximal clarity.

(1) 'x's aren't mentioned so I left that one out.' 'What do you expect to find on the other side of y?' 'Well, if it is an x, the sentence is false.'

(2) 'x has got nothing to do with it. There has to be a y under z for the sentence to be true.' 'What if there is an x under y?' 'Then the sentence would be false.'

These dialogues can be appreciated as abstract formulae, but an important additional clue to their meaning is provided, if it is known that y (and in the second example, y and z) had been selected initially, and x omitted. In other words, a subject will tend to make an inference from the uppermost symbol on a selected card to a possible symbol assumed to be underneath it. But he does not readily make the same inference (or even sanction its validity) in the reverse direction from a symbol uppermost on an *unselected* card. The selection of a card confers meaning on it; the omission of a card divests it of meaning. A subject ensnared in this way will contradict himself, over and over again, unless the independent assessment of the cards overcomes the domination exerted by the initial selection, and illuminates the contradiction in his own thought.

The other main component of error, *denial*, is even more surprising and frequent than irreversibility. It pervaded the responses in the original experiment (Wason, 1968a), but even in the tightly controlled, binary experiment (Wason, 1969b), exactly half the subjects manifested it before the relevant cards were actually turned over. Denial is apparent when a subject agrees that not-q associated with p would (or does) falsify the rule, but then fails to select not-q as relevant; and similarly, when he agrees that q associated with not-p is irrelevant, but then fails to dismiss q. The following dialogues (Wason and Johnson-Laird, 1970), again presented in symbolic terms, illustrate its manifestation. The subjects have just agreed that x verifies and y falsifies, both cards having been fully revealed. x had been selected and y omitted.

(1) 'The only way you can verify the sentence is to look at x and z. y is totally useless, as it doesn't have z on it so it doesn't matter.' 'You have seen that y does have x on it. Do you still think it doesn't matter?' 'Yes, I do.'

(2) 'Well, you've just said that y makes it false.' 'It hasn't got z on it, so it doesn't matter.'

(3) 'y makes it false. But I'd still choose x and z.'

We may now look more closely at the correction process,

implicit in the contradictions imposed on the subjects, and ask the psychologically pertinent question why they do not always work. In order to do this, it is helpful to distinguish two processes: (a) the selection process, which is an initial intention to turn over certain cards in accordance with the task, and (b) the evaluation process, which is an independent evaluation of specific cards, under the guidance of the experimenter, in relation to the truth and falsity of the rule. At first, the selection process tends to dominate the evaluation process so that the contradictions fail to modify the initial choice of cards. One possible explanation of these phenomena points to affective causes: the subjects know that they are wrong, but are reluctant to admit it. This is very implausible because, for highly intelligent subjects, it would be an admission of stupidity. A more subtle possibility is that the subjects may feel that their initial selections are threatened by the contradictions, but refuse to admit their fallibility to themselves. They suffer from self-deception, and hence strengthen their hold on their initial selections. Such an explanation is clearly speculative, and not particularly parsimonious.

A more testable explanation is in terms of attention. We may assume that the subjects' attention is concentrated on those cards which have been initially selected—the others are often said 'to have nothing to do with it'. But the intention to turn over the selected cards is frequently frustrated by the experimenter, who may begin to talk about another card, e.g. not-q, which has already been dismissed from consideration. Our supposition, postulated in the previous chapter, is that (without insight) the subjects' selection of cards is not consistent with the instructions, i.e. 'to find out whether the rule is true *or* false', but is governed solely by a need to *verify* the rule. It is plausible to assume that the combination of a frustrated intention, which would be expected to create unusually high motivation, and a self-instruction to verify the rule, results in a 'funnelling' of attention which excludes the unselected cards. Hence, the selection process tends to become dissociated, or internalized, so that it functions at a conceptual level which renders it relatively immune from subsequent verbal processes designed to modify it.

This sometimes has the bizarre effect of making the same individual begin to sound almost like two different people talking. The subjects frequently do not reject the falsifying card (not-q) for rational reasons, even when they have just said it falsifies the rule, They never say, 'That card only falsifies the rule but I want to find out if it is true.' They say, 'It is totally useless', and 'It doesn't matter.' The critical card simply does not exist at the level of the selection process, but the experimenter's tiresome questions about it have to be answered in some fashion. Hence their talk comes to resemble some of the phenomena of post-hypnotic suggestion, but it is, of course, unclear whether such a resemblance indicates a real similarity in the underlying processes involved.

These manifestations of different components, or levels, within an error may be revealed only when the problem is very difficult. Our other main attack is to see what happens when we radically change the problem in order to make it easier. One way of doing this was to present it in different (although equivalent) logical terms, and the other way was to reduce the logical values from four (p, not-p, q, not-q) to two (q and not-q).

The disjunctive expression, 'Either not-p or q, or both', does not, at first blush, seem to mean the same thing as the conditional, 'If p then q.' In fact, it is a more adequate formulation of material implication (see Table on p. 88). Both propositions are false only when p is true and q is false.

The first experiment (Wason and Johnson-Laird, 1969) utilized the disjunctive expression of material implication, and in the selection task compared performance between this expression and an unnegated disjunction (either p or q, or both). A variety of stimulus material was used, e.g. 'Every card has a square which isn't black on one side, or it has a line which is crooked on the other side', where 'white square' is p, 'black square' is not-p, 'crooked line' is q, and 'straight line' is not-q. In this example the correct solution would be to select 'white square' (p) and 'straight line' (not-q). 'Black square' and 'crooked line' obviously provide no information: the rule could not be falsified by whatever is on their other side. Unlike the previous experiments, the subjects were restricted to selecting only two cards under each condition. A simple decision procedure, which could be used, whether the expression is negated or unnegated in its first term, is to select only values not explicitly mentioned in the rule.

About half the subjects were able to solve the problem when material implication was expressed in disjunctive terms, and when the disjunction was not negated, it was significantly easier. The errors were primarily due to 'matching' the selected cards with values explicitly mentioned in the rule. For example, if the rule mentioned an 'even number', they would wrongly select a card showing such a number rather than a card showing an odd number.

The main difference, however, between behaviour in this task and behaviour in the previous experiments, when material implication was expressed in a conditional rule, was not reflected in the error scores. With the disjunctive expression of implication, the subjects more often tended to be right, but were unconfident about their solution; with the conditional expression they more often tended to be wrong, but were confident they were right. With the disjunctive expression the very act of choice sometimes spontaneously made the subjects repudiate it. Labile reasoning of this kind could have been due to the disjunctive expression *per se*, or to the presence of an explicit negative, or to the restriction of having to select only two values. It is plausible to suppose that these factors broke off that strong and misleading positive connotation of the conditional. Doubts and misgivings seldom occurred with a conditional rule. The disjunctive expression evidently liberated the subjects from the deep fixations which were so typical of the conditional, but at the cost of some confusion. It may be concluded that such an expression of material implication does make the 'selection task' easier by removing the deceptive characteristics associated with the conditional. But it does so at a price.

The second experiment maintained the rule in a conditional form, but it made the choice lie only between values of q and not-q (which we know are crucial with respect to error). In addition, concrete objects were substituted for cards, which made it possible for the different combinations of logical values to cohere in single stimuli, rather than being positioned on either side of a card. Thirdly, the problem was posed as a serial task which has the considerable advantage that the subjects' solution does not rest on a single decision.

In the experiment (Johnson-Laird and Wason, 1970b) the rule was, 'All the triangles are black', and under one condition it had to be proved true, and another false, in both cases as economically as possible. At each trial the subject could ask to be given either a *black* shape (of which he knew there were 15 in a box marked 'black'), or a *white* shape (of which he knew there were 15 in a box marked 'white'). In addition, he knew that the only shapes involved were triangles and circles. But, of course, he could only request the colour of a shape, and not its form.

Whether the sentence has to be proved true or false, the completely correct solution is to ask to see only the shapes in the white box (not-*q*). It is only the total absence of a white triangle which could prove the rule true, and it is only the presence of at least one which could prove it false. As predicted, the problem was much easier when the instructions were to prove the rule false.

But the more important comparison is with the earlier 'selection task' experiments in which the subjects had to solve the problem by making a single decision about selecting four available cards, each representing a different logical value. In the present experiment no subject requested more than nine of the 15 possible black shapes, and in every case they requested all the 15 white shapes. Thus, without any intervention from the experimenter, the subjects spontaneously appreciated at some stage that not-*q* (white) was more relevant than *q* (black) for proving the rule. If the task is made simple enough; if the 'cognitive load' on the subject is reduced, then insight will be spontaneously gained into its logical structure.

This conclusion is unfortunately open to question because of a further experiment reported in the same paper (see also Johnson-Laird, 1970b). The conditional was not presented as an explicit statement, but was an intrinsic part of the structure of a sorting-task. This had the advantage that the cognitive load imposed on the subject could be systematically varied by altering the complexity of the decisions which had to be made in performing the sorting. It was found that after insight seemed to have been gained, it might suddenly vanish when the task became more difficult, only to reappear again when more simple decisions had to be made.

These results suggest that insight is by no means an 'all-or-none' matter. It may fluctuate when extra work, or computation, is imposed on the organism. Indeed, the experiment by Goodwin and Wason (1972), discussed in the previous chapter, confirms that insight may exist in 'degrees'. It is a commonplace feeling to have 'half understood' an argument, or a lecture, and our results suggest that half understanding may be a psychological fact.

All these modifications to the original problem do evidently make the task easier for the subject. But from our point of view, it is failure in the task, and the nature of the errors which are revealed which are of greater interest. The present 'selection task' problem is a deductive one in which all the evidence is available for its solution. Its main interest lies in the fact that subjects tend to structure it in the wrong way, to 'freeze' it impulsively into a particular aspect, so that gain of insight may occur only after a lengthy process of trying to see the problem material in a different way. We now turn to a looser problem in which the evidence for the solution has to be generated by the subjects themselves. And here we may see cases in which individuals tend to form beliefs which seem inviolable because they have unwittingly assembled only evidence which supports them.

In the last three chapters the deductive component of scientific inference was investigated in a miniature task. The subjects were presented with a hypothesis, and had to decide what items of evidence were relevant for testing its truth. In spite of the difficulties of the task, it could be argued that, as an analogy to scientific research, half the work had already been done for them. In doing research one has to postulate a hypothesis, collect the evidence which would be relevant to it, and then evaluate this evidence in order to modify the initial hypothesis. The experiments reported in this chapter simulate this activity in an abstract task. More specifically, they seek to examine the adequacy of the tests to which hypotheses about an unknown rule are subjected. At least two factors may be important: (a) the ability to think up hypotheses, and (b) the ability to relinquish hypotheses. These factors are likely to interact. The ability to conceive a hypothesis which seems to 'work', in the sense that it fits the data, may make the individual reluctant to abandon it. On the contrary, he may simply try to strengthen it by adducing more confirming evidence for it. The experiments were designed to investigate the propensity of individuals to offer premature solutions based on such evidence. In this way, they are related to tolerance for uncertainty.

These interests demand a task with a much looser structure and with fewer constraints than those which have been used in experiments discussed previously. But before we consider it we must discuss in some detail the 'concept attainment' task (mentioned in Chapter 7), which has been the traditional method for investigating the process of generalization. This task is basically one of discrimination learning. The subject is presented with a series of stimuli, and is told each time whether they exemplify the concept which the experimenter has in mind. Thus, in discovering the concept, the subject has to attend to what is relevant and irrelevant in these positive and negative instances. Bruner, Goodnow and Austin (1956) liberated the subjects from an imposition of a sequence of instances by presenting them all simultaneously in an array, and allowing the subjects to choose which ones they wanted to test. Thus in this task the number of instances considered relevant, and the order in which they are tested, is under the subject's control. The experimenter simply points out an initial instance, and thereafter tells the subject each time whether the instances, which he selects, are positive or negative. This important innovation brings the concept attainment task one step closer to the thought processes which occur in research. Bruner *et al.* postulated a number of 'ideal' strategies which could be used, and they were able to show how variation in the presentation of the material (e.g. random versus ordered array) affected the subject's tendency to approximate to them.

In one experiment the material consisted of 81 instances made up from all the combinations of four 'attributes', each exhibiting one of three 'values', i.e. *shape* (cross, square, circle), *colour* (green, red, black), *number of figures* (one, two, three) and *number of borders* (one, two, three). Thus, every instance has one value of each of the four attributes, e.g. 'two green squares with three borders', and the possible concepts consist of any set of particular values of some, or all, of the attributes, e.g. 'squares' (27 positive instances), 'green circles' (9 positive instances), 'two crosses with one border' (3 positive instances). It should be noted, for future reference, the more specific the concept, the smaller the number of instances which satisfy it.

One very economical 'ideal' strategy (which is only relevant for conjunctive concepts) is known as 'conservative focusing'. It is governed by the following simple algorithmic rule: vary only one value at a time in the initially presented positive instance; if the outcome is a positive instance, then the value varied (and its attribute) is irrelevant to the concept; if the outcome is a negative instance, then the value varied is part of the concept. The following example illustrates how the consistent use of this strategy allows the concept to be derived.

Given: '3 green circles with 2 borders' $(+)$[1]

(1) '2 green circles with 2 borders' $(+)$ ∴ 'Number of figures' is irrelevant.

(2) '3 green *squares* with 2 borders' $(-)$ ∴ 'Circles' is part of the concept.

(3) '3 green circles with *3* borders' $(+)$ ∴ 'Number of borders' is irrelevant.

(4) '3 *red* circles with 2 borders' $(-)$ ∴ 'Green' is part of the concept.

All the necessary evidence has been acquired, and the concept must be 'green circles'. A more primitive and wasteful 'ideal' strategy is known as 'successive scanning'. It consists in formulating a hypothesis about the concept from the initial positive instance, and then seeking to confirm it by searching for more positive instances. This strategy (which is closely analogous to Bacon's 'induction by simple enumeration') entails that if a negative instance is encountered, then the subject must start to develop a new hypothesis all over again because he uses only positive instances to corroborate his hypothesis.

A more detailed analysis of this strategy is needed before we introduce our task. Any one of four contingencies may occur when a subject engages consistently in 'successive scanning'. Let us assume that the initial positive instance designated by the experimenter is '3 red squares with 1 border'.

First, the experimenter might have in mind the concept '1 border' (27 positive instances), but the subject might start to confirm the hypothesis, 'red squares' (9 positive instances). It is evident that he will soon encounter a negative instance, and in consequence have to start all over again with a new hypothesis.

Second, the concept might be 'red squares', and the subject might start to confirm the hypothesis 'red squares'. He will discover the concept after testing its nine positive instances, but he will be correct without justification. The concept might instead have been 'squares', and his strategy fails to discriminate between these two possibilities.

[1] $(+)$ and $(-)$ denote positive and negative instances, respectively.

Third, the concept might be 'squares', and the subject might start to confirm the hypothesis 'squares'. He will be right again, after testing its 27 positive instances, but this time he can *prove* he is right because no more general concept could hold.

Fourth, the concept might be 'squares', and the subject might start to confirm the hypothesis 'red squares'. After encountering nine positive instances, and no negative instances, he will announce the concept to the experimenter, and be told he is wrong.

It is this fourth contingency which we attempted to capture in our task. The others do not reveal the logical fallacy of induction by simple enumeration.

In our first experiment (Wason, 1960) the subjects were told that the three numbers, 2 4 6, conformed to a simple relational rule which the experimenter had in mind, and that their task was to try to discover it by generating successive triads of numbers. After each triad they were told whether, or not, the numbers conformed to the rule. They were allowed to keep a written record of their numbers, and their hypotheses, but were strictly instructed to show the rule to the experimenter ('announce the rule') only when they were highly confident that they had discovered it. If they announced a hypothesis other than the rule, they were told they were wrong and instructed to proceed with the task. The rule was: *numbers increasing in order of magnitude*. But the real point of the experiment was not to see whether the subjects discovered it, but to see how they set about trying to discover it. A very general rule was deliberately chosen so that positive instances of it would also tend to be positive instances of the more restricted hypotheses which would be likely to occur first of all to the subjects, e.g. 'intervals of two between increasing numbers'. In a strict sense, of course, the task is impossible if 'high confidence' were to be equated with proof. The rule cannot be proved, but it will be demonstrated subsequently how any more specific (sufficient) hypotheses can be disproved. This task, which relaxes the constraints in the conventional concept attainment task, has three distinctive features.

First, the subject is not presented with all the available evidence at the start. He has to generate both his own instances and his own hypotheses. In Bruner's task all the available evidence is presented, and the subject knows in principle all the possible concepts.

Second, the universe of instances is potentially infinite, and hence the number of instances which exemplify any hypothesis can never be exhausted. For example, an endless number of instances, exemplifying a sufficient hypothesis such as 'intervals of two between increasing numbers', can be generated without forcing the subject to generate an instance which does not exemplify it. It follows that if a subject only verifies, or confirms, his hypothesis, he will be forced to announce it to the experimenter as the only way of finding out whether it is the rule. As we have seen, this does not necessarily occur in Bruner's task because the universe of instances is finite, and the degree of generality of the possible concepts is correlated with the number of instances which satisfy them.

Third, the subjects do not have to remember either their previous instances, or their previous hypotheses, but can refer to their record sheet. In nearly all traditional concept attainment tasks memory has been a factor. It may, of course, be of considerable interest to investigate the interaction between reasoning and memory (e.g. Whitfield, 1951), but often memory has been a gratuitous variable without specific predictions being made about it. The use of paper and pencil is not denied in real life as an aid to thinking and planning.

It is evident that there are three strategies which a subject could adopt in the present task. The first one is to try to *verify* a hypothesis, and, if it is confirmed, to announce it as the rule. As we have seen, the task is biased so that this strategy will almost certainly lead to plausible but wrong conclusions.

The second strategy is to try to *falsify* a hypothesis. The strictest criterion for this strategy is when a subject generates an instance which is *inconsistent* with the hypothesis he is entertaining. For example, he might generate the instance, 3 6 10, and write down on the record sheet, 'to see if the rule is successive multiples of the first number'.

The third strategy is to *vary* his current hypothesis instead of trying to confirm it, or deliberately falsify it. Unlike the second strategy, this one is particularly interesting because it is consistent with Kuhn's (1962) thesis that scientists only relinquish a theory when an alternative theory, or hypothesis, is available. In the present context it entails that the subject will only abandon a hypothesis when another one is conceived.

Both the second and third strategies share the common factor that the rule will probably be discovered without announcing any incorrect hypotheses, and the aim of the experiment was primarily to investigate the extent to which procedures of this kind were used. It is simplest to show how the third strategy might achieve its end.

Suppose a subject has entertained the hypothesis, 'intervals of two between ascending numbers', on the strength of the positive instances, 8 10 12, 14 16 18, he might then consider the more general hypothesis, 'an equal interval between ascending numbers' (arithmetic progression). And in doing this, he might generate 7 11 15. Since that instance turns out to be a positive instance of the rule, he has disproved at a stroke his former hypothesis, 'intervals of two between ascending numbers'. Similarly, his new hypothesis of arithmetic progression could be disproved by finding out that an instance such as 1 6 7 is also positive. Thus the strategy of varying a hypothesis, which has been confirmed, will gradually purge the initial instance, 2 4 6, of all the surplus meaning inherent in it, and inexorably tend to lead the subject towards a consideration of the rule. It should be noted that there is a pertinent psychological distinction between the strategy of varying (falsifying) hypotheses on the one hand, and the strategy of verifying hypotheses on the other hand. When hypotheses are varied the work involved in discovery is internalized; but when hypotheses are only verified on the basis of confirming evidence the subject is forced to appeal to an external authority (the experimenter) to find out if his conclusions are correct.

In the exploratory experiment (Wason, 1960) only 21 per cent of the subjects discovered the rule without making any announcements of incorrect hypotheses, and the results showed that these subjects varied their hypotheses significantly more often than the remainder. They did not hit on the rule by chance. There was, however, very little evidence for the use of the falsification strategy, and hence the main interest lies between the variation of hypotheses (which of course, frequently leads to implicit falsification of former hypotheses), and the verification of hypotheses by piling up confirming evidence for them. This provides some corroboration, in an artificial task, for Kuhn's (1962) view that beliefs, or hypotheses, are only abandoned (if at all) when more adequate alternatives become available. But even the spontaneous variation of hypotheses is rare in the present experiment. The majority of subjects announced at least one incorrect hypothesis, and one subject only discovered the rule after making four incorrect announcements. However, only 28 per cent failed to discover the rule by whatever strategy. The two protocols which follow illustrate the difference between trying out alternative hypotheses and the failure to do so. The first is derived from a subject who made no incorrect announcement ('immediate correct announcement'), and the second from a subject who made four incorrect announcements.

No. 1. Immediate correct announcement. Female. Psychology undergraduate.

Instances			Hypotheses
2	4	6 (+) (Given)	
3	6	9 (+)	Three goes into the second figure twice and into the third figure three times.
2	4	8 (+)	Perhaps the figures have to have an L.C.D.
2	4	10 (+)	Same reason.
2	5	10 (+)	The second number does not have to be divided by the first one.
10	6	4 (−)	The highest number must go last.
4	6	10 (+)	The first number must be the lowest.
2	3	5 (+)	It is only the order that counts.
4	5	6 (+)	Same reason.
1	7	13 (+)	Same reason.

Announcement: *The rule is that the figures must be in numerical order.* (Correct: 16 min.)

It is apparent that this subject does spontaneously vary her hypotheses, and hence avoids getting entangled in her own thought. It is also clear that with one instance she does attempt the falsification strategy: she generates the instance 10 6 4, and cites a hypothesis inconsistent with it, 'the highest number must go last'.

No. 2. Four incorrect announcements. Female. Psychology undergraduate.

Instances	Hypotheses
2 4 6 (+) (Given)	
8 10 12 (+)	Two added each time.
14 16 18 (+)	Even numbers in order of magnitude.
20 22 24 (+)	Same reason.
1 3 5 (+)	Two added to preceding number.

Announcement: *The rule is that by starting with any number two is added each time to form the next number.* (Incorrect)

| 2 6 10 (+) | The middle number is the arithmetic mean of the other two. |
| 1 50 99 (+) | Same reason. |

Announcement: *The rule is that the middle number is the arithmetic mean of the other two.* (Incorrect)

| 3 10 17 (+) | Same number, seven, added each time. |
| 0 3 6 (+) | Three added each time. |

Announcement: *The rule is that the difference between two numbers next to each other is the same.* (Incorrect)

| 12 8 4 (−) | The same number is subtracted each time to form the next number. |

Announcement: *The rule is adding a number, always the same one, to form the next number.* (Incorrect)

| 1 4 9 (+) | Any three numbers in order of magnitude. |

Announcement: *The rule is any three numbers in order of magnitude.* (Correct: 17 min.)

A protocol like this poses a large number of crucial questions. First, it might be argued that the subject announced hypotheses in order to get feedback in the most direct fashion from the experimenter. In other words, the instruction to announce a hypothesis, only when there is a high degree of confidence that it is correct, is violated. At the moment, it should be pointed out that such a procedure would logically confer no advantage. In fact, the generation of an instance consistent with a new hypothesis provides more information than announcing the old hypothesis. It would show decisively whether the old hypothesis is incorrect (if the instance is positive), and it would also show whether the new hypothesis is at least on the right lines. Hence, if anything, the announcement of a hypothesis suggests that the subject really believes that it is correct rather than incorrect. On the other hand, the subject might be able to proceed in no other way. If it is assumed, and there is some evidence for this assumption, that only the strategy of verification is available to the subject, then the announcement of hypotheses is the only way of finding out whether they are correct. A speculative possibility, which remains untested at this point, is that a subject may vary aspects of a hypothesis about which he is doubtful, but is severely inhibited from varying hypotheses which he believes to be true.

This protocol is an extreme example of a trend which was apparent throughout the experiment. In fact, over all the subjects, as many as 51·6 per cent of the instances, which were generated immediately after an incorrect announcement, remained consistent, rather than inconsistent, with the hypothesis just announced. On more than half the possible occasions the hypothesis is not relinquished, even when it is known to be wrong. Time is needed to find a new idea in a large number of cases—a point which is again in conformity with Kuhn's (1962) views. Typical incorrect announcements were fairly stereotyped, e.g. 'arithmetic progression' (constant interval between ascending numbers), 'increasing intervals of two', 'successive multiples of the first number', 'consecutive even numbers', etc. A few were more idiosyncratic, e.g. 'arithmetic or geometric progression', and the relation between such hypotheses and pathological thinking will be discussed in Chapter 18.

It seems a reasonable conclusion from this exploratory experiment that most highly intelligent adults, in an abstract task, tend to use only a verification strategy in attempting to discover an unknown rule. It is supported by a similar study carried out by G. A. Miller (1967) in which the subjects had to discover the rules governing artificial grammars. According to Miller (personal communication): 'Once a subject finds a rule that seems to work, he is unlikely to suspect the existence of other positive instances that lie beyond the scope of his particular rule.'

The general conclusion from our experiment, however, should be viewed with some caution because it is open to a considerable number of objections, and until these have been met not much progress has really been made. First, it could be claimed that a positive instance of the rule would reinforce the hypothesis which is also exemplified by it. The conflation between hypothesis and rule, wedded by the same positive instance, would tend to reward the generation of incorrect hypotheses. Miller (1967) has argued cogently, and at length, against this criticism, and we were able to adduce some empirical evidence to support his arguments. In a subsequent experiment, Angela Fine (reported in Wason, 1971) delayed telling her subjects whether their instances were positive or negative until they had been generated in blocks of varying sizes. If a reinforcement principle had been responsible for the failure to vary hypotheses, then it would be predicted that generating (say) eight instances in a block, before receiving feed-back about them, would lead to more variation of hypotheses than would immediate feed-back, given after each instance. In fact, no increase in variation of hypotheses was observed. Feed-back does not function simply as reward; if subjects are going to stick to their hypotheses, they will do so in any case. Fine's study, incidentally, also provided the comforting evidence that 75 per cent of the subjects (27 out of 36) rated the task subsequently as either 'enjoyable', or 'very enjoyable'. Furthermore, all the subjects said afterwards that they considered the rule was perfectly fair: they did not feel cheated.

Second, it could be claimed that the results were a function of the material used in the task. More specifically, the charge might be that students would be familiar with the 'number series' type of intelligence test item, in which a unique continuation is assumed correct, and hence extrapolate this knowledge to the supposition that only the most 'fitting' rule was correct. However, J. Penrose (1962) substituted verbal material for numbers, and devised a sort of inverted game of 20 questions. The subjects were given an instance, e.g. 'Siamese cat', and had to discover a class under which it fell ('living things'), and which the experimenter had in mind. They did this by generating instances, and were told each time whether they were included, or not included, in this class. Very similar effects were obtained. For example, one subject only changed his hypothesis from 'domestic pets' to 'animals' after generating 12 instances. Tirril Gatty (reported in Wason, 1968b) adopted a different approach. She retained numerical material, but tried to alert the subject to a variety of different possible rules. The main instruction was to discover 'rules which *could be* the correct one, but were not the one the experimenter had in mind', and a subsidiary instruction was to announce the correct rule if this was discovered, as a by-product of the main task. The results showed no difference in the number of incorrect hypotheses, announced as the rule, compared with a control group who were instructed to discover the rule in the ordinary way. In the experimental group, six out of the 11 subjects announced at least one incorrect hypothesis as the rule, and only two apparently appreciated that a single instance was sufficient to prove conclusively that a hypothesis was incorrect. A particularly interesting finding was that five out of the 11 subjects first of all generated instances to confirm a hypothesis (in contradiction to their instructions), and only then attempted to eliminate them. This confirms, yet again, Kuhn's (1962) argument that the scientist carries out research with reference to a pre-existing 'paradigm'. Even in an artificial task, in which no particular values are invested, the technique of deliberately trying to disconfirm a hypothesis, in accordance with explicit instructions, would seem to be a logically possible, but deviant procedure. Penrose's and Gatty's studies suggest respectively that neither the material used in our original experiment, nor the possible belief that only one rule is appropriate, could explain our results.

Third, it could be claimed that the subjects in the original experiment were merely announcing incorrect hypotheses in order to remove themselves from the experimental situation as quickly as possible. This seems unlikely because they were highly motivated, and were very surprised when told that their first incorrect announcement was not the rule. However, a modest study (reported in Wason, 1968b) was carried out to try to determine whether subjects were unwilling, or unable, to adopt the appropriate strategy. One group was given ten shillings (50p) initially, and told that they would lose half a crown (12·5p) for every incorrect announcement. A control group was not given this incentive. There were no differences between the groups in the number of incorrect announcements made; the incentive only had the effect of increasing the number of confirming instances generated before making an announcement. The study suggested that the strategy of varying hypotheses does not exist in the repertoire of most subjects, rather than that the effort of using this strategy is too onerous.

Fourth, it was pointed out that if a subject can only use the verifying strategy, then he must announce that hypothesis, which he verifies, in order to find out whether it is the rule. The present task provides no objective information about whether a subject 'really' believes his hypothesis is the rule. Strategy and belief are confounded, and subjective confidence ratings could be merely artefacts. They would be expected to increase as a function of the need to find out about a hypothesis rather than provide an independent criterion of the strength of belief. An experiment carried out in collaboration with Martin Katzman (reported in Wason, 1968b) modified the task in order to try to clarify this issue. The subjects were told that they would be given only one opportunity to announce the rule. If an incorrect hypothesis was announced, they were not told it was wrong but were asked: 'If you were wrong, how could you find out?' In response to this question, nine out of the 16 subjects, to whom it was asked, replied that they would continue to generate instances consistent with their hypothesis, and wait for one to be a negative instance of the rule. Four replied that they would either vary their hypotheses, or generate instances inconsistent with them. Three gave the revealing answer that no other rules were possible, e.g. 'I can't be wrong since my rule is correct for those numbers'; 'Rules are relative—

if you were the subject and I were the experimenter, then I should be right.' It is evident that some subjects at any rate, not only believe that their hypotheses are the rule, but also believe that they have logical reasons for supposing that they cannot be mistaken. This phenomenon, in which subjects seem to identify with their hypotheses, is presumably the most extreme consequence of the verifying strategy. One other subject, who broke down completely and appeared to exhibit psychotic symptoms, will be discussed in Chapter 18.

The research described above does not, of course, conclusively settle potential criticisms of our exploratory experiment, but it does considerably weaken them. It is at least evident that the predominant tendency to adopt the verifying strategy is to a large extent impervious to the manipulation of task variables.

We shall now ignore such variables and attempt to analyse the most pervasive and distinctive qualitative feature in the protocols. It will be noted that in No. 2 the second, third and fourth incorrect announcements are all consistent with the rule of arithmetic progression $(a, a + d, a + 2d)$: *The rule is that the middle number is the arithmetic mean of the other two; The rule is that the difference between two numbers next to each other is the same; The rule is adding a number, always the same one to form the next number.* The subject is logically re-formulating virtually the same hypothesis in different terms, rather than conceiving a different hypothesis. However, it became apparent that the subjects who do this genuinely believed at the time that they had conceived, and announced, different hypotheses. They did not assume that the verbal expression of a hypothesis counted towards its correctness. It is worth one more clear-cut example. The subject had announced the hypothesis of successive multiples in the following terms: *The rule is to start with a basic number, then double it and thirdly multiply it by three.* On being told it was wrong she proceeded as follows:

14	28	42 (+)	The first number being a half of the second and a third of the third.
7	14	21 (+)	Same reason.
8	16	24 (+)	Same reason.

9   18   27 (+)   Same reason.
50 100 150 (+)   Same reason.

Announcement: *The rule is that the second number is double the first and two-thirds of the third.*

There are two interpretations of this phenomenon. The first is that the reason the 'new' hypothesis is logically equivalent to its predecessor is largely coincidental: the urge to discover the rule blinds the subject to the identity between his hypotheses. This interpretation is tenable in spite of the fact that a characteristic of many subjects, after making an incorrect announcement, was to ponder on their previous hypothesis before generating new instances. They might simply have failed to realize the logical equivalence between two hypotheses because of an unduly high motivation to succeed.

The second interpretation is that the underlying concept, represented in a former incorrect announcement, continues to exert a selective effect upon the choice of a 'new' hypothesis. In several cases a more dramatic effect was observed, which enhances this interpretation: two logically equivalent announcements were made contiguously without generating any new instances between them, e.g.

(1) (*i*) *Any number*, (*ii*) *Twice the number*, (*iii*) *Sum of* (*i*) + (*ii*)
(2) (*i*) *Any number*, (*ii*) *Twice the number*, (*iii*) *Three times* (*i*)

Again, it is difficult to imagine that the following announcements, which have a strong flavour of asseveration about them, and which were also made without any intervening instances, were supposed to be different hypotheses:

(1) *The rule is that the three numbers must be in an ascending series and separated by regular step intervals.*
(2) *The rule is that the first number can be arbitrarily chosen; the second number must be greater than the first and can be arbitrarily chosen; the third number is larger than the second by the same amount as the second is larger than the first.*

This, more speculative, interpretation is related to observations by Gestalt psychologists, such as Maier (1931), who have shown that an action may be performed without the subject being able to give a verbal account of its cause, and to the findings of Hull (1920) and Smoke (1932) who showed that a concept may be correctly discriminated before it can be described. In a more general way, it is also consistent with psychoanalytic theory, and with the 'New Look' research, concerned with effects of motives on perception (e.g. Allport, 1955), in the sense that they presuppose, or suggest, that what the individual reports is governed by underlying motives of which he is unaware. In fact, it seems likely that there is a continuum between the inability to verbalize a concept and the production of multiple descriptions of a concept, when these are demanded by the task. In both, the possession of a concept either renders a description psychologically redundant, or elicits spurious descriptions which seem genuinely different, and which may change without forcing any modification in the subject's fundamental thought process. In this way, such descriptions act as compromises which minimize frustration, fulfil the obligation to the experimenter, and conceal from the subject the repetitive nature of his thinking by granting the illusion of progress. These repetition phenomena are the most distinctive qualitative feature of behaviour in this task, but they should not obscure its even more pronounced quantitative feature: the proclivity to offer premature solutions to the problem based on confirming evidence.

The results, taken as a whole, seem to have more than a superficial resemblance to the results obtained with the 'selection task', described in the three previous chapters. In the 'selection task', the subjects without insight seek only to verify the rule by matching those values, explicitly mentioned in it, with the cards on the table. The remaining cards are regarded as meaningless. In the present discovery task, the subjects show a strong tendency to match their instances with their hypotheses (or vice versa). In both tasks, too, verbal response often seems to be processed at a relatively superficial level. In the 'selection task' a card may be acknowledged to falsify the rule, and then dismissed with rationalizations; in the present task two logically equivalent hypotheses may not be recognized as identical because of a difference in their expression.

There are two reasons why behaviour in the present task is more incorrigible. In the 'selection task' a single hypothesis is presented for testing, but in the present task the subjects are free to generate both their own instances, and their own hypotheses. The looseness of these constraints tends to make the subjects, and indeed some psychologists who have criticized the experiments, mistake the task for the creative one of confirming the products of their own ingenuity. Second, no conceptual incongruity is deliberately imposed in the present experiments. In fact, the biased nature of the task, in which potential confirmations are abundant, may create a system of positive feedback in which thought either becomes increasingly stereotyped and conventional, or idiosyncratic and bizarre, and in both cases detached from reality. These matters will be discussed in more detail in Chapter 18.

One last point does deserve a mention. I. M. L. Hunter (personal communication) has pointed out that children do not know enough about numerical relationships to make the mistakes, so typical in the task with adults, and hence they often hit on the rule immediately. They have not yet learnt to erect their own obstacles against finding it.

In previous chapters we have been primarily concerned with academic and theoretical questions. We now turn to a practical problem which affects us all in our everyday lives: the understanding of rules and regulations.

A simple regulation poses no difficulty. 'Keep off the grass' states unequivocally that a certain action is prohibited. But the matter is not so straightforward when rules are logically interrelated. It is highly probable that the reader will at some time have been baffled by instructions for working, or maintaining domestic equipment, e.g. 'The best method of determining the size of main jet is to use a jet which is one size larger than the size which produced the above symptoms.' It is even reputed that the cause of a plane crash was due to an ambiguity in the maintenance manual. At the court of enquiry the man in charge of maintenance was asked what the manual said, and he replied, 'Remove the pin, examine it, and if it is bent replace it.' He was then asked what he did, and he said, 'I removed the pin, examined it, saw that it was bent and replaced it.' It would have been more redundant, but evidently more prudent to have changed the words, '. . . replace it', to '. . . replace it with a new pin'. Everybody will have their favourite examples, but the most notorious ones concern, not so much instructions, but official rules and regulations, concerned with social security, pension schemes, etc., which are issued by government departments in a form which is supposed to be intelligible to every rational person. These are not easy to understand, and the problem is likely to become even more acute in the future. It is particularly insidious because it is not usually recognized as a problem which is solvable, but is treated as a joke, or the sort of irritant to which we have all got used. Let us look at two examples.

'A Class 1 contribution is not payable for employment by any one employer for not more than 8 hours in any week— but if you normally work for more than 8 hours in any week for any one employer, a Class 1 contribution is payable except for any week when you do not do more than 4 hours work for that employer.'

'Contributions paid late cannot normally count for death grant (other than towards the test of yearly average) unless they were paid before the death on which the grant is claimed and before the death of the insured person if that was earlier. But if the insured person died before the person on whose death the grant is claimed, contributions which, although paid late, have already been taken into account for the purpose of a claim for widow's benefit or retirement pension, will count towards death grant.' (One begins to wonder *who* has died.)

In all such cases the applicant who wants to know how he stands, unaided by official help, will have to tread his way through a maze of conditions, guided only by his own circumstances. He may have to exercise a fine degree of deductive skill in coming to a conclusion. Sometimes, however, even a single sentence can cause a strange state of puzzlement:

'If any part of the property is NOT occupied by the person shown above as occupier, please give the names of the other occupiers.'

It is clear what is wrong: the sentence carries the preconception that property unoccupied by someone is necessarily occupied by someone else. But without benefit of a linguistic analysis, the effect is confusing in exactly the same way as if a friend had said, 'I shan't go to Peking tomorrow', when we had no reason to suppose he would (see Chapter 4).

The main source of trouble in such documents, however, is due to the concatenation of qualifying clauses, linked by words such as 'but', 'unless', 'except', etc., which probably seem completely arbitrary to most people. A great deal of effort has gone into the task of explaining the law to the man in the street, without finding out whether he wants it explained. It is a more plausible and modest assumption that he is not interested in the law *per se*, but only in how he, and his family, stand in relation to it. After all, even if he did understand the law, it is bound to seem arbitrary to him. However, for the moment, we shall not rule out the possibility that he wants it explained. Paradoxically, he may not want to know about it if the attempt is made to explain it, but he may want to know about it if no attempt is made to explain it. This issue is not relevant to our aims.

Our fundamental assumption is that the writers of these non-statutory leaflets are not to be blamed if their products are largely incomprehensible. On the contrary, we shall argue that the logical relations involved in many inter-related regulations are just too complex to be adequately reflected by the syntax of continous prose. Hence, in collaboration with A. R. Jonckheere, we proposed that such regulations should be expressed in the form of algorithms, or 'logical trees', which resemble computer programs, treating the individual as a computer (Wason, 1962). This is best explained by an example. Consider the following passage, taken from an official leaflet.

'The earliest age at which a woman can draw a retirement pension is 60. On her own insurance she can get a pension when she reaches that age, if she has then retired from regular employment. Otherwise she has to wait until she retires or reaches age 65. At age 65 pension can be paid irrespective of retirement. On her husband's insurance, however, she cannot get a pension, even though she is over 60, until he has reached age 65 and retired from regular employment, or until he is 70 if he does not retire before reaching that age.'

This information can be expressed in two forms of 'logical tree': (a) as a 'visual graph' (or flow diagram), which directly reveals the inter-connections between the propositions, but which may consume considerable space, or (b) as a 'list structure', which is more compact, but conceals the inter-connections. Both forms of representation share considerable advantages over continuous prose. The visual graph is presented in Figure 20, and the list structure in Figure 21.

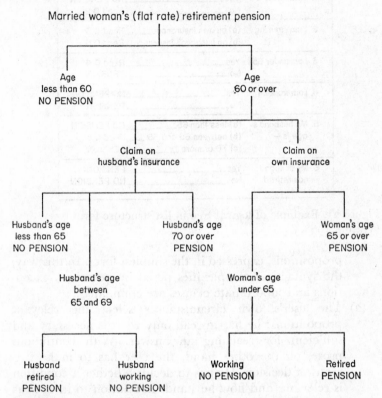

Figure 20. Example of logical tree in visual graph form (Wason, 1968c)

The visual graph is self-explanatory. With the list structure, all that the user has to do is to answer the first question, and then answer *only* the questions to which he is referred. The advantages of both modes of representation over continuous prose are:

(1) The user has to make a series of explicit decisions, which are usually binary ('Yes', 'No'), based on questions, or

Married woman's (flat rate) retirement pension		
1. I am under 60	Yes	NO PENSION
	No	Read Q.2
2. I am claiming	(a) on own insurance	Read Q.3
	(b) on husband's insurance	Read Q.5
3. I am under 65	Yes	Read Q.4
	No	PENSION
4. I am working	Yes	NO PENSION
	No	PENSION
5. My husband's age is —	(a) less than 65	NO PENSION
	(b) between 65 and 69	Read Q.6
	(c) 70 or more	PENSION
6. My husband has retired	Yes	PENSION
	No	NO PENSION

Figure 21. Example of logical tree in list structure form (Wason, 1968c)

propositions, expressed in the simplest form. In this way, the syntactical complexities posed by negatives, exceptions and subordinate clauses are eliminated.

(2) The user's own circumstances select the relevant propositions: he has to read only what is necessary and sufficient for reaching an answer. With continuous prose, on the other hand, the user has to make two kinds of decision. He has to decide whether a condition is relevant, and how he stands in relation to it. It is as if he had to find his own way through a maze rather than being asked to check its relevant choice points.

(3) Progress through a logical tree does not involve memory in any way. After a decision has been made, it can be forgotten. With continuous prose there may be a constant searching back and forth so that the user can ensure that he is on the right track.

These advantages appear unassailable, but it is only fair to point out possible disadvantages. First, if an erroneous decision is made at any point, or the user inadvertently reads a wrong proposition, then, of course, a wrong conclusion may be drawn. This could be overcome (if necessary) by inserting an 'error-correcting code' into the program. Second, as hinted earlier, the public may develop an emotional reaction to being treated as computers who only make binary decisions. They may want to know the grounds for the decisions, and these are not provided by the logical tree. However, since these grounds often seem incomprehensible, in any case, this may not be a serious objection. Third, the public may have acquired a stereotyped image of the government as 'them', as opposed to 'us', and this could disrupt the purely cognitive task of understanding official sentences. One can only say that this possible effect would be likely to be much more pronounced with continuous prose, which imposes other burdens, than with logical trees.

In collaboration with Sheila Jones (Jones, 1968b), (Wason, 1968c), we tested the list structure on a group of Executive Class officers within the Civil Service. An extremely complex document, concerned with the authorization of private vehicles on official business, was selected as the experimental material. None of the subjects were acquainted with the document. Half were given the material in the form of continuous prose, and half as a 'list structure'. In both groups, five problems were presented, in the form of hypothetical cases, and the task was to determine their outcome as accurately, and quickly, as possible. On all five problems, the subjects, who had been given the 'list structure', performed faster (4·6 min. on average) than those who had been given the continuous prose (7·1 min. on average). Moreover 86 per cent of the solutions were correct in the 'list structure' group, compared with 79 per cent in the continuous prose group. Subsequent comments revealed 13 favourable remarks, and one unfavourable one, about the 'list structure', compared with one favourable, and 13 unfavourable remarks, about the continuous prose.

This demonstration was really more of a propaganda exercise than a scientific experiment because it could hardly fail. It merely showed the feasibility of a new technique, that it did not result in more error, and that its professional users very much approved of it. There are several non-trivial aspects to 'logical trees', however, which have not yet been tested.

It would be of interest to know whether a 'logical tree', especially one represented as a 'visual graph', enables a set of regulations to be learnt more readily. Hypothetical cases could be presented for solution, and then further cases presented to be solved from memory of the material. An alternative test might involve the recall of the material in continuous prose. It might be expected that the 'visual graph' representation would facilitate the use of visual imagery, and hence lead to greater accuracy when cases are solved from memory.

A quite different problem would be to invert the procedures which have been discussed. Instead of constructing 'logical trees' from continuous prose regulations, we could investigate the writing of continuous prose, guided only by a 'logical tree' representation of the regulations. A 'visual graph' might provide a standard, or model, to generate clear continuous prose. Indeed, it might even be possible to standardize types of verbal expression in the form of connectives which mirror the structure of the tree. This would have some practical applications in the drafting of rules (Wason, 1968c), although, from the user's point of view, a 'logical tree' would be superior. But from a theoretical point of view, it would be of interest to know the point at which the logical complexity of the rules forces a departure from standard expressions which may suffice in simpler cases. Consider first the following 'logical tree', expressed as a 'visual graph' (Figure 22), and then the prose versions which were constructed directly from it (Wason, 1962).

Prose versions based on logical tree

(1) Less than 13 Class 1 contributions, paid or credited in the preceding year, gives no benefit. If there are more than 12 Class 1 contributions, paid or credited in the preceding year, (a) a total of more than 49 contributions of any kind, paid or credited for that year, gives full benefit; (b) a total of more than 25 and less than 50 gives reduced benefit; and (c) a total of less than 26 gives no benefit. (76 words)

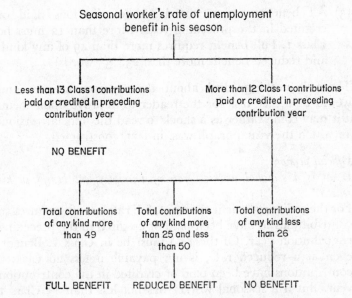

Figure 22. Example of a logical tree used as a standard from which to construct continuous prose versions (Wason, 1962)

(2) Less than 26 contributions of any kind, paid or credited in the preceding year, gives no benefit. If there are more than 12 Class 1 contributions, paid or credited in the preceding year, a total of more than 49 contributions of any kind, paid or credited, for that year, gives full benefit, and a total of more than 25 and less than 50 gives reduced benefit. (68 words)

(3) Full benefit requires more than 49 contributions of any kind, paid or credited in the preceding year, and more than 12 must be Class 1. Reduced benefit requires more than 25 and less than 50 contributions, paid or credited in the preceding year, and more than 12 must be Class 1. (53 words)

(4) For any benefit, more than 12 contributions, paid or credited in the preceding year, must be Class 1. Full benefit requires more than 49 contributions of any kind, and reduced benefit more than 25 of any kind. (36 words)

(5) All benefits are reckoned on contributions paid or credited in the preceding year. More than 12 must be Class 1. Full benefit requires more than 49 of any kind, and reduced benefit more than 25. (35 words)

There is nothing ideal about these prose versions, and it would be a nice task for the reader to improve upon them. But it may come rather as a shock to read the 'official version' from which the visual graph was, in fact, constructed.

Official version
What is a seasonal worker's rate of unemployment benefit in his season?
For the ordinary benefit claimant, full rate benefit requires 50 contributions to have been paid or credited in the preceding contribution year. Of these 39 must be in Class 1. Benefit, even at a reduced rate, is not payable unless 26 Class 1 contributions have been paid or credited in the contribution year. But if a seasonal worker has not less than 13 Class 1 contributions paid or credited in a contribution year, he may count as Class 1 contributions any other contributions paid or credited in that year for the purpose of determining his rate of benefit if he is unemployed during his season. Thus if he should become unemployed in that part of the year when he is normally working for an employer, he should be entitled to full rate benefit so long as he has contributed according to his class of insurance throughout the preceding contribution year. (150 words, 105 without last sentence)

The economy achieved in the 'visual graph', derived from this passage, which is reflected in the constructed prose versions, is due mainly to the exclusion of (a) the 'contrast case', i.e. the situation of the 'ordinary benefit claimant', and (b) the exemplar of the typical seasonal worker. But we would argue, in the absence of contrary evidence, that this information is of no interest whatsoever to a seasonal worker who suddenly finds himself unemployed. Indeed, it might even irritate him. If it is argued that such information *ought* to be important to a seasonal worker, then a clear case could be made for presenting it in a brief preamble, in a different portion of the leaflet from the information which concerns the technical regulations, i.e. the conversion of 'contributions of any kind', which is specifically relevant to the seasonal worker.

The 'visual graph' and 'list structure' representations of complex inter-related rules do not exhaust the possible devices for easing comprehension. Another method, which has not yet been tested, is to present a string of necessary conditions for a specific benefit, without which it cannot be granted. If an applicant satisfies these conditions, then he could be referred to lists of sufficient conditions, any one of which would enable the benefit to be granted. Such a method lacks the economy of the 'logical tree' presentations because it does not reflect the logical structure of the rules. But it has the advantage that it is less novel, and it retains the property of eliminating connections between clauses which we noted as a potential stumbling block to comprehension. The applicant simply has to scan the elements in a finite number of lists, and it seems likely that the number of such lists would be small in most cases. They could also be ordered in increasing length of items, so that if an applicant's conditions are satisfied by a list of n elements, he would not have to scan a list of $n + 1$ elements.

It is gratifying to note that the Civil Service are now presenting some of their leaflets in these forms, and the thought arises that analogous techniques could replace, or augment, other kinds of expository writing. In our view this would be dubious. We have noticed that some people are so concerned with making their prose run on in a logical way that they have great difficulty in writing down anything at all. It seems possible that the attempt to impose a logical structure on their thought may result in constraining it so that it is not open to subsequent modification. Accordingly, we have argued elsewhere (Wason, 1970) that writing should not necessarily be regarded as a strictly linear process, but that it should first aim to exteriorize thought, in any fashion, without regard to internal coherence or optimal sequence. In our experience, this allows the writer to discern an appropriate form, or logical structure, which emerges from it. The creative products of thought can then more easily be fashioned in accordance with this structure by a process of successive re-drafting.

The algorithmic procedures which we have discussed are almost certain to be helpful for elucidating complex interconnected rules and regulations. Their application to other kinds of discourse may be detrimental.

In some of our research we were forcibly reminded of pathological phenomena which are not usually found, or looked for,
in psychological experiments. Repetition, asseveration, self-
contradiction, outright denial of the facts, and ritualistic
behaviour became quite typical in some tasks. We do not, of
course, suggest that the subjects concerned were suffering from
any kind of pathological thought disorder. On the whole, they
appeared reasonably sane. Rather it would seem that the interaction between the demands of the task and their own reasoning
processes sometimes created something analogous to evanescent
'miniature psychoses', like those which have been induced by
psychiatrists in order to study the processes assumed to occur
spontaneously in real psychoses. In other words, these symptoms
were reflections of reasoning under mildly stressful conditions,
induced by the subjects' own approach to the rather unusual
tasks.

The present chapter is concerned with tracing resemblances
between our data and real pathological phenomena. In this
way, each may illuminate the other. It would, however, be
premature to do more than hint that there may be a real
similarity in the antecedents of the behaviour in the two cases.
Clearly, there is not enough evidence to make any strong
claims. Instead, our aim in drawing out resemblances is to show
both the experimentalist and the clinician that they could have
more in common than they seem to suppose. In the present
state of psychology these specialists speak a different language,
and are preoccupied by different kinds of problem. Perhaps
each would benefit if they were to get more familiar with the
problems and skills of the other.

The first experimental case which we shall discuss concerns data which hardly seem pathological at all. And yet it is just here that clinical observations seem relevant to one of our hypotheses. In Chapter 3 we postulated an emotional inhibition, associated with negative sentences, as one possible explanation of the difficulty which subjects experienced in handling them. The experimental evidence, however, was equivocal, but clinical evidence is both dramatic, and much more convincing. In his essay on Negation, Freud (1925), pointed out that the analyst, in interpreting a patient's associations, should ignore the negative, and simply pick out the subject-matter of the utterance. The patient says: 'You ask who this person in the dream can have been. It was *not* my mother.' Freud remarks: 'We amend this: so it was his mother.' In our terms, the analyst concentrates upon the preconception of the negative, since it is this which constitutes the repressed material: 'The subject-matter of a repressed image or thought can make its way into consciousness on condition that it is negated.' The following dialogue between therapist and patient, transcribed from Sullivan (1962), illustrates this perfectly in the case of a young man with paranoid symptoms.

THERAPIST It seems always to be the case with people of your age who are brought to hospital that there is some difficulty in the field of sex.

PATIENT No, I have never been interested in anything but women.

THERAPIST Oh, is that so?

PATIENT Yes.

THERAPIST Well, have you had sexual relations?

PATIENT Yes, but only with women.

THERAPIST Is it that you wish to emphasize to me that you have not had homosexual affairs?

PATIENT Never—I hate it.

The patient clearly protests too much, but it is not his actual words which give him away. They can obviously mean exactly what they say, and it would be absurd to interpret all negatives as signs of repression. What then is the diagnostic cue? One simple criterion is the lack of an appropriate context—the statements negate preconceptions which have not been stated. And it was, of course, precisely such negatives, lacking in an appropriate context for the subjects, which proved to be difficult in the laboratory setting. (It is not easy to say quickly whether, 'seven is not even', is true or false, but it is much easier with, 'ten is even and seven is not even'.) Freud infers that the pre-conception which is denied in the utterance must exist in the mind of the speaker, and this suggests that a negative, lacking an appropriate context, may have a special emotional signi-ficance in daily life.

A quite different aspect of our results, which may have some clinical relevance, concerns the '2 4 6' experiments described in Chapter 16. It was pointed out that in this task the thought processes tended to become conventional or stereotyped, and a considerable repetition of the same hypotheses occurred. On the whole, the subjects obviously found it hard to discard their own hypotheses, when they had thought them up, and con-firmed them. But it was also suggested that the task may create a system of positive feed-back in which thought may become bizarre or idiosyncratic, and increasingly detached from reality. The subjects' hypotheses then resemble self-fulfilling prophecies which, like many religious and political ideologies, are immune to correction. Only when an individual ventures to offer a formulation of the general rule does he encounter, in principle, a correction. But all too frequently it fails in its effects. It does not always make the subject change his strategy; like punish-ment, it sometimes makes him commit the same offence again.

It is well worth quoting, in full, two sharply contrasting protocols, and it is tempting to regard them as if they were intellectual Rorschach Tests which reveal, not the subject's personality traits, but some aspects of 'cognitive style'.

1. Subject: Male (Arts undergraduate). Experimenter: Tirril Gatty 1960.

Instances			Hypothesis
2	4	6 (+) (Given)	
8	10	12 (+)	A series of alternates.
7	9	11 (+)	No change.
7	5	3 (−)	Hypothesis abandoned.

Instances					Hypothesis
13	26	28	(+)	(Given)	Second number is first times two, third is second times two.
8	16	18	(+)		No change.
49	58	100	(+)		No change.
8	13	15	(+)		No relation between first and second, but third is second plus two.
1	2031	2033	(+)		Same reason.

The rule is that the first and second numbers are random, and the third is the second plus two. (Incorrect)

7	5	7	(−)	—
1	5	7	(+)	—
5	5	7	(−)	—
4	5	7	(+)	—
9	5	7	(−)	—
263	364	366	(+)	First and second numbers are random, but first is smaller than the second, and the third is the second plus two.

The rule is that the first and second numbers are random, but the first is smaller than the second, and the third is the second plus two. (Incorrect)

261	263	101	(−)	Relation between second and third numbers is in octals (*sic*).
3	17	17	(−)	—
51	53	161	(+)	—
671	673	3	(−)	—
671	673	900	(+)	—
42	43	45	(+)	—
41	43	42	(−)	—
41	43	67	(+)	—
67	43	45	(−)	—

The rule is that the second number is random, and either the first number equals the second minus two, and the third is random but greater than the second; or the third number equals the second plus two, and the first is random but less than the second. (Incorrect)

(Subject gives up. Time: 50 min.)

It is not difficult to detect strong obsessional features in this protocol. There is a meticulous choice of instances, in which certain numbers are held constant while others are varied, and in which the positions of constants appear to be varied systematically within the triads. There is also a cautious tenacity in the conjectures about the general rule. He offers merely three formulations of it within a space of 50 minutes, and finally arrives at a complex disjunction which largely preserves the remnants of previous hypotheses. These are strong hints that his fertile imagination, and intense preoccupation with original hypotheses, has narrowed his field of appreciation to the point where he has become blind to the obvious. The nine instances which follow his second formulation of the rule (four positive and five negative) would surely enable 'another' subject to derive the rule fairly quickly. It seems so obvious that all the positive instances, and none of the negative ones, increase in magnitude. However, the subject who generated these instances did so with a higher purpose in mind, and hence completely misses the point. Excessive scrupulousness in one direction goes hand in hand with excessive carelessness in another—a typical obsessional syndrome (Fenichel, 1946, p. 280). For example, the sixth instance, 49 58 100 (+), is inconsistent with his very first announcement of the rule: 'The rule is that the first and second numbers are random, and the third is the second plus two.' In general, the performance of this subject reminds one of the 'system building' of metaphysicians who sometimes mistake the products of their own brain for reality.

In sharp contrast, it is hard to believe that the subject who was responsible for the next protocol was 'really' confident (as he claimed) that each of his announcements represented the rule.

2. Subject: Male (Science undergraduate). Experimenter: Angela Fine 1967.

Instances			Hypotheses
2	4	6 (+) (Given)	
4	6	8 (+)	Add two to the first number
6	8	10 (+)	and carry on as above.

The rule is add two to the first number and two to the second one. (Incorrect)

8   10   12 (+)   The progression of positive
                                       integers.

The rule is the progression of even positive integers. (Incorrect)

Instances   *Hypothesis*
13   15   17 (+)   Any three positive integers.

The rule is any three positive integers. (Incorrect)

3   5   7 (+)   Any three numbers.

The rule is any three numbers. (Incorrect)

3   5 $22\frac{1}{2}$ (M)   Any three numbers.

-11 $0 \cdot 999$ $\dfrac{22}{7}$ (+)   Any group of numbers with
                                       or without modifying signs.
                                       Reverse of original instance.

The rule is any group of numbers with or without modifying signs.
(Incorrect)

8   6   4 (−)   Reverse of original instance.

The rule is any three increasing numbers. (Correct)

The experimenter notes that the requirement of being highly
confident before announcing the rule was repeated to this
subject during the session, and that at each announcement he
claimed that he *was* highly confident. The protocol gives the
impression of an individual who is singularly impatient, and
unable to learn that his hunches are likely to be incorrect: he
is in need of immediate and external reassurance about each of
his conjectures. Such impulsiveness is a common characteristic
of people who cannot tolerate the uncertainty of knowing
whether they are right or wrong. This subject would not
allow himself the time to work out whether his conjectures
were correct—a simple matter of generating appropriate instances. He seemed to mind less being told that he was wrong
(did he even enjoy it?) than finding out for himself by systematic tests. It seems quite clear that he enjoyed gambling on
the basis of minimal information, and that he relied on
intuition rather than upon any rational procedures to guide his
thought.

Clearly the '2 4 6' experiments could be said to illustrate

prejudice in an abstract task because so many of the subjects tended to ignore alternatives, and seek merely to confirm their own particular hypotheses. Our 'selection task', discussed in Chapters 13, 14 and 15, shows quite clearly how it is possible for an individual to seek out confirming evidence, without having first to deliberate upon whether he should pay attention to it. The essential point can be illustrated by considering how a prejudice is likely to be rendered immune from contradictory evidence. A prejudice such as, 'all actors are effeminate', has an underlying logic of the form, 'if x is an actor, then x is effeminate'. The selection task showed that subjects, lacking in insight, often attempt to test a rule in the form, 'if p then q', by examining p and q (rather than the correct test of p and not-q). This suggests that a prejudiced person, on encountering someone effeminate, will enquire whether he is an actor. If he is, then the prejudice is confirmed; if he is not, then the information is irrelevant. In this way, the prejudice is proof against disconfirmation. It could only be truly tested if the prejudiced person were to check up on the occupation of the non-effeminate, or mix freely with actors (a policy which his prejudice would make him reluctant to pursue).

But our tasks revealed analogies to pathological thinking of a more serious kind than prejudice. And in one case it was no analogy at all, but a direct manifestation of thought disorder. In the '2 4 6' experiments, somewhat to our surprise, hardly any subjects felt 'cheated' by the generality of the rule. On the contrary, even after an indifferent performance, they frequently seemed curiously elated at the end. However, out of the several hundred tested, one subject broke down completely. Our assistant, Martin Katzman, entered the room and informed us, quite politely, that the subject, whom he was testing, was 'behaving like a lunatic'. And, indeed, he was certainly behaving in a strange way. On the one hand, he would not allow the experimenter to persuade him to break off the task, because 'he could do wonderful things with numbers', and on the other hand, he constantly engaged in self-recriminations. What was more disconcerting, however, was that he was apparently unable to stand up, and had to be carried bodily down the stairs, and taken to the Harvard Health Center.

It seemed extremely likely that, in fact, he was predisposed to psychosis, and that a task involved with numbers precipitated an acute schizophrenic crisis. This seems all the more plausible because it is known that numbers have a peculiar fascination for certain kinds of schizophrenics and schizoid individuals. Nathan (1967), for example, describes a patient who perpetually performed nonsensical calculations aloud, e.g. 'One times 4 is 90, 2 times 3 is 72 . . . etc.' In our experiment, what seemed like a perfectly innocent task, which most people found enjoyable, apparently assumed a more menacing quality, and signalled a mental illness.

It is rather more strange that some of the behaviour, which we observed in our tasks, and which seemed to us perfectly normal, is evidently assumed by some authorities to be indicative of thought disturbance. Von Domarus (1944), for instance, claims that the logic of schizophrenic thought is governed by the principle that two classes are identical, or at least related, if they have some attribute in common. A patient described by Searles (1961) thought that people who were similar were identical, and that her stockings were her glasses, since she derived the same feeling of security from both. The error is precisely that which occurs in the following inference:

Certain Indians are swift.

Stags are swift.

Therefore, certain Indians are stags.

Yet this fallacy is just an example of what Chapman and Chapman (1959) call 'probabalistic inference'—an error which normal subjects often make when an argument lacks thematic content. In rather the same way, Matte-Blanco (1965) argues that the root of the disordered thought process in schizophrenia is that all relational terms are treated as if they were symmetrical. In other words, 'illicit conversions' are made which, as we saw in Chapter 6, frequently occur when the tasks are abstract. Our subjects were not suffering from schizophrenia, and yet they performed in accordance with a principle which is assumed to be fundamental in schizophrenic thought. It would seem to follow that this principle, in itself, is not a very satisfactory criterion of schizophrenia.

It is in schizophrenic delusions, however, that we find the

most clear-cut resemblances to some of our experimental data. Anyone who has ever mistakenly tried to argue a paranoid individual out of his delusions can vouch for the persistence of a stubbornly dogmatic, but strangely logical vein of thought. There may be mysterious jumps in the argument, but some kind of internal coherence is maintained. Consider this dialogue, recorded by Federn (1953).

THERAPIST How do you know that you are poisoned?
PATIENT My bed was smelling mysteriously.
THERAPIST What kind of smell?
PATIENT Lavender.
THERAPIST Is lavender a poison?
PATIENT In the movies poisonous plants are put in the bedroom to poison her.

Now compare it with the following two excerpts from the '2 4 6' experiments.

EXPERIMENTER If you were wrong, how could you find out?
SUBJECT A I can't be wrong since my rule is correct for those numbers.
SUBJECT B Rules are relative. If you were the subject, and I were the experimenter, then I would be right.

But it is not only by asseveration and dogmatic repetition that delusions are maintained intact. Every device, ranging from self-contradiction to denial, is brought into the service of self-deception. The point is succinctly put by McReynolds (1960):

'How can the patient so convincingly overlook contrary evidence, evidence which in many instances is seemingly obvious? There are two answers here, I think: the patient avoids percepts incongruent with his delusion, and he seeks percepts congruent with it—or, to put it another way, he avoids percepts contradictory to his delusioned beliefs, and he seeks percepts supportive of them. I know of no experimental evidence bearing directly upon this hypothesis, but many behavioural characteristics of paranoid schizophrenics appear to be in accord with it.'

This account of the maintenance of delusions fits rather well the behaviour of some of our undeluded subjects in the 'selection task' (Chapters 13, 14, 15). Consider again these examples of denial.

(1) 'This card tells me it's true. That card [which falsifies the rule] has nothing to do with it because I wasn't interested in it at the beginning.'

(2) 'Well, you've just said this card makes it false?'
   'It hasn't got a squiggly border round it so it doesn't matter.'

(3) 'But you just said, when the red circle was turned over, the sentence was false.'
   'That is doing it the other way round.'

Or consider this more insidious example of self-contradiction.

(4) 'Can we consider triangles and two borders?'
   'Triangles aren't mentioned, so I left that one out.'
   'What do you expect to find on the other side of two borders?'
   'Well, if it's a triangle the sentence is false.'

These subjects are not deluded in their daily lives, and yet in these experiments they evade the truth, and talk in every respect like a deluded person. In this task the initial instructions to select specific cards, as relevant to turn over in order to decide whether the sentence is true or false, forces an intention which seems to have a fundamental effect upon their capacity to distribute their attention over the other cards, i.e. those not selected as relevant. It seems likely that a similar mechanism, connected with attention, may govern the delusions of schizophrenics. And yet, of course, there is a difference, and it lies in the content of the discourse. The schizophrenic is likely to be affected in a deleterious way about encapsulated spheres of interest which have developed into complexes, and these are likely to concern problems of human relationships. The normal individual, on the contrary, is affected by the 'concreteness' of the material. When it consists of simple, familiar statements from daily life, little difficulty occurs. The difficulties occur when it is abstract. It is as if such material is too tenuous and arbitrary to manipulate mentally; it provides no intrinsic check to error, and no reassuring contact with reality. And hence, like the hallucinations which subjects are reported to experience under conditions of sensory deprivation, the subject talks as if he were deluded; his attention is funnelled on his first decision; he contradicts himself in a way in which he would not do ordinarily; and he even denies the very facts which confront him. But he leaves the room, at the end of the experiment, in a perfectly normal state.

These considerations suggest the tentative conclusion that it is not just particular mechanisms and logical factors which are diagnostic of thought disorder. We have demonstrated that such effects can readily be induced in normal individuals under rather special tasks. Different ways of evading reality are not the prerogative of the mentally ill. On the contrary, we suggest that the distinguishing features of pathological thought are to be looked for in the combination of these mechanisms and specific types of content, or universes of discourse. The clinician presumably wants to know both what is being evaded, and why it is being evaded. The method of evasion, we should be inclined to argue, is of lesser importance.

The importance of certain variables, which fall under the broad headings of structure and content, emerge when we draw the threads of our work together. The most important, and well entrenched, finding is that it is difficult to understand negative statements, when they do not occur in an appropriate context. Apart from our early studies, this difficulty is most clearly shown when a negative premise has to be subsequently contradicted in order to make a valid deduction. It is hardly surprising that most of our own work, and more recently, the work of others, has been devoted to this problem.

The complementary case of the ease of handling affirmative statements, which frequently tempted our subjects into making fallacious inferences, is illuminated especially in the 'selection task' and the '2 4 6 experiments', described in Chapters 13 to 16. Just as a negative statement, out of context, proves difficult, so we find an often overwhelming tendency for our subjects to try to verify generalizations rather than to try to falsify them. It was quite a common occurrence to present a generalization, or hypothesis, to a subject and ask him to do something to find out whether it was true or false. Not only would he frequently try simply to verify it, he would sometimes behave as if it couldn't be false: he would presuppose its truth. When a subject has succeeded in arriving at a generalization, which has been supported by confirming evidence, he seems to exert a propriety right over it—it is his own creation. We see here, in a very exaggerated form, an analogy to the difficulty of understanding a negative statement, and the reluctance to test the negation of a proposition. As Bruner et al. (1956, p. 93) have aptly pointed out, people have a

'thirst for confirming redundancy'. They may not simply want
to know that a proposition is true; they feel the need to convince themselves of its truth, over and over again.

This strong bias towards verification is reflected in another
tendency. Our subjects, when they solve problems, often tend
to be riveted by those terms explicitly mentioned in the rules,
or generalizations, which they are required to test. Very often
they consider the unmentioned terms to be literally meaningless—they have 'nothing to do with the problem', even when,
in fact, they are crucial to its solution. This concentration on
what is mentioned also underlies the phenomenon of 'illicit
conversion'. The subject's universe of discourse is limited by the
terms mentioned, especially by the major terms, e.g. given
the sentence, 'All A are B', he will often conclude, 'All B are A.'
The terms, A and B, are made to coincide because they are
taken to exhaust the universe: it is as if B cannot be allowed
to be anything except A because no other possibility is
envisaged.

All of these factors which we have discussed seem to be consequences of one general principle: *whenever two different items,
or classes, can be matched in a one-to-one fashion, then the process of
inference is readily made, whether it be logically valid or invalid.*
Hence, affirmatives are easy because they assert a one-to-one
relation between a statement and a state of affairs, whereas
negatives (out of context) involve an extra step in order to
establish this relation. Similarly, individuals will attempt to
establish such a relation in dealing with the world, and will
accordingly be biased towards verifying, rather than falsifying,
their beliefs. And when a putative generalization is presented
to them their general strategy will be to try to match its terms
with the real world. In exactly the same way, the illicit conversion of statements is equivalent to assuming that the classes
involved are related in a one-to-one fashion. In all our research
we have been struck by the excessive attention and deference
paid to what is in black and white.

The idea that a one-to-one relation is easy is so fundamental
that one can hardly ask for a psychological justification for it.
On the analogy with perception, we generally see what we
expect to see; we don't see what we don't expect. What more

basic principle could there be? It is here that one senses the prescience of Piaget, who first appreciated that, in postulating a psychological theory of knowledge, there are times when the theorist can do no other than appeal to mathematical simplicity. A one-to-one relation is the simplest relation that can exist between two classes, and hence the ability to appreciate, or construct, such a relation must be a prerequisite for rational thought. One might ask a comparative psychologist at what point in the phylogenetic scale such a skill emerges, and at what point sub-human animals can operate with relations which violate the one-to-one constraint. Without benefit of language, can primates understand and use some equivalent to negation and class inclusion? What is truly remarkable is not that intelligent human beings can appreciate and use negatives, or that in their daily lives they can grasp implicitly more complex logical relations, but that in experimental situations they readily fall back to operating with a one-to-one relation. When they are required to demonstrate an explicit knowledge of their powers, it is as if they had suddenly unlearnt all that they knew. This characteristic is one reason why man has so often been considered to be irrational, and it is of course epitomized by pathological thought. It would, however, be a mistake to conclude that such lapses from rationality can be attributed to the constraints of the experimental situation, and to the fact that our subjects are 'under test'. And it is at this point that the content of the problem becomes of overriding importance.

Contrary to our expectation, the content of the material, about which inferences are made, gradually began to assume increasing significance. There is a sort of hierarchy in the degree of abstractness of content. The material may be so abstract that it is almost impossible to give it an intuitive representation. For example, initially, certain mathematical problems in n-dimensional space can be manifested only in a symbolic way. Miller's (1967) *Grammarama Project* is the best example of a psychological investigation at this level of abstraction. It proved most difficult for subjects to discover the rules of artificial grammars until the strings of symbols, which conformed to the grammar, were related to geometrical configurations. It is this level of abstraction, involving the use of arbitrary geometric shapes, etc., which we have defined as abstract. It is only when there is a familiar, everyday relationship involved that we speak of concrete material. The most concrete material of all consists of actual objects used in a familiar situation, e.g. the envelopes used in the 'selection task' (Chapter 14), which make an extremely difficult problem almost trivial.

When the material is abstract in our experiments the subjects tend to succumb to the effect of all the structural variables which we have considered. They will concentrate on what is mentioned in the premises; they will make illicit conversions; they will be blocked by negatives; they will be biased towards verification. When the material is concrete, on the other hand, there are characteristic changes in performance. The advantage of such material is that it helps the individual to appreciate when there isn't a one-to-one relation between the classes, or items, concerned. It will be easier for him to remember such a state of affairs, and to use it correctly in his inferences. Moreover, he is likely to have experienced a variety of different connections with such material, and hence find it easier to generate and assess hypothetical connections between the facts. This applies particularly with causal events because much of his behaviour and thought in everyday life is of a causal kind. It confers upon him a natural facility in making assumptions and deductions, but whether such facility is to be turned to advantage depends precisely upon the structural requirements of the task. When the two coincide, as in the vast majority of our studies and those of others (e.g. Inhelder and Piaget, 1958), then the reasoning is relatively easy. When the two conflict, then causality tends to win, to the detriment of logical performance.

Another aspect of concrete material, of course, is the individual's emotional attitude towards it. It has been claimed that such attitudes, or even prejudices, distort the reasoning process. However, we know of no study which demonstrates this unequivocally. The studies which purport to show the phenomenon suffer from the limitation that they have required the subject merely to evaluate a given conclusion, and hence it is by no means certain that he has been engaged in the process of deduction. The studies which fail to show the phenomenon, on the other hand, suffer from another limitation: they contain no independent measure of emotional arousal. Hence, it is uncertain whether the subjects did feel strongly about the content of the problem. Nevertheless this hypothesis is plausible, and quite compatible with the interaction between structure and content which we have observed. Of course, different individuals may be more affected by the specific nature of the content than others.

Indeed, this interaction would seem to heighten the difficulty of constructing valid intelligence tests, in a rather unexpected way. If it is true that the content of a problem exerts a decisive influence on how easy it is to solve, then it would seem that familiarity with the content should also create a distinct advantage. Hence, in trying to design a fair cross-cultural test, it would be necessary to ensure that all the individuals to be tested were equally familiar with the content of the test items. The last thing we would wish to recommend is that the material be abstract because people from different cultures may be differentially familiar with abstract patterns, etc. And, of course, abstract material leads to all the lapses from rationality which we have demonstrated. On some of our tasks even professional logicians have gone wrong in ways indistinguishable from those of the most naive subjects.

These reflections force us to take a somewhat radical view about the relationship between formal logic and ordinary inference. Bar-Hillel (1969) has pointed out that it is one of the greatest scandals of human existence that logicians have been so little interested in arguments in natural language. The emphasis which we have placed on the importance of content in reasoning shows that a purely formal, or syntactic, approach to it may suffer from severe limitations. Perhaps the aversion of logicians (although not philosophers) to this task reflects a deep, intuitive appreciation of this point. But one can turn this argument round, and examine the usefulness of formal logic in constructing psychological models of reasoning. For some considerable time we cherished the illusion that this was the way to proceed, and that only the structural characteristics of the problem mattered. Only gradually did we realize first that there was no existing formal calculus which correctly modelled our subjects' inferences, and second that no purely formal calculus would succeed. Content is crucial, and this suggests that any general theory of human reasoning must include an important semantic component.

In the Introduction we questioned the extent to which man is a rational thinker. In the broadest sense of this question, few would disagree with Freud that our behaviour is controlled by motives of which we are unaware. These clearly lack a logical foundation, and moreover they may be irrational in the sense that they conflict with one another. But our research has suggested that the individual's logical competence may be either enhanced, or limited by performance variables. And, of these, content has turned out to be vitally important for revealing, or obscuring, structure. At best, we can all think like logicians; at worst, logicians all think like us.

References

Abelson, R. P. and Kanouse, D. E. (1966) 'Subjective acceptance of verbal generalizations', in Feldman, S. (ed.), *Cognitive Consistency*, New York: Academic Press

Allport. F. H. (1955) *Theories of Perception and the Concept of Structure*, New York: Wiley

Bar-Hillel, Y. (1969) Colloquium on the role of formal languages (International Congress for Logic, Methodology and Philosophy of Science, Amsterdam, 1968), *Foundations of Language*, **5**, 256–84

Begg, I. and Denny, J. P. (1969) 'Empirical reconciliation of atmosphere and conversion interpretations of syllogistic reasoning errors', Journal of Experimental psychology, **81**, 351–4

Beth, E. W. and Piaget, J. (1966) *Mathematical Epistemology and Psychology* Dordrecht: Reidel

Brown, R. and Gilman, A. (1966) 'Personality and style in Concord', in Simon, M. and Parsons, T. H. (eds.), *Transcendentalism and its Legacy*, University of Michigan Press; reprinted in *Psycholinguistics: Selected Papers by Roger Brown*, New York: Free Press, 1970

Bruner, J. S. (1964) 'The course of cognitive growth', *American Psychologist*, **19**, 1–15; reprinted in Wason, P. C. and Johnson-Laird, P. N. (1968)

Bruner, J. S., Goodnow, J. J. and Austin, G. A. (1956) *A Study of Thinking*, New York: Wiley

Burt, C. (1919) 'The development of reasoning in school children', Journal of Experimental Pedagogy, **5**, 68–77 and 121–7

Carroll, J. B. (1958) 'Process and content in psycholinguistics', in Glaser, R. *et al.* (eds.), *Current Trends in the Description and Analysis of Behavior*, Pittsburgh: University Press

Chapman, L. J. and Chapman, J. P. (1959) 'Atmosphere effect re-examined', *Journal of Experimental Psychology*, **58**, 220–6; reprinted in Wason, P. C. and Johnson-Laird, P. N. (1968)

Chomsky, N. (1957) *Syntactic Structures*, The Hague: Mouton

Chomsky, N. (1965) *Aspects of the Theory of Syntax*, Cambridge, Mass.: M.I.T. Press

Church, A. (1936) 'A note on the Entscheidungsproblem', *Journal of Symbolic Logic*, **1**, 40–1, and 101–2

Clark, H. H. (1969a) 'Linguistic processes in deductive reasoning', *Psychological Review*, **76**, 387–404

Clark, H. H. (1969b) 'The influence of language in solving three term series problems', *Journal of Experimental Psychology*, **82**, 205–15

Clark, H. H. (1972) 'Semantics and comprehension', in Sebeok, T. A. (ed.), *Current Trends in Linguistics, Vol.* **12**: *Linguistics and Adjacent Arts and Sciences*. The Hague: Mouton (in press)

Clark, H. H. and Card, S. K. (1969) 'The role of semantics in remembering comparative sentences', *Journal of Experimental Psychology*, **82**, 545–53

Collins, A. M. and Quillian, M. R. (1969) 'Retrieval time from semantic memory', *Journal of Verbal Learning and Verbal Behavior*, **8**, 240–7

Cornish, E. R. (1971) 'Pragmatic aspects of negation in sentence evaluation and completion tasks', *British Journal of Psychology*, **62**, 505–11

De Soto, C. B., London, M. and Handel, S. (1965) 'Social reasoning and spatial paralogic', *Journal of Personality and Social Psychology*, **2**, 513–21; reprinted in Wason, P. C. and Johnson-Laird, P. N. (1968)

Dollard, J. and Miller, N. E. (1950) *Personality and Psychotherapy*, New York: McGraw-Hill

Donaldson, M. (1963) *A Study of Children's Thinking*, London: Tavistock

Donaldson, M. (1970) 'Developmental aspects of performance with negatives', in Flores D'Arcais, G. B. and Levelt, W. J. M. (eds.), *Advances in Psycholinguistics*, Amsterdam: North-Holland

Donaldson, M. and Wales, R. J. (1970) 'On the acquisition of some relational terms', in Hayes, J. R. (ed.), *Cognition and the Development of Language*, New York: Wiley

Eifermann, R. R. (1961) 'Negation: a linguistic variable', *Acta Psychologica*, **18**, 258–73

Evans, J. St. B. T. (1972a) 'Reasoning with negatives', *British Journal of Psychology*, **63** (in press)

Evans, J. St. B. T. (1972b) 'Deductive reasoning and linguistic usage (with special reference to negation)', unpublished University of London Ph.D thesis

Evans, J. St. B. T. (1972c) 'Interpretation and "matching bias" in a reasoning task', *Quarterly Journal of Experimental Psychology*, **23**, (in press)

Federn, P. (1953) *Ego Psychology and the Psychoses*, London: Imago

Fenichel, O. (1946) *The Psychoanalytic Theory of Neuroses*, London: Routledge

Flavell, J. H. (1963) *The Developmental Psychology of Jean Piaget*, Princeton: Van Nostrand

Flores D'Arcais, G. B. (1970) 'Linguistic structure and focus of comparison in processing comparative sentences', in Flores D'Arcais, G. B. and Levelt, W. J. M. (eds.), *Advances in Psycholinguistics*, Amsterdam: North-Holland

Freud, S. (1925) 'Negation', in Strachey, J. (trans.), *Complete Psychological Works of Sigmund Freud*, **19**, *The Ego and the Id and Other Works*, London: Hogarth

Gilson, C. and Abelson, R. P. (1965) 'The subjective use of inductive evidence', *Journal of Personality and Social Psychology*, **2**, 301–10; reprinted in Wason, P. C. and Johnson-Laird, P. N. (1968)

Goldman Eisler, F. and Cohen, M. (1970) 'Is N, P, and PN difficulty a valid criterion of transformational operations?', *Journal of Verbal Learning and Verbal Behavior*, **9**, 161–6

Goodwin, R. Q. and Wason, P. C. (1972) 'Degrees of insight', *British Journal of Psychology*, **63** (in press)

Gough, P. B. (1965) 'Grammatical transformations and speed of understanding', *Journal of Verbal Learning and Verbal Behavior*, **4**, 107–11

Greene, J. M. (1970a) 'The semantic function of negatives and passives', *British Journal of Psychology*, **61**, 17–22

Greene, J. M. (1970b) 'Syntactic form and semantic function', *Quarterly Journal of Experimental Psychology*, **22**, 14–27

Greene, J. M. and Wason, P. C. (1970) 'Negation: a rejoinder to Wales and Grieve', *Perception and Psychophysics*, **8**, 238–9

Handel, S., De Soto, C. B. and London, M. (1968) 'Reasoning and spatial representation', *Journal of Verbal Learning and Verbal Behavior*, **7**, 351–7

Haygood, R. C. and Bourne, L. E. Jr. (1965) 'Attribute- and rule-learning aspects of conceptual behavior', *Psychological Review*, **72**, 175–95; reprinted in Wason, P. C. and Johnson-Laird, P. N. (1968)

Henle, M. (1962) 'On the relation between logic and thinking', *Psychological Review*, **69**, 366–78; reprinted in Wason, P. C. and Johnson-Laird, P. N. (1968)

Hughes, M. A. M. (1966) 'The use of negative information in concept attainment', unpublished University of London Ph.D thesis

Hull, C. L. (1920) 'Quantitative aspects of the evaluation of concepts' *Psychological Monographs*, **28**, no. 123

Humphrey, G. (1951) *Thinking*, London: Methuen

Hunt, E. B. (1962) *Concept Learning: an Information Processing Problem*, New York: Wiley

Hunter, I. M. L. (1957) 'The solving of three term series problems', *British Journal of Psychology*, **48**, 286–98

Huttenlocher, J. (1968) 'Constructing spatial images: a strategy in reasoning', *Psychological Review*, **75**, 550–60

Huttenlocher, J., Eisenberg, K. and Strauss, S. (1968) 'Comprehension: relation between perceived actor and logical subject', *Journal of Verbal Learning and Verbal Behavior*, **7**, 527–30

Huttenlocher, J. and Strauss, S. (1968) 'Comprehension and a statement's relation to the situation it describes', *Journal of Verbal Learning and Verbal Behavior*, **7**, 300–4

Huttenlocher, J., Higgins, E. T., Milligan, C. and Kauffman, B. (1970) 'The mystery of the "negative equative" construction', *Journal of Verbal Learning and Verbal Behavior*, **9**, 334–41

Inhelder, B. and Piaget, J. (1958) *The Growth of Logical Thinking*, New York: Basic Books

Inhelder, B. and Piaget, J. (1964) *The Early Growth of Logic in the Child*, London: Routledge

James, W. (1890) *The Principles of Psychology*, Vol. **2**, New York: Holt

Janis, I. L. and Frick, F. (1943) 'The relationship between attitudes toward conclusions and errors in judging logical validity of syllogisms', *Journal of Experimental Psychology*, **33**, 73–7

Johnson-Laird, P. N. (1967) 'An experimental investigation into one pragmatic factor governing the use of the English language', unpublished University of London Ph.D thesis

Johnson-Laird, P. N. (1968a) 'The choice of the passive voice in a communicative task', *British Journal of Psychology*, **59**, 7–15

Johnson-Laird, P. N. (1968b) 'The interpretation of the passive voice', *Quarterly Journal of Experimental Psychology*, **20**, 69–73

Johnson-Laird, P. N. (1969a) 'On understanding logically complex sentences', *Quarterly Journal of Experimental Psychology*, **21**, 1–13

Johnson-Laird, P. N. (1969b) 'Reasoning with ambiguous sentences,' *British Journal of Psychology*, **60**, 17–23

Johnson-Laird, P. N. (1970a) 'The interpretation of quantified sentences', in Flores D'Arcais, G. B. and Levelt, W. J. M. (eds.), *Advances in Psycholinguistics*, Amsterdam: North-Holland

Johnson-Laird, P. N. (1970b) 'Linguistic complexity and insight into a deductive problem', in Flores D'Arcais, G. B. and Levelt, W. J. M. (eds.), *Advances in Psycholinguistics*, Amsterdam: North-Holland

Johnson-Laird, P. N. (1972) 'The three-term series problem', *Cognition*, **1** (in press)

Johnson-Laird, P. N. and Tagart, J. (1969) 'How implication is understood', *American Journal of Psychology*, **82**, 367–73

Johnson-Laird, P. N. and Wason, P. C. (1970a) 'A theoretical analysis of insight into a reasoning task', *Cognitive Psychology*, **1**, 134–48

Johnson-Laird, P. N. and Wason, P. C. (1970b) 'Insight into a logical relation', *Quarterly Journal of Experimental Psychology*, **22**, 49–61

Johnson-Laird, P. N., Legrenzi, P. and Sonino Legrenzi, M. (1972) 'Reasoning and a sense of reality', *British Journal of Psychology*, **63** (in press)

Johnson-Laird, P. N. and Tridgell, J. (1972) 'When negation is easier than affirmation', *Quarterly Journal of Experimental Psychology*, **24**, 87-91

Jones, S. (1966a) 'The effect of a negative qualifier in an instruction', *Journal of Verbal Learning and Verbal Behavior*, **5**, 497–501

Jones, S. (1966b) 'Decoding a deceptive instruction', *British Journal of Psychology*, **57**, 405–11

Jones, S. (1968a) 'Instructions, self-instructions and performance', *Quarterly Journal of Experimental Psychology*, **20**, 74–8

Jones, S. (1968b) *Design of Instruction*, London: H.M.S.O.

Jones, S. (1970) 'Visual and verbal processes in problem-solving', *Cognitive Psychology*, **1**, 201–14

Just, M. A. and Carpenter, P. A. (1971) 'Comprehension of negation and quantification', *Journal of Verbal Learning and Verbal Behavior*, **10**, 244–53

Kaufmann, H. and Goldstein, S. (1967) 'The effects of emotional value of conclusions upon distortion in syllogistic reasoning', *Psychonomic Science*, **7**, 367–8

Klima, E. S. (1964) 'Negation in English', in Fodor, J. A. and Katz, J. J. (eds.), *The structure of language: Readings in the philosophy of language*, Englewood Cliffs, N.J.: Prentice Hall

Kneale, W. and Kneale, M. (1962) *The development of logic*, Oxford: Clarendon Press

Kuhn, T. S. (1962) *The structure of scientific revolutions*, Chicago: University of Chicago Press

Lefford, A. (1946) 'The influence of emotional subject matter on logical reasoning', *Journal of General Psychology*, **30**, 127–51

Legrenzi, P. (1970) 'Relations between language and reasoning about deductive rules', in Flores D'Arcais, G. B. and Levelt, W. J. M. (eds.), *Advances in psycholinguistics*, Amsterdam: North-Holland

Legrenzi, P. (1971) 'Discovery as a means to understanding', *Quarterly Journal of Experimental Psychology*, **23**, 417–22

Lovell, K., Mitchell, B. and Everett, I. R. (1962) 'An experimental study of the growth of some logical structures', *British Journal of Psychology*, **53**, 175–88

250 References

Lyons, J. (1968) *Introduction to theoretical linguistics*, Cambridge: Cambridge University Press

McMahon, L. E. (1963) 'Grammatical analysis as part of understanding a sentence', unpublished University of Harvard Ph.D thesis

McReynolds, P. (1960) 'Anxiety, perception and schizophrenia', in Jackson, D. D. (ed.), *The etiology of schizophrenia*, New York: Basic Books

Maier, N. R. F. (1931) 'Reasoning in humans: 2. The solution of a problem and its appearance in consciousness', *Journal of Comparative Psychology*, **12**, 181–94; reprinted in Wason, P. C. and Johnson-Laird, P. N. (1968)

Matalon, B. (1962) 'Étude génétique de l'implication', *Études d'épistémologie génétique*, **16** : *Implication, formalisation et logique naturelle*, 69–95

Mates, B. (1961) *Stoic logic*, Berkeley: University of California Press

Matte-Blanco, I. (1965) 'A study of schizophrenic thinking: its expression in terms of symbolic logic and its representation in terms of multi-dimensional space', *International Journal of Psychiatry*, **1**, 91–6

Michotte, A. (1963) *The perception of causality*, London:Methuen

Miller, G. A. (1951) *Language and communication*, New York: McGraw Hill

Miller, G. A. (1962) 'Some psychological studies of grammar', *American Psychologist*, **17**, 748–62

Miller, G. A. (1967) 'Project Grammarama', in *The psychology of communication*, New York: Basic Books

Miller, G. A., Galanter, E. and Pribram, K. H. (1960) *Plans and the structure of behavior*, New York: Holt

Miller, G. A. and McKean, K. O. (1964) 'A chronometric study of some relations between sentences', *Quarterly Journal of Experimental Psychology*, **16**, 297–308

Miller, G. A. and McNeill, D. (1969) 'Psycholinguistics', in Lindzey, G. and Aronson, E. (eds.), *The handbook of social psychology*, second edition, Vol. 3, Reading, Mass: Addison-Wesley

Nathan, P. E. (1967) *Cues, decisions, and diagnoses*, New York: Academic Press

Newell, A., Shaw, J. C. and Simon, H. (1958) 'Elements of a theory of human problem-solving', *Psychological Review*, **65**, 151–66

Peel, E. A. (1967) 'A method for investigating children's understanding of certain logical connectives used in binary propositional thinking', *British Journal of Mathematical and Statistical Psychology*, **20**, 81–92

Penrose, J. (1962) 'An investigation into some aspects of problem-solving behaviour', unpublished University of London Ph.D thesis

Piaget, J. (1921) 'Une forme verbal de la comparaison chez l'enfant', *Archives de Psychologie*, **18**, 141–72

Piaget, J. (1928) *Judgment and reasoning in the child*, London: Routledge

Polya, G. (1954) *Mathematics and plausible inference*, Vol. **2**: *Patterns of plausible inference*, Princeton: Princeton University Press

Polanyi, M. (1958) *Personal knowledge*, London: Routledge

Quine, W. V. O. (1952) *Methods of logic*, London: Routledge

Reich, B. (1970) 'Affective constraints on the generating of speech', unpublished University of London Ph.D thesis

Rescher, N. (1968) *Topics in philosophical logic*, Dordrecht: Reidel

Revlis, R., Lipkin, S. G. and Hayes, J. R. (1971) 'The importance of universal quantifiers in a hypothetical reasoning task', *Journal of Verbal Learning and Verbal Behavior*, **10**, 86–91

Russell, B. (1948) *Human knowledge: its scope and limits*, London: Allen and Unwin

Russell, B. (1957) 'The existence of God—a debate between Bertrand Russell and Father F. C. Copleston, S.J., in *Why I am not a Christian*', London: Allen and Unwin

Searles, H. F. (1961) 'Schizophrenic communication', *Psychoanalysis and the Psychoanalytic Review*, **48**, 3–50; reprinted in Searles, H. F. (1965) *Collected papers on schizophrenia and related subjects*, London: Hogarth

Sells, S. B. (1936) 'The atmosphere effect: an experimental study of reasoning', *Archives of Psychology*, **29**. 3–72

Sells, S. B. and Koob, H. F. (1937) 'A classroom demonstration of "atmosphere effect" in reasoning', *Journal of Educational Psychology*, **28**, 514–18

Simpson, M. E. and Johnson, D. M. (1966) 'Atmosphere and conversion errors in syllogistic reasoning', *Journal of Experimental Psychology*, **72**, 197–200

Slobin, D. I. (1966) 'Grammatical transformations in childhood and adulthood', *Journal of Verbal Learning and Verbal Behavior*, **5**, 219–27

Smithies, B. and Fiddick, P. (1969) *Enoch Powell on Immigration*, London: Sphere Books

Smoke, K. L. (1932) 'An objective study of concept formation', *Psychological Monographs*, **42**, no. 191

Strawson, P. F. (1950) 'On referring', *Mind*, **59**, 320–44; reprinted in Flew, A. (ed.), *Essays in conceptual analysis*. (1956), London: McMillan

Sullivan, H. S. (1962) *Schizophrenia as a human process*, New York: Norton

Suppes, P. (1965) 'On the behavioral foundations of mathematical concepts', in Morrisett, L. N. and Vinsonhaler, J. (eds.), *Mathematical Learning, Child Development Monographs*, **30**, 60–96

Tanner, J. M. and Inhelder, B. (1960) (eds.), *Discussions on child development*, Vol. 4, London: Tavistock

Trabasso, T., Rollins, H. and Shaughnessy, E. (1971) 'Storage and verification stages in processing concepts', *Cognitive Psychology*, **2**, 239–89

Von Domarus, E. (1944) 'The specific laws of logic in schizophrenia', in Kasinin, J. S. (ed.), *Language and thought in schizophrenia*, Berkeley: University of California Press

Wales, R. J. and Grieve, R. (1969) 'What is so difficult about negation?' *Perception and Psychophysics*, **6**, 327–32

Wang, H. (1963) 'Dominoes and the AEA case of the decision problem', in Fox, J. (ed.), *Proceedings of the symposium on mathematical theory of automata*, Brooklyn. N.Y.: Polytechnic Press

Wason, P. C. (1959) 'The processing of positive and negative information', *Quarterly Journal of Experimental Psychology*, **11**, 92–107

Wason, P. C. (1960) 'On the failure to eliminate hypotheses in a conceptual task', *Quarterly Journal of Experimental Psychology*, **12**, 129–40

Wason, P. C. (1961) 'Response to affirmative and negative binary statements', *British Journal of Psychology*, **52**, 133–42

Wason, P. C. (1962) *Psychological aspects of negation*, London: Communication Research Centre, University College London

Wason, P. C. (1964) 'The effect of self-contradiction on fallacious reasoning', *Quarterly Journal of Experimental Psychology*, **16**, 30–4; reprinted in Wason, P. C. and Johnson-Laird, P. N. (1968)

Wason, P. C. (1965) 'The contexts of plausible denial', *Journal of Verbal Learning and Verbal Behavior*, **4**, 7–11; reprinted in *Language*, Oldfield, R. C. and Marshall, J. C. (eds.) (1968), Harmondsworth: Penguin

Wason, P. C. (1966) 'Reasoning', in Foss, B. M. (ed.), *New Horizons in Psychology*, Harmondsworth: Penguin

Wason, P. C. (1968a) 'Reasoning about a rule', *Quarterly Journal of Experimental Psychology*, **20**, 273–81

Wason, P. C. (1968b) ' "On the failure to eliminate hypotheses . . ."—a second look', in Wason, P. C. and Johnson-Laird, P. N. (1968)

Wason, P. C. (1968c) 'The drafting of rules', *New Law Journal*, **118**, 548–9

Wason, P. C. (1969a) 'Structural simplicity and psychological complexity: some thoughts on a novel problem', *Bulletin of the British Psychological Society*, **22**, 281–4

Wason, P. C. (1969b) 'Regression in reasoning?' *British Journal of Psychology*, **60**, 471–80

Wason, P. C. (1970) 'On writing scientific papers', *Physics Bulletin*, **21**, 407–8

Wason, P. C. (1971) 'Problem solving and reasoning', in *Cognitive Psychology*, Summerfield, A. (ed.), British Medical Bulletin. **27**

Wason, P. C. (1972) 'In real life negatives are false', *Logique et Analyse* (in press)

Wason, P. C. and Jones, S. (1963) 'Negatives: denotation and connotation', *British Journal of Psychology*, **54**, 299–307

Wason, P. C. and Johnson-Laird, P. N. (1968) (eds.), *Thinking and reasoning*, Harmondsworth: Penguin

Wason, P. C. and Johnson-Laird, P. N. (1969) 'Proving a disjunctive rule', *Quarterly Journal of Experimental Psychology*, **21**, 14–20

Wason, P. C. and Johnson-Laird, P. N. (1970) 'A conflict between selecting and evaluating information in an inferential task', *British Journal of Psychology*, **61**, 509–15

Wason, P. C. and Shapiro, D. (1971) 'Natural and contrived experience in a reasoning problem', *Quarterly Journal of Experimental Psychology*, **23**, 63–71

Whitfield, J. W. (1951) 'An experiment in problem solving', *Quarterly Journal of Experimental Psychology*, **3**, 184–97; reprinted in Wason, P. C. and Johnson-Laird, P. N. (1968)

Wilkins, M. C. (1928) 'The effect of changed material on the ability to do formal syllogistic reasoning', *Archives of Psychology*, **16**, no. 102

Wood, D. J. (1969) 'The nature and development of problem-solving strategies', unpublished University of Nottingham Ph.D thesis

Woodworth, R. S. (1938) *Experimental psychology*, New York: Holt

Woodworth, R. S. and Sells, S. B. (1935) 'An atmosphere effect in formal syllogistic reasoning', *Journal of Experimental Psychology*, **18**, 451–60

Name Index

Subject Index

256 Subject Index

84778119
535K